Cybersecurity in
Our Digital Lives

PROTECTING OUR FUTURE, SERIES IN CYBERSECURITY
Editor, Jane LeClair

Protecting Our Future: Educating a Cybersecurity Workforce, Vol. 1
Examines 7 of the 16 Homeland Security Critical
Infrastructure Sectors, in addition to other workforce needs.
Edited by Jane LeClair

Cybersecurity in Our Digital Lives
Looks at evolving operational needs in areas that
affect our daily digital lives.
Edited by Jane LeClair and Gregory Keeley

Protecting Our Future: Educating a Cybersecurity Workforce, Vol. 2
Examines 9 of the 16
Homeland Security Critical Infrastructure Sectors.
Edited by Jane LeClair

Cybersecurity in Our Digital Lives

edited by

JANE LeCLAIR

and

GREGORY KEELEY

HUDSON
WHITMAN
EXCELSIOR COLLEGE PRESS

Published in the United States by
Hudson Whitman/ Excelsior College Press
7 Columbia Circle, Albany, NY 12203
www.hudsonwhitman.com

Printed in the United States of America
Book design by Sue Morreale
Cover design by Phil Pascuzzo

Library of Congress
Cataloging-in-publication data

LCCN 2014958091

ISBN: 978-0-9898451-4-4 (paperback)

Contents

Acknowledgments

Writing a book about a topic that one enjoys is always a pleasure, but it is never written in a vacuum. There are always countless individuals who contribute their time and talents to making sure it reaches the finish line. Greg and I would like to thank everyone who helped us to accomplish this work. Naturally, we wish to thank the authors of the various chapters for their participation, hard work, and diligence in providing their valuable insights. Without question, the information they have provided will go a long way to helping the reader better understand the multiple issues involved in cybersecurity. Hudson Whitman/ Excelsior College Press, in particular Susan Petrie, should be thanked for valuable inputs to the final product. The support staff at our National Cybersecurity Institute (NCI) has been essential in completing this work. And, as always, Dr. John Ebersole, the president of Excelsior College, must be thanked for his ongoing support of the NCI, and for his encouragement of our efforts. Finally, we wish to extend our appreciation to former U.S. Attorney General John Ashcroft for taking time from his busy schedule to write the foreword. It is deeply appreciated.

Foreword

As U.S. Attorney General, I witnessed first-hand the consequences of being unprepared to defend against attacks—be they attacks of rogue states or commercial criminals. The cyber threats to our national security grow day by day.

Whether cyber attacks are launched to gain a marketplace edge or to impair the security of the United States, their impacts always reverberate broadly. The pervasive use of information technology in the digital age has fostered unparalleled productivity. Unfortunately, it has also exposed new avenues for espionage and disruptive malicious acts.

While systems, tools, and rules can help build a bubble of defense against cyber attack, the deployment of these measures is often too late. In the end, the most important resources for threat prevention and attack mitigation are found in the preparedness of trained professionals. This book examines how individuals and organizations can be better prepared.

Industry and governments have developed a wide variety of measures to evaluate disparate risks to their cyber infrastructure. As a result, they can estimate various risks. However, bad actors massage the data and develop strategies to penetrate existing defenses.

There are those who see cybersecurity as simply the new technology "buzz" word. However, as major breaches of the government health care system, Veterans Affairs, Gmail, and major retailers attest, the negative impacts on compromised systems are most serious and significantly damaging. The National Cybersecurity Institute (NCI) at Excelsior College has considered these issues and the challenges we face as a nation. The NCI has assembled a valuable set of tools to help students, government, and commercial enterprises both understand and address the serious threat to our cybersecurity.

John Ashcroft
79th U.S. Attorney General

Introduction

Jane LeClair and Gregory Keeley

We are a connected people. Daily, our dependence on computers, mobile devices, and digital systems increases for business, personal transactions, social media, education, entertainment, communication, and a host of other purposes, some vital to our wellbeing and some insignificant and perhaps frivolous. We are a connected society—a "digital people" with our fame and fortune a click away on the Internet. With so much of our daily life dependent on digital systems, we need to insure that our dependence on those systems is secure and safe from mischief. Despite our reliance on information technology, most people are naïve as to the threats and the security required to combat malicious actions. People have placed their digital security in the hands of others and in many respects have relinquished control of their personal and commercial data and information.

Cybersecurity, simply stated, is the process by which we guard our data at any level—personal, organizational, or governmental information in the digital world. Information—data—is valuable not only to us personally, but to our national interest. Our personal computers and mobile devices are being assaulted by viruses, the digital networks of the banking systems are attacked regularly, and every minute of every day those with malicious intent attempt to breach the cyber defenses of our government agencies. Bad actors, both state and criminal, seek to steal our personal information from social media outlets, gain access to financial information through social engineering, and harm businesses from the inside. Cybersecurity seeks to guard against such intrusions as well as losses.

Cybersecurity continues to be one of the most important issues confronting the connected planet. If we recognize the value and importance of information in the digital age, then it is essential to appreciate just how crucial cybersecurity is to us as individuals, organizations, and most crucially to the sectors we highlight in this book. The globe is now linked in ways unimaginable little more than a decade ago. We are sharing enormous amounts of information and data sometimes willingly, but often times unwittingly. We operate in a knowledge economy where information and the exploitation of that information are incredibly valuable. Nefarious actors, be they state or criminal, strive to access commercial information for competitive advantage, personal data which is exchanged and exploited by criminals for financial gain, and of course government databases affecting everything from health care to national defense.

While we like to believe that our data is secure, rarely a day passes without news of a major cybersecurity breach. Seemingly cutting-edge organizations such as Target, Home Depot, Amazon, Pinterest, Tumblr, Airbnb, Facebook, Google, Twitter, Adobe, the Washington State Courts, and J. P. Morgan have all been compromised. The new national health care system, the national power grid, numerous government agencies, schools, social media, the defense industry, and financial institutions have all been assaulted by those with malicious intent (Marks, 2014). Sensitive data has been lost, businesses compromised, personal lives exposed, credit card numbers stolen, and health and well-being endangered through threats to our major networks and infrastructures.

We have gained much through technology; we now have the ability to: transmit huge amounts of data over the Internet, complete limitless electronic transactions on a daily basis, and compile increasingly large amounts of sensitive information for our business organizations. Some estimate that each day nearly three quintillion bytes of data are generated online. Digital technology has given us the ability to utilize social media and chat with our friends, shop online, read magazines, enjoy the news, monitor our finances, and secure our homes. We spend billions of dollars online each year and send countless tweets and e-mails. The convenience and advances have come with a hefty price—security (Indvik, 2013).

Technologies are rapidly evolving with enormous change having occurred during the past decade; this has created a great sense of urgency to protect our systems. Experts are increasingly strident in urging that our cyber infrastructure be strengthened to meet mounting challenges. As we seek to strengthen our defenses, it is imperative that we recognize the importance of educating our workforce so that there is a seamless transition between educational facilities and industry (Pawlenty, 2014).

While our reliance on technology has grown, so have our many vulnerabilities, and often there are individuals and foreign powers actively seeking to do us and our systems harm. With seeming regularity, there are reports of cyber attacks on our financial institutions, government agencies, defense contractors, and our own personal computers. Millions of dollars have been lost to cybercrime; increasingly sophisticated viruses attack our personal systems, social networks, and mobile devices (Strohm, 2014).

Much is at risk and expenditure on solutions is ballooning. Corporations and government agencies globally are scrambling to harden computer systems from outside attack and increasingly seek protection by storing data in 'the cloud' (Strickland, 2014). Computers and systems are being constantly upgraded with new virus protection and much has been done to educate those who care for our systems. This effort to safeguard our data has resulted in cybersecurity becoming one of the fastest growing and crucial areas in information technology.

There has been a good deal written on the topic of cybersecurity, but much remains to be addressed. There is a scarcity of information about the topics covered in this text and even less regarding the urgent need to develop the cyber workforce, particularly in numerous sub-sectors. There are unique challenges in the areas of specialization addressed here. The National Cybersecurity Institute (NCI) at Excelsior College in Washington, D.C., has called upon experts in these unique topics to provide insight aimed at filling the gaps. The special topics examined in this book are cybersecurity as it relates to: the supply chain, the Internet of things, social media, the cloud, mobile devices, the law, social engineering, insider threats, C-Suite, and future trends in education.

Dave Chesebrough begins this work with his essay on cybersecurity in the supply chain. Threats from malware introduced along the chain are too often ignored. Dave illustrates just how crucial securing the supply chain is to our daily lives. We have all heard the term "The Internet of Things," but do we really understand what it is all about? Justin Zeefe gives us an overview of just what these 'things' mean and how catastrophic a compromise of the system could be. A huge portion of our population is using social media despite the ongoing concerns over its security. Ron Carpinella takes a close look at the interesting phenomena of social media and cybersecurity. One of the growing aspects of technology is the secure storage of data. Diana Burley discusses this issue with her essay on cloud storage and the dilemmas surrounding it. Thomas Malatesta and James Swanson have extensive, hands-on experience with cyber issues related to mobile devices and provide many interesting and expert perspectives into this rapidly expanding technology. Andrew Proia and Drew Simshaw combine their talents to give insight into the complex issues of cybersecurity and the legal profession, a sector that continues to grow in importance with each breach of security. Reg Harnish has some excellent thoughts on one of the biggest problems in cybersecurity—social engineering. Training is invaluable in overcoming this threat and Reg shares his expertise in training opportunities. Derek Smith offers insight on the vitally important aspect of insider threats to an organization's cybersecurity. Peter O'Dell offers his expertise on cybersecurity at the upper management levels of organizations in the C-Suite. Finally, Kevin Jackson concludes with a discussion of future trends in educating a cybersecurity workforce. He points out that the trend is toward cloud computing and the workforce of the future will need to be well versed on its capabilities and constantly be upgrading their skills.

Government agencies and private organizations spend billions to protect their digital assets, yet nearly every day we hear of another major data breach. Each subsequent attack seems to be bolder, bigger, and more complex. Advanced persistent threats (APTs) are highly complex, targeted advanced malware that once inside an IT infrastructure will mutate and remain undetected for extended periods while stealing assets and data. During the last few years, technology has had a staggering and disruptive influence on society with burgeoning accessibility to our personal data. In just 24 hours nearly one billion files are uploaded to 'Dropbox' (thenextweb.com), half a billion tweets are sent, and approximately 140,000 hours of video are posted to YouTube (internetlivestats.com). The more information we share, the more we expose ourselves to threats, fraud, and exploitation. Cybercriminals generally follow broad trends. Therefore, organized criminals are increasingly engaging social engineering and social networks to perpetrate targeted cybercrime. The more we share information via social networks the more exposed and vulnerable we become.

As our technologies rapidly evolve, an increasing amount of data is generated and available with no more than the click of a mouse or the touch of a finger. A great deal of that information is sensitive, valuable, and needs to be effectively secured. From our own mobile devices and personal computers to business and government networks, data needs to be safely guarded. The National Cybersecurity Institute (NCI) in Washington, D.C., continues to assist in the ongoing battle against illegal and intrusive activities in cyberspace through research and the development of cybersecurity programs. The Institute, in conjunction with Excelsior College, is pleased to present this latest informative text offering the knowledge of experts in the various topics that have been neglected in the cybersecurity field. Cybercrime, cyber terrorism, and cybersecurity are all important topics in our current society. Henry Ford once said, "The only real security that a man [sic] can have in this world is a reserve of knowledge, experience and ability" (brainyquote.com). This book examines the cybersecurity issues faced by society across a broad spectrum of perspectives and offers information for practitioner use. In addition, it seeks to tap the knowledge of cybersecurity experts and provide readers with the ability to act in their own cyber defense.

References

Indvik, L. (2013). Forrester: U.S. online retail sales to hit $370 billion by 2017. Retrieved from http://mashable.com/2013/03/12/forrester-u-s-ecommerce-forecast-2017/.

Marks, G. (2014). Why the Home Depot breach is worse than you think. Retrieved from http://www.forbes.com/sites/quickerbettertech/2014/09/22/why-the-home-depot-breach-is-worse-than-you-think/.

Pawlenty, T. (2014). Time to strengthen our collective cyber defenses. Retrieved from http://fsroundtable.org/time-strengthen-collective-cyber-defenses-american-banker-op-ed/.

Strickland, J. (2014). How cloud storage works. *How Stuff Works*. Retrieved from http://computer.howstuffworks.com/cloud-computing/cloud-storage.html.

Strohm, C. (2014, June 9). *Cybercrime remains growth industry with $445 billion lost*. Business week.com Bloomberg Anywhere. Retrieved from http://www.bloomberg.com/news/2014-06-09/cybercrime-remains-growth-industry-with-445-billion-lost.html.

Summers, N. (2013, February 27). Dropbox: 1 billion files are now being uploaded every day. *TNW Blog*. Retrieved from http://thenextweb.com/insider/2013/02/27/1-billion-files-are-now-being-uploaded-to-dropbox-every-day/.

Chapter 1

Cybersecurity in Supply Chains

DAVE CHESEBROUGH

Introduction

Complex, interconnected supply chains dominate the vast majority of businesses. They provide the mechanisms to deliver product and the flexibility and cost control necessary for competitive success in modern markets. Understanding cybersecurity in a supply chain requires examining the present state of supply chains, the vulnerabilities created by modern approaches to supply chain information exchanges, and the extent of IT application within this environment. In today's business environment there are very few, if any, products that are produced completely, beginning to end, by a single company. In fact, the modern archetype for production has been to reduce costs, increase flexibility, and increase speed by outsourcing pieces, parts, and components to other companies. This is particularly true of multi-national corporations operating in international markets. Boeing does not manufacture a 787; it assembles the pieces from its lean, global supply chain. Dell does not take silicon, copper, and petroleum in one end of a building and ship finished computers out of the other. Supply chains are mostly global, with vast, incredibly complex, and interconnected networks of production, distribution, and sourcing across multiple nations.

1

A Mobile Device Example

Perhaps you are reading this on an iPhone or an iPad. Since Apple completely outsources its manufacturing, your device contains components from upwards of 700 suppliers, most of them in Asia. This device is far more complicated than even the best devices were just a few years ago. It includes a powerful operating system, high definition display, responsive touch screen, fast processors, more memory, broadband connectivity, third-party applications, and a high-quality camera. The Samsung Galaxy SIII has over 1,033 discrete components, more than triple the best phone from six years ago (Gharibjanian, 2014). These devices are produced in mass quantities, with 990 million units shipped in 2013 (Hyer, 2014). Apple and Samsung manage high volumes of components sourced from a global supply chain. The trend toward lean and just-in-time processes means the probability is quite high that a disturbance anywhere in the supply chain will disrupt product delivery schedules, and impact market share and profitability. Larry Page, CEO at Google, came forward in 2013 to address the supply chain issues that were delaying delivery of the NEXUS 4 device, saying that fixing the Nexus supply line would be a goal for the company's team (Eadicicco, 2013). Not the kind of message a company at the leading edge of innovation wants its CEO to deliver.

Growth of Global Supply Chains

What is the evidence of this ubiquitous reliance on complex, global supply chains? Tom Friedman, in his book *The World is Flat*, analyzed globalization in the 21st century and identified ten "flatteners" that are factors impacting international commerce. He correctly identified that technology adoption requires a perceptual shift on the part of countries, companies, and individuals if they are to remain competitive in global markets. Three of these relate directly to the growing global supply interdependence: outsourcing enabled by global expansion of information and communications technology; offshoring of manufacturing or other processes to take advantage of lower costs; and advanced supply chains that enable mass customization and proliferation of product choices to win market share. Friedman pointed to Walmart as an example of a company using technology to streamline sales, distribution, and shipping. In 2005 this may have been best commercial practice, but today it is commonplace (Friedman, 2005).

The Organisation [sic] for Economic Cooperation and Development (OECD) said, in a report in May 2010, that "intermediate goods and services—that is, products used as inputs to produce other products—dominate international trade flows, representing 56% of trade in goods and 73% of trade in services in OECD member countries" (OECD, 2010). This is an indicator of the expansion of global markets and supply chains that has become a dominant feature of the international business landscape. The cybersecurity implications are significant when considering the vast array of digital networks that enable these business arrangements.

A lean supply chain is a fragile one, and supply chain visibility is a key item on the agenda of supply chain management (SCM) professionals. SCM software connects suppliers and bridges visibility gaps with information exchanges. For example, Levi Strauss & Co. reduced manual tracking and tracing of inbound shipments by 98% by implementing a supply chain visibility platform supporting the EDI transaction Advanced Shipping Notification (CapGemini, 2013).

Complexity in Traditional Supply Chain Concepts

The concept of a supply chain is most often described in two-dimensional terms. The Michigan State University Department of Supply Chain Management (SCM) defines a supply chain as "an integrated approach to planning, implementing and controlling the flow of information, materials and services from raw material and component suppliers through the manufacturing of the finished product for ultimate distribution to the end customer" (MSU, 2014). Supply chain descriptions also include the various stages of distribution channels that actually make the product available to the end consumer. Each of these tiers and stages has value, transactions, and information flows enabled by digital business systems and networks.

This two-dimensional concept is, however, insufficient to describe the cyber environment that surrounds these complex supply chains created by the relentless adoption of information technology across all functions of an enterprise. Businesses and governments have turned to the best available information technology and digital networks to speed the flow and accuracy of information. This, in turn, has created and internal and external environment where risk of cyber attack has grown to an alarming level and the security of any participant is dependent on the security of all. The Business Continuity Institute reports in its Supply Chain Resilience study for 2013 that once again the most frequent causes of disruption were unplanned outages of telecommunications (networks) and IT systems (Business Continuity Institute, 2013). If an adversary wants to halt production, it just needs to bring down a critical supplier.

Cyber: The Third Dimension

The need for cybersecurity across supply chains has never been more important. Cyber introduces a third dimension to the supply chain problem. Vulnerabilities are created when any aspect of a supply chain is connected to a network, connected to the Internet, or connected to another company's network. The sources of these vulnerabilities are:

- Intra-supply chain—systems that process and control supply chain interactions, including demand and resource planning, inventory control, ordering systems, etc.

- Cyber-physical components—process and plant control systems that rely on networks and computers to control industrial processes in process and manufacturing industries as well as the embedded electronics, processors, and software designed into the products themselves.

- Extra-supply chain—the interconnected business systems that may exist at any tier or stage of a supply chain that provided networked access to critical systems where attackers can do damage, or simply steal information.

Products with embedded processors, supply chain transactional systems, even third-party suppliers who do not directly participate in the flow of goods through the supply chain are vulnerable to cyber attack. Communications among the participants of many supply chains have become almost exclusively network-based. For example, suppliers to Lockheed Martin receive purchase orders by connecting to a supplier portal to receive and accept purchase orders and submit invoices. Many major corporations have similar systems. Bringing suppliers into such a close relationship through online systems has clear competitive advantages, but it also presents increased vulnerability to cyber attacks. But that is not the whole of it. Consumer products, critical infrastructure, manufacturing processes, security and military systems have increasingly integrated physical, electronic, and information system components to form capabilities essential to product and process quality. As more and more products introduce networked connections, the number of vulnerable areas, or what is called the attack surface, is increasing rapidly.

The Target data breach in 2013 is an example of how supply chain vulnerabilities now extend beyond the supply chain interactions and into the interconnected corporate information world. The *Wall Street Journal* reported that the Target attackers were able to steal, through a phishing campaign, the credentials of an employee at a vendor that supplied HVAC services to Target stores (Yadron, Ziobro, & Levinson, 2014). Once access was gained to Target networks, attackers were able to plant malware in point-of-sale devices, skimming credit and debit card transactions from about 40 million customers. They also were able to access a Target database to steal personal information on 70 million people.

Growth of Cyber-Physical Systems

Consumers demand through their spending habits ubiquitous access to the Internet. This demand is driving manufacturers to build "e-enabled" cars, trains, and commercial aircraft with embedded computers. Most people are not aware that their cars incorporate already high-tech computers. And now manufacturers are networking them by giving them wireless connectivity. Research has shown that all major car manufacturers, led by BMW, have as central to their strategy the goal of bringing connected cars to market (Machina, 2014).

These cars will offer services ranging from complete on-board diagnostics that can communicate problems to dealerships and manufacturers, to streaming audio, Wi-Fi, communication with home systems, and connected navigation (Muller, 2013). Low-end models may have a few dozen micro-processors, while luxury models can have a hundred or more. More features and functions mean more computers on-board that are linked to an on-board backbone network, and more opportunities for hacking. During a presentation at DEFCON 21 in 2013, two hackers demonstrated how they were able to control a car through a laptop hacked into the car's network, making it alter its speed, change direction, and even tighten the seat belts (Rosenblatt, 2013).

Obviously embedded computers use software. The Apollo 11 spacecraft had roughly 145,000 lines of computer code. The Android operating system has 12 million. Today's luxury vehicle can easily have 100 million lines of code (Pagliery, 2014). Much of this comes from the supply base. Manufacturers must assure that there is no malware or backdoor programmed into this code that provides unauthorized access to systems. Commercial aviation is also moving into connected platforms with e-enabled aircraft. Driven more by the search for efficiency than consumer demand, digitally connected aircraft will have major benefits for airline operations. The aviation community, which is quite capable of managing risks of aircraft and operations, has no common roadmap or international policy for cybersecurity (AIAA, 2013). These are examples of the growing connection between the cyber and physical domains. The blending of cyber and physical systems—where a network-connected processor controls a physical aspect of a product, facility, or system—adds another dimension to the supply chain cybersecurity problem.

Businesses employ automation and networks to increase efficiency and reduce costs across business functions that do not directly participate in the flow of the supply chain. These support functions—from point-of-sale systems, to building security, to plant operations, to mobile connectivity—also introduce additional sources of vulnerability. The reliance on digital technology in nearly every functional business area creates an interconnected, highly complex fabric from which a clever adversary can launch an attack in any direction in a supply chain once it gains access.

The Impact of Lean Production

Driven by competitive pressures, manufacturers have increasingly incorporated the principles and techniques of lean production into their processes, and have integrated suppliers into production scheduling systems and resource planning. While technology has enabled adoption of these lean manufacturing strategies, it has also created very complex relationships and dependencies. For example, there are about 3,000,000 parts in a Boeing 777 supplied by 500 companies from around the world (Boeing, 2014). The Boeing 787 program suppliers have been connected directly into production systems through lean principles of just-in-time ordering and point-of-use delivery (Arkell, 2005). The digital fabric of complex supply chains is necessary because, without it, no producer has the ability to give customers what they want, when and where they want it, at an acceptable price.

Fundamental Issues Unique to the Supply Chain

> The cyber threat is one of the most serious economic and national security challenges we face as a nation—America's economic prosperity in the 21st century will depend on cybersecurity.
>
> —President Barack Obama

Can there be any doubt that the Internet has become one of the greatest engines for innovation and productivity the world has ever known? This disruptive force is changing traditional equations of economics and social structures across the globe. As the use of the Internet and the World Wide Web has evolved, the nature of the threat continues to evolve. Sophisticated and inventive professionals, drawn by the enormous value of the data and information contained in networks, continually change the threat landscape.

The Executive Imperative

Cybersecurity must be an executive concern. It must be addressed in the Boardroom and the C-Suite as a corporate priority. Believing the threat is not real, or that somehow your company is not a target, is a mistake. Executives who have fallen into this trap have placed their organizations in serious jeopardy. Cybersecurity is an enterprise risk to be dealt with by executive management and corporate governance. It should not be viewed as the sole responsibility of the CIO, the CISO, or the IT organization. Cyber breaches impact shareholder value, tarnish the brand, require expensive mitigation efforts to protect customers, and expose companies to litigation. See Chapter 9, "Cybersecurity in the C-Suite," for a full discussion of this issue.

Three Challenges for Supply Chains

There are many challenges facing organizations that participate in modern supply chains. Perhaps the most important of these is to be aware of and acknowledge the risks inherent in doing business in a highly networked world. Another fact to acknowledge is that a chain is only as strong as its weakest link. The weakest link may be the unaware or incautious employee ensnared by a social engineering attack, or one that intentionally ignores security rules, having insufficient appreciation for the consequences.

The three main challenges to the supply chain are:

Knowing your suppliers and the inherent risk they bring: As the computer network defenses of larger corporations and government organizations get stronger and harder to penetrate, attackers are seeking the easier targets. These may be suppliers without adequate knowledge or resources to protect their networks. Smaller firms that offer the innovative or specialized capabilities and products essential to maintaining a competitive edge are often not financially positioned to afford adequate defenses, especially if they are being squeezed by customers to lower costs. A recent survey of small and medium-sized enterprises (SMEs) by security firm Kaspersky Lab revealed that 75% believe they are not at real risk of cyber attack because of their size, and 59% said the information they hold is not of interest to cyber-criminals. This results in an insufficient investment in security and ignores the very real possibility that cybercriminals will target SMEs to get information that will enable them to access a larger company's infrastructure (Ashford, 2014). Their customers would do well to take an active role in helping them defend their networks and data.

Knowing your complete risk environment: Supply chain connections are but one part of an organization's cyber profile. Every system that connects to a network and eventually to the Internet introduces a degree of vulnerability and risk. Phishing schemes invariably use e-mail as the delivery mechanism. Weak controls on access in one part of an organization can lead to compromise and eventual loss in another. It likely never occurred to anyone at Target that a successful phishing attack on an HVAC contractor combined with weak access control for their point-of-sale systems would result in the breach they experienced in 2013.

Developing organizational competence and resilience: We now well understand the importance of internal processes and procedures that maintain cyber defenses. Firewalls, access controls, software patching and updates, password adequacy and changes, two-factor authentica-tion, data at rest encryption, network controls, and continuous moni-toring are just some of the cyber-hygiene tools every organization needs to instill in its culture. Employees along with key supplier and vendor personnel must be made aware of the potential risks and the responsi-bilities they have to help defend against attack. Help them understand that phishing, spear phishing, and watering-hole attacks are attempts to trick staff into giving away confidential information which could help grant a cybercriminal access to the company's networks and sensitive information. They must learn to recognize these and resist them.

Where IS the Weakest Link?

Unfortunately, the answer to this question today may not be the same tomorrow. Both supply chains and the cyber domain are dynamic; they continually experience software and system changes, new vulnerabilities, new attack methods, new suppliers, and new technology. The dynamic cyber environment surrounding an organization requires constant attention if security is to be maintained.

Cybersecurity Threats that Challenge Supply Chains

> We don't fully understand the economics and psychology of cybersecurity.
>
> —Michael Daniel, White House Cybersecurity Coordinator

In an ever-more networked world, cyber vulnerabilities pose challenges to governments and industries in every sector and across the globe and it is unlikely that any meaningful legislation will be passed to assure the integrity and availability of key U.S. industries. We are vulnerable, and adversaries and criminals understand the interconnected nature of our economy and know that coordinated attacks on financial institutions or critical infrastructure would wreak havoc on the economy and weaken our ability to respond to a nation-state threat to our national security. Moreover, as the cost of technology decreases, the barriers to entry are lowered and the lucrative market for stolen data serves as profit incentive for a cybercrime "growth industry."

Cybercrime is Big Business

There is no accurate way to determine the annual cost of cybercrime and cyber espionage. However, by all estimates, it is substantial. At an American Enterprise Institute event in 2012 General Keith B. Alexander (then Commander of U.S. Cyber Command and Director of the NSA) called cybercrime "the greatest transfer of wealth in history" (Protalinski, 2012). A report authored by McAfee and the Center for

International Studies in 2014 estimated the annual cost to the global economy resulting from cybercrime to be $400 billion (CSIS, 2014). The accuracy of these numbers is sometimes questioned because they are usually generated by surveys and not rigorous analyses. Moreover, companies are normally reluctant to be forthcoming about incidents when they might be damaging to corporate image. Nevertheless, there is plenty of evidence that the consequences of successful attacks have a high cost to the affected companies, their customers, and society in general.

Scope of the Problem

> There are two types of companies in this country, those who know they've been hacked, and those who don't know they've been hacked.

> —Chairman Mike Rodgers, House Intelligence Committee

Digital technology is woven throughout the fabric of society. Business systems, accounting and banking, engineering and product design, command and control, manufacturing operations, communications, supply chains, air traffic control, unmanned vehicles—all make extensive use of digital technology, and the dependence is deepening.

The connected lifestyle is a given (IDC, 2014). The growth of mobile devices and applications that enhance the consumer experience present vulnerabilities and avenues of attack: A capability or convenience that may be seen as desirable may be the one thing that the adversary sees as an exciting opportunity. Information residing in a network that is connected to or transverses the Internet is vulnerable: data can be erased or altered, keystrokes and online behaviors can be tracked, account information and passwords can be stolen, identities can be stolen, physical operations can be sabotaged through their computer controls, intelligence can be gathered, and malware can be inserted that lays dormant and undetected until activated. The threats are constantly morphing, and smart phones, tablets, and ubiquitous wireless networking have exponentially increased the opportunities available to criminals and spies.

Adversaries know that harnessing the power of the Internet's infrastructure yields far more benefits than simply gaining access to individual computers. Attackers are using malicious exploits and social engineering attacks (phishing and spear-phishing e-mails sent to employees is a favorite technique) to gain access to web hosting servers, name servers, and data centers with the goal of taking advantage of the tremendous processing power and bandwidth they provide. Through this approach, exploits can reach many more unsuspecting computer users and have a far greater impact on the organizations targeted, whether the goal is to make a political statement, disable an adversary, or generate revenue (CISCO, 2014).

Sources of the Threat

> John Dillinger couldn't do 1,000 robberies in one day in 50 states while wearing his pajamas, but that's what we deal with today.
>
> —James Comey, Director, Federal Bureau of Investigation

Today's cybercriminals are highly motivated professionals—often well-funded by criminal organizations or nation-states—who are far more patient and persistent in their efforts to break through an organization's defenses. They do extensive research to identify targets and vulnerabilities, and they use sophisticated attack processes and social engineering.

Any or all of these may have the intent, motivation, and means to do harm to any organization. According to the Open Security Foundation, there were 669 incidents reported during the first three months of 2014, exposing 176 million records. Of these, the business sector accounted for the largest reported incidents (57.5%), followed by Government (15.7%) (Risk Based Security, 2014).

The rise in frequency and breadth of cyber attacks can be attributed to a number of factors. Unfriendly nation-states attack systems to gather intelligence or steal intellectual property. Hacktivists aim to make political statements through systems disruptions. Organized crime groups, cyber gangs, and other criminals breach systems for monetary gain. Nation-states seek to take intellectual property or trade secrets to bolster their national businesses, conduct espionage on governments and militaries, and potentially plant malware that could be activated to do damage at a later time, perhaps as a part of a coordinated attack. The Department of Homeland Security Industrial Control Systems Cyber Emergency Response Team describes sources of cyber threats (ICS-CERT, 2014):

Nation-States: Nations, both friendly and unfriendly, have cyberwarfare programs that pose serious threats. Government-sponsored cyber warfare programs are oriented to cause widespread disruption and long-duration damage. Presently nations are the only institutions with the resources and motivation necessary to create and sustain advanced persistent threats.

Terrorists: Terrorists, despite their intentions, are less developed in their computer network capabilities and resources. Their propensity is to pursue attacks that garner immediate attention. They are likely, therefore, to pose only a limited cyber threat.

Organized Crime and Industrial Spies: Corporate spies and organized crime pose a serious threat because of their ability to conduct industrial espionage and large-scale monetary theft as well as their ability to hire or develop hacker talent. They are considered to be high intent and high impact threats.

Insider Threat: There are essentially two types of insider threat—malicious and accidental. Malicious insiders can be employees, former employees, contractors, or business associates who have inside information concerning the organization's security practices, data and computer systems, and a personal motivation to harm the organization or achieve personal gain. An accidental insider threat results from an employee unwittingly victimized by a phishing e-mail campaign that results in downloading malware to an organization's networks. This social engineering approach has become quite sophisticated and is a favorite tactic of an advanced, persistent threat.

Hacktivists: Hacktivists are small groups of hackers with political motives. Hacktivists appear to desire propaganda victories rather than damage to critical infrastructures or high-impact theft. Their goal is to support their political agenda, and to inflict damage to achieve notoriety for their cause.

Contaminated Parts: This is a critical supply chain assurance issue. Supply chain assurance involves validating the authenticity of parts and components as they flow into products. The concern is two-fold—counterfeit parts/assemblies with potential for inserted malware, and assurance of the IT supply chain, to include the computers and the software they run. While "knock offs" pose certain threats to businesses through patent infringement and loss of sales, they may also often have inferior specifications and quality, which may represent a hazard if incorporated into critical systems. However, for many parts or assemblies that contain processors and embedded software, the concern is over the insertion of malware.

Advanced Persistent Threats: Advanced Persistent Threat (APT) usually refers to a well-funded, highly organized group, such as a government or criminal gang, with both the capability and the intent to persistently and effectively target a specific entity. This targeting can be general, such as a type of company or industry, or specific, based on the goals of the attack. An APT uses multiple phases to break into a network, avoid detection, and harvest valuable information over the long term. The APT usually targets organizations and/or nations for business or political motives, and it depends on not being detected over a long period of time. APT attacks consist of several stages or steps: targeting, reconnaissance, infiltration, control, discovery, and exfiltration. APT attacks are not random, but are part of a well-conceived plan to accomplish strategic goals.

Understanding the Risk

Identifying and managing cyber risk originates at the top of the organization through its recognition and inclusion in Enterprise Risk Management. It is never a matter purely for the IT team, although they clearly play a vital role. An organization's risk management function needs a thorough understanding of the constantly evolving risks as well as the practical tools and techniques available to address them. What do we mean by cyber risk? Cyber risk means any risk of financial loss, disruption, or damage to the reputation of an organization from some sort of failure of its information technology systems (IRM, 2014).

Specific risks resulting from cyber vulnerabilities include:

- Disruption—Disruption to operations can come from intentional acts against an organization or the loss of services such as electrical power from cyber attacks on critical infrastructure. A cyber attack on a critical supplier that interrupts the flow of components can be just as devastating to a supply chain as a natural disaster.

- Theft—Financial institutions are constantly on guard against cybercriminals whose goals are to penetrate systems and transfer wealth. While stealing money is an obvious objective, intellectual property and trade secrets are also prime targets.

- Alteration—Design data in supply chains is most often exchanged through computer-aided design and manufacturing systems. As we embrace new technologies such as additive manufacturing, the unauthorized alteration of the process, material, or physical dimensions of a design can result in sub-standard components.

- Degradation of Function—Supervisory control and data acquisition (SCADA) networks perform key control functions in process and manufacturing industries. Losing control to outside hackers can mean degradation of function or even physical destruction of equipment being controlled.

- Damage to Reputation—When loss of customer information, whether retail, industrial, or government, is publically revealed companies must then conduct damage control to retain positive image and avoid lasting negative press and loss of business.

- Loss of Competitive Advantage—Theft of intellectual property and trade secrets means competitors can leapfrog companies in product design, bringing to market equivalent products and erasing the premium created by getting to the market first with an innovative product. According to the U.S. Commerce Department, intellectual property theft costs domestic industries $250 billion annually (Burgess & Power, 2010).

- Nullification of Investment—The loss of competitive data (which was developed with internal funds or external investments) that accompany the theft of data can be devastating. Those expenditures and the advantage they created in terms of potential investor or shareholder value become nullified when the sensitive information is stolen in a cyber-intrusion. What is worse, the company may not even know until it sees a competitor's product that its sensitive information has been compromised.

Cybersecurity Laws and Policies Relevant to Supply Chain

There is little in the way of current law and regulation that specifically addresses cybersecurity in supply chains. The lack of comprehensive cybersecurity legislation stems from the disagreements over information sharing mechanisms, civil penalties, lawsuit protection, and the interests of those who favor privacy safeguards. In 2013, the House passed the Cyber Intelligence Sharing and Protection Act (CISPA), but it was met with substantial opposition over a perceived lack of privacy protections. The Senate Select Committee on Intelligence voted in 2014 to approve a cybersecurity bill known as the Cyber Information Sharing Act (CISA). The bill is intended to help companies and the government combat cyber attacks. Civil liberties advocates have opposed CISA, arguing that it fails to adequately shield Americans' privacy. Proponents of the bill say it will help stop attacks by encouraging data-sharing between businesses and the government.

In the absence of legislation, and faced with an onslaught of attacks against companies who have sensitive defense information in their networks, the Defense Department published DFARS subpart 234.73 in November 2013. This rule addresses the safeguarding by contractors of unclassified controlled technical information (UCTI). The rule, implemented in contract clauses, requires DoD and its contractors and subcontractors to provide adequate security safeguards to prevent unauthorized access and disclosure of UCTI resident on their unclassified information systems. It further requires that those contractors, and their subcontractors, report to DoD cyber incidents that affect unclassified controlled technical information on their unclassified information systems (DFARS Subpart 204.73, 2013).

In that same month DoD published an interim rule, Subpart 239.73, that addresses requirements for information related to supply chain risk. This rule allows DoD to exclude a company from any covered procurement related to a national security system that fails to meet supply chain risk qualification standards, or fails to achieve an acceptable rating for supply chain risk. The rule implements the authority of Section 806 of the National Defense Authorization Act for Fiscal Year 2011, and allows DoD to direct a contractor to exclude a particular source from consideration for a subcontract (DFARS Subpart 239.73, 2013).

DoD and the U.S. General Services Administration (GSA) jointly released a report "Improving Cybersecurity and Resilience through Acquisition," in January 2014 with six planned reforms to improve the cybersecurity and resilience of the Federal Acquisition System (Hagel & Tangerlini, 2014). The reforms outlined in this joint report are currently being evaluated for implementation across the Federal government. These reforms include:

- Institute baseline cybersecurity requirements as a condition of contract award for appropriate acquisitions.

- Cybersecurity must be included in acquisition training.

- Develop common cybersecurity definitions for federal acquisitions.

- Institute a federal acquisition cyber risk management strategy.

- Include a requirement to purchase from original equipment manufacturers, their authorized resellers, or other trusted sources.

- Increase government accountability for cyber risk-management.

Cybersecurity concerns have changed the way DoD is doing business with industry. Breaches and vulnerabilities now have significant consequences for DoD contractors. Not taking cybersecurity seriously could result in being eliminated as a source of supply for the DoD, and perhaps for the entire Federal government. While some regulatory efforts today are aimed at voluntary compliance, such as the NIST Framework for Cybersecurity, the time is coming when more mandatory regulations will be in place because of the reluctance by many to invest in cybersecurity.

For supply chain managers concerned with risk management there is other applicable Federal guidance, and a comprehensive Supply Chain Risk Management program can be largely modeled after these programs. This approach aligns commercial and federal operations with the most up-to-date cybersecurity, supply chain risk management, and ICT management directives. These documents include:

- Comprehensive National Cybersecurity Initiative (CNCI);

- National Institute of Standards and Technology (NIST) IR 7622, *National Supply Chain Risk Management Practices;*

- NIST Special Publication (Draft) 800-161, *Implementation of the Supply Chain Risk Management Framework;*

- Committee on National Security Systems (CNSS) Directive 505, *Supply Chain Risk Management;*

- FIPS Pub 199, *Standards for Security Categorization of Federal Information and Information Systems;*

- Public Law 113-76 Section 515, Sets conditions for the use of funds by the Departments of Commerce and Justice, NASA, or NSF to acquire a high-impact or moderate-impact information system;

- DFAR SUBPART 239.73, *DFAR Requirements for Information Relating to Supply Chain Risk;*

- DoD Instruction 5200.44, *Protection of Mission Critical Functions to Achieve Trusted Systems and Networks;*

- DOE Order 205.1B, *DOE Cybersecurity Program;*

- Customs and Border Protection's C-TPAT Program;

- National Defense Authorization Act (NDAA) 2013;

- Defense Information Systems Agency (DISA) Security Technical Implementation Guides (STIGs);

- National Security Agency (NSA) Systems and Network Analysis Center (SNAC) Guides;

- ISO/IEC 27036-1:2014, *Information Technology—Security Techniques—Information security for supplier relationships;* and

- The Open Group, Open Trusted Technology Provider Standard (O-TTPS).

Cybersecurity Skills Necessary in the Supply Chain Workforce

Workers with cybersecurity skills and knowledge are critical to protecting the digital infrastructures on which much of modern society is built. Industries as diverse as retail, health care, manufacturing, and energy all depend on the security and reliability of cyberspace. With the nation facing new and dynamic risks, threats, and vulnerabilities, a highly skilled cybersecurity workforce capable of responding to these challenges is needed now more than ever.

Non-cyber Workforce

The vast majority of workers in supply chains are not cybersecurity, or even IT, professionals. They are clerks, office workers, accountants, administrators, warehouse managers, logistics specialists, plant floor operators, design and manufacturing engineers, maintenance technicians, etc. Yet, they are the first line of defense against some of the most threatening cyber attacks. They need to be equipped to recognize and deal with policies and procedures that help make their organizations safe and dependable participants in supply chains. They need to be trained and educated in the following areas:

- Awareness of the risk and consequences.
- Acceptable and unacceptable workplace practices.
- Fundamentals of proper safeguarding and cyber-hygiene.

Cyber Workforce

For larger companies such as financial institutions, retail chains, integrators, manufacturers, infrastructure operators, etc. there are increasing demands for properly skilled and educated cybersecurity professionals. Many of these will need advanced degrees and certifications. The National Cybersecurity Workforce Framework has been developed as a foundational guide for increasing the size and capability of the U.S. cybersecurity workforce. The Workforce Framework is a national resource that categorizes, organizes, and describes cybersecurity work. The National Initiative for Cybersecurity Education (NICE) developed the Workforce Framework to provide educators, students, employers, employees, training providers, and policy makers with a systematic way to organize the way we think and talk about cybersecurity work, and what is required of the cybersecurity workforce (DHS, 2014).

The cybersecurity profession is maturing and growing and cyber-security roles are becoming more distinct and defined. In the past, employers had to develop customized position descriptions to fill existing capability gaps. Some large employers followed certain standards, but different employers followed different standards. This resulted in:

- A disorganized job market with uncoordinated standards and descriptions.

- Colleges not having programs that were aligned to industry needs and jobs.

- Employers needing to retrain new hires in the specific skills required.

- Students not having clear job prospects and career opportunities.

To effectively coordinate the cybersecurity job market, colleges, educators, employers, employees, and training vendors need a standardized way to describe the work encompassed by the term "cybersecurity." The Workforce Framework is an organized, comprehensive description of the work done by cybersecurity professionals. It is the foundation for increasing the size and capability of the U.S. cybersecurity workforce.

There are also a number of professional certifications that are valuable in the cyber workforce. These indicate that the holder has gained a specific level of knowledge and professional experience in cybersecurity. Certifications can be obtained in three general types: Knowledge Based—certifying an individual's knowledge and skills; Organizational Based—certifying that an organization has reached certain standards; and Product Based—certifying that a product or system has been accredited at a certain standard. Some of the better known certifications for professionals include:

- CISSP—Certified Information Security Professional.

- CISM—Certified Information Security Manager.

- GIAC—Global Information Assurance Certificate.

- CISA—Certified Information Systems Auditor.

- CSFA—Certified Security Forensic Auditor.

- CBCP—Certified Business Continuity Professional.

- CPP—Certified Protection Professional.

- CPTC—Certified Penetration Testing Consultant.

- CPTE—Certified Penetration Testing Engineer.

- CompTIA—Security+.

- CSTA—Certified Security Testing Associate.

- OSCP—Offensive Security Certified Professional.

- CEH—Certified Ethical Hacker.

- ECSA—EC-Council Certified Security Analyst.

- CEPT—Certified Expert Penetration Tester.

- MCSE Security—Microsoft Certified Systems Engineer (Security).

This is by no means an exhaustive list, and many vendors offer certifications in their specific products.

Recommendations for Supply Chain Cybersecurity Best Practices

Best practices for supply chain cybersecurity are developed or addressed in the context of Supply Chain Risk Management, which in turn ought to be considered an element of Enterprise Risk Management. Enterprise Risk Management (ERM) addresses methods and processes to identify and manage risks and seize opportunities related to the achievement of their objectives. It provides a framework for identifying events or circumstances relevant to the organization's objectives (risks and opportunities), assessing them in terms of likelihood and magnitude of impact, determining a response strategy, and monitoring progress. By identifying and proactively addressing risks and opportunities through ERM, organizations protect and create value for their stakeholders, including owners, employees, customers, and compliance regulators. ERM is also a risk-based approach to managing an organization through integrating internal control, Sarbanes–Oxley compliance, and strategic planning.

Best practices for cybersecurity in supply chains begin with awareness and strong cybersecurity on the part of individual participants, with some unique activities focused on suppliers. Supply chain participants should develop strong cybersecurity policies and processes following applicable guidance. These include:

- Maintaining good hardware and software updating procedures.

- Enforcing cyber-hygiene.

- Training employees.

- Using appropriate security technologies such as firewalls, malware scanners, e-mail scanners, network segmentation, data encryption, etc.

- Implementing continuous monitoring for critical high-risk, high-impact areas.

- Participating in information sharing organizations such as the voluntary DoD Defense Industrial Base Cybersecurity/Information Assurance Program, the FBI InfraGard, industry sector ISACs, and regional efforts such as the Arizona Cyber Threat Response Alliance.

- Maintaining thorough ERM and SCRM programs.

- Instituting cyber auditing and penetration testing to assure adequate defenses, much like external audits assure adequate financial controls.

Supply chains must also develop strong cyber processes specifically intended to strengthen all suppliers, including:

- Regular visits and communication with suppliers.

- Regular internal and third-party penetration testing with suppliers.

- Promoting specific security requirements and best practices with suppliers.

- Information sharing and threat alerts.

- Support for supplier networks in need of technology or capabilities.

- Education and training.

Supply Chain Risk Management (SCRM) can be viewed as a subset, or component, of ERM. SCRM attempts to reduce supply chain vulnerability through a coordinated approach, involving all supply chain stakeholders, which identifies and analyzes the risk of failure points within the supply chain. Mitigation plans to manage these risks can involve logistics, finance, and risk management disciplines; the ultimate goal being to ensure supply chain continuity in the event of a scenario which otherwise might have interrupted normal business and, thereby, profitability. Because supply chains are now complex and inherently dependent on IT, the cybersecurity component of an SCRM program is becoming vitally important. The National Institute of Standards and Technology has issued a draft report to help organizations mitigate supply chain risks. The NIST Special Publication 800-161, Supply Chain Risk Management Practices for Federal Information Systems and Organizations (2ndDraft) (Boyens, Paulsen, Moorthy, & Bartol, 2014), is an update of NIST Interagency Report 7622, Notional Supply Chain Risk Management Practices for Federal Information Systems (Boyens, Paulsen, Bartol, Moorthy, & Shankles, 2012). It identifies supply chain risks to include insertion of counterfeits, unauthorized production, tampering, theft, insertion of malicious software, as well as poor manufacturing and development practices in the supply chain. These risks are realized when threats in the supply chain exploit existing vulnerabilities.

Draft SP 800-161 offers a comprehensive approach to designing best practices for cybersecurity in supply chains and integrating cybersecurity risk management into ERM. It includes the following continuous and iterative steps:

- Frame the risk—establish the context for risk-based decisions and the current state of the system or IT supply chain infrastructure.

- Assess the risk—review and interpret criticality threat, vulnerability, likelihood, impact, and related information.

- Respond to risk—select, tailor, and implement mitigation controls.

- Monitor risk—on an ongoing basis, including changes to an information system or IT supply chain infrastructure, using effective organizational communications and a feedback loop for continuous improvement.

To integrate risk management throughout an organization, NIST SP 800-39 describes three organizational tiers, which address risk at the organization level, mission/business process level, and information system level. NIST indicates IT risk management requires the involvement of all three tiers. While this publication is aimed at Federal agencies, it can be useful as a foundation for any supply chain approach to cybersecurity risk management.

Future Trends in Supply Chain Cybersecurity

Attacks on supply chain participants will likely increase as supply chains continue to be targets of cybercriminals and spies. Certain nation-states will continue their attempts to create advantages for their industries over the global competition through theft of intellectual property and trade secrets. Industries doing business with governments, particularly in the defense and security markets, will continue to see relentless attacks, as will firms that provide critical infrastructure services. Simultaneously, supply chains will continue to adopt advanced technology to increase/retain customer value and to improve efficiency; in addition, new vulnerabilities will be introduced that will need to be identified and managed. Collaboration will increase as the benefits of cooperative information sharing begin to outweigh the risk many perceive in acknowledging vulnerabilities. Risk management becomes an increasingly critical aspect of supply chains. In the future, supply chains will face new cybersecurity challenges as they transform operations and seek new ways to use technology to achieve agility and efficiency.

Small and Medium Businesses in the Crosshairs

Smaller companies will continue to be the focus of targeted attacks to be used as stepping stones to larger companies. The September 2013 Symantec Intelligence Report showed a marked increase in attacks targeted to companies with 250 or less employees; these accounted for 48% of all unique attacks. "Much of this could be related to supply chain attacks, where attackers look for the easiest point of entry and work their way up the chain," Symantec said (Symantec, 2013). Tactics are likely to remain largely the same: a mixture of spearphishing attacks with malicious e-mail attachments, watering hole campaigns attempting to target regular visitors of a website, and reinforcement of these with direct calls to targets to get them to open up a malicious file attachment. For supply chains, it will be even more critical to know their small business suppliers and perhaps even support them in strengthening their defenses.

New Technological Advances

Technology will continue to be used to achieve better supply chain performance. Low cost and reliable cloud solutions for global supply chains are starting to emerge that will transform how supply chains interact and collaborate. Driven by ERP vendor migrations of capability into cloud and mobile offerings, supply chains will be able to take advantage of the "network effect."

Cloud-based supply chain strategies that have the greatest potential to deliver the network effect throughout a supply chain compare the sensitivity of sharing data with the benefit of a large number of suppliers having rapid access to information. However, as has been recently noted, cloud providers can be susceptible to hacking, and implementation of this technology must consider cybersecurity and risk implications. Large organizations will continue to migrate away from e-mail/phone/fax communications toward some form of network-based unified communications. Some will reside in cloud technology, while some will make use of vendors offering Internet-based services. In either case, the security of these communications will be an important aspect.

The intersection of business intelligence with mobile devices and fast wireless connections will continue to transform the supply chain management landscape bringing SCM apps to smartphones and tablets, improving precision and flexibility. This will also bring a new set of vulnerabilities making endpoint security and network segmentation important aspects of supply chain cybersecurity.

The "Internet of Things" (intelligent devices networked together) will transform supply chains in unexpected ways from both the supplier and consumer perspectives, and create a network rich with information allowing supply chains to assemble and communicate in new ways. Gartner forecasts a 30-fold increase in Internet-connected physical devices by 2020, significantly altering supply chain information access and cyber-risk exposure (Gartner, 2014). An example of this is the use of commercial telematics to improve logistics' efficiency in the trucking industry. Cyber-physical products, such as connected cars, will also alter how consumers interact with producers and the resulting impacts will ripple down the supply chain. Connected technology is always accompanied by unintended and often unknown cyber vulnerability.

Data analytics can unlock rich troves of useful information residing in supply chain systems. As ERP and other legacy enterprise vendors respond to market demands and make information that resides in their systems available, big data will become an important tool in understanding consumer and supplier trends. This will give rise to third-party analytics providers, who will analyze supply chain data to provide information on what happens in supply chains and why. But like cloud computing, the supply chain data will be held by various analytics and IT experts, data brokers, software vendors, and solutions consultantsthus creating a potential vulnerability (remember the Target breach?).

Collaboration

Not only is working together an important element of efficient supply chains, it is a crucial element of cybersecurity. Supply chain efficiency, which is directed at improving a company's financial performance, is different from supply chain resilience, whose goals are risk reduction, the avoidance of disruption, and fast recovery when a disruption occurs. Supply chains will develop communal resources where cyber threat information and best practices can be shared and the resilience of the entire chain can be improved. Supply chains will increase their engagement with industry and sector-specific organizations that share information on collective risk. As an example, the Department of Homeland Security Industrial Control System's Cyber Emergency Response Team (ICS-CERT) works across all critical infrastructure sectors, coordinating efforts for threat and risk identification among control systems owners, operators, and vendors. ICS-CERT also collaborates with international and private sector Computer Emergency Response Teams (CERTs) to share control systems-related security incidents and mitigation measures.

Theft of Organizational Identity

Identity theft is typically associated with individuals. However, there is an emerging source of fraud that is based on the theft of organizational identity. Both corporations and governments can be affected. Criminals can research elements of identity (people, brand images, DUNS number, Employer Identification Number, etc.) and pose as a legitimate legal entity for the purpose of conducting a transaction. This erodes the trust fabric of an economy or society and is leading to the call for development of authoritative sources of organizational registry data where the identity and qualifications of a legal entity can be verified. Currently focused in the European market, momentum is building for addressing this emerging threat.

Emphasis on Risk Management

Tighter control of risk exposure in supply chains will mean regionalization and segmentation as product developers seek to limit exposure and maximize security of the supply base. Supply chain complexity can mean reduced efficiency as companies struggle to deal with delays and fluctuations. Dependencies on single source suppliers can mean everything comes to a halt when a disruption occurs. Controlling the amount of complexity can, therefore, lead to higher cost efficiency and reduced risk, and executives need to ensure that the impact of supply chain disruptions can be contained within a portion of the supply chain. Supply chains will continue to trade off efficiency and resilience to find optimal balance. Diversity of supply becomes more important so that a disruption of one part of a supply chain can be contained in a region or segment and then quickly mitigated. Standard cybersecurity and risk identification and management approaches across regional and segmented parts of supply chains will be necessary to assure security. This may be more complex for multi-national companies as supply chains that cross international borders will be subject to differing cybersecurity rules and privacy laws.

Conclusion

It is hard to imagine a more fertile area for cyberattackers than a poorly defended supply chain. It is unreasonable to think that this problem will go away or somehow be solved by others. Every supply chain participant, from raw material producer to retail outlet, needs to understand how to protect their supply chains, limit damage, and recover quickly from disruptions from cyber attacks. Maintaining a strong and resilient cybersecurity posture avoids the shock of serious security breaches, helps with recovery from attack, and ultimately assures business continuity.

Sources of Further Information

Brown, Evelyn. Proposed Risk Management Guidelines Aim to Bolster Security of Federal ICT Supply Chains. NIST Information Technology Laboratory, 2014. http://www.nist.gov/itl/csd/risk-060314.cfm.

Goertzl, Karen Mercedes et al. Security Risk Management for Off-the shelf Information and Communications Technology Supply Chain. Information Assurance Technology Center, Defense Technology Information Center, 2010.

LeClair, Jane et al. *Protecting Our Future: Educating a Cyber Workforce*. Albany, NY: Hudson Whitman/Excelsior College Press, 2013.

Manners-Bell, John. *Supply Chain Risk: Understanding Emerging Threats to Global Supply Chains*. Philadelphia: Kogan Page, 2014.

Moeller, Robert. *IT Audit, Control and Security*. New Jersey: John Wiley & Sons, 2010.

Statement before the Senate Judiciary Committee, Subcommittee on Crime and Terrorism, Washington, D.C. Gordon M. Snow, Assistant Director, Cyber Division, Federal Bureau of Investigation, April 12, 2011. http://www.fbi.gov/news/testimony/cybersecurity-responding-to-the-threat-of-cybercrime-and-terrorism.

Touhill, Gregory J., and Touhill, C. Joseph. *Cybersecurity for Executives: A Practical Guide*. American Institute of Chemical Engineers: John Wiley & Sons, 2014.

Waters, Donald. *Supply Chain Risk Management: Vulnerability and Resilience in Logistics*. Philadelphia: Kogan Page, 2011.

References

AIAA. (2013, August). *The connectivity challenge: Protecting critical assets in a networked world*. Retrieved May 14, 2014, from The American Institute of Aeronautics and Astronautics: https://www.aiaa.org/uploadedFiles/Issues_and_Advocacy/AIAA-Cyber-Framework-Final.pdf.

Arkell, D. (2005, March). The evolution of creation. *Boeing Frontiers On-line*, 3(10). Retrieved July 17, 2014, from http://www.boeing.com/news/frontiers/archive/2005/march/mainfeature1.html.

Ashford, W. (2014, March 17). *SMEs believe they are immune to cyber attack.* Retrieved September 1, 2014, from Computer Weekly: http://www. computerweekly.com/news/2240216202/SMEs-believes-it-is-immune-to-cyber-attack-study-shows.

Boeing. (2014). *Boeing 777 family facts.* Retrieved July 17, 2014, from http:// www.boeing.com/boeing/commercial/777family/pf/pf_facts.page.

Boyens, J., Paulsen, C., Bartol, N., Moorthy, R., & Shankles, S. (2012, October). *Notional supply chain risk management practices for federal information systems.* Retrieved September 1, 2014, from http://nvlpubs. nist.gov/nistpubs/ir/2012/NIST.IR.7622.pdf.

Boyens, J., Paulsen, C., Moorthy, R., & Bartol, N. (2014, June). *Supply chain risk management practices for federal information systems and organizations.* NIST Special Publication 800-161. Retrieved September 1, 2014, from http://csrc.nist.gov/publications/drafts/800-161/sp800_161_2nd_draft. pdf.

Burgess, C., & Power, R. (2010, July 6). *How to avoid intellectual property theft.* Retrieved September 1, 2014, from CIO: http://www.cio.com/ article/2445646/security0/how-to-avoid-intellectual-property-theft.html.

Business Continuity Institute. (2013). *5th annual survey on supply chain resilience 2013.* Retrieved 2014, from http://www.thebci.org/index.php/supply-chain-continuity/cat_view/24-supply-chain-continuity/33-supply-chain-continuity/140-bci-resources.

CapGemini. (2013). *Operational excellence through digital in manufacturing industries.* CapGemini Consulting. Retrieved August 8, 2014, from http:// www.capgemini.com/resource-file-access/resource/pdf/operational_ excellence_goes_digital_29_07_final.pdf.

CISCO. (2014). *CISCO 2014 Midyear Security Report.* CISCO. Retrieved August 29, 2014.

CSIS. (2014). *Net losses: Estimating the global cost of cybercrime.* Retrieved July 17, 2014, from http://csis.org/files/attachments/140609_rp_economic_ impact_cybercrime_report.pdf.

DFARS Subpart 204.73. (2013, November 18). Safeguarding unclassified controlled technical information. United States Government. Retrieved August 12, 2014, from http://www.acq.osd.mil/dpap/dars/dfars/html/ current/204_73.htm#204.7303.

DFARS Subpart 239.73. (2013, November 18). Requirements for information relating to supply chain risk. November. Retrieved August 12, 2014, from http://www.acq.osd.mil/dpap/dars/dfars/html/current/239_73.htm.

DHS. (2014). *National cybersecurity workforce framework.* Retrieved from Department of Homeland Security, National Initiative for Cybersecurity Careers and Studies: http://niccs.us-cert.gov/training/ national-cybersecurity-workforce-framework.

Eadicicco, L. (2013, January 28). *Google CEO says supply shortages are a 'priority' for the Nexus team.* Retrieved from International Business Times: http://

www.ibtimes.com/nexus-4-sold-out-again-us-google-ceo-says-supply-shortages-are-priority-nexus-team-1042598.

Friedman, T. (2005). *The world is flat: A brief history of the twenty-first century.* New York: Farrar, Straus and Giroux.

Gartner. (2014, March 24). *Gartner says a thirty-fold increase in internet-connected physical devices by 2020 will significantly alter how the supply chain operates.* Retrieved September 2, 2014, from Gartner: http://www.gartner.com/newsroom/id/2688717.

Gharibjanian, V. (2014, April). *Billions served (in secret): How their mobile supply chains give Apple and Samsung an edge.* Retrieved August 29, 2014, from Endeavor Partners: http://endeavourpartners.net/billions-served-in-secret-how-their-mobile-supply-chains-give-apple-and-samsung-an-edge/.

Hagel, C., & Tangerlini, D. (2014). *Improving cybersecurity through resilience and acqusition—Final Report of the Department of Defense and General Services Administration.* Retrieved August 12, 2014, from https://acc.dau.mil/adl/en-US/694372/file/75816/IMPROVING_CYBERSECURITY_AND_RESILIENCE_THROUGH_ACQUISITION.pdf.

Hyer, K. (2014, January 27). *Global smartphone shipments reach a record 990 million units.* Retrieved from Strategy Analytics.

ICS-CERT. (2014). *Industrial control systems cyber emergency response team.* Retrieved September 3, 2014, from Department of Homeland Security: https://ics-cert.us-cert.gov/content/cyber-threat-source-descriptions.

IDC. (2014, January 27). *Worldwide smartphone shipments top one billion units for the first time, according to IDC.* Retrieved August 8, 2014, from IDC: http://www.idc.com/getdoc.jsp?containerId=prUS24645514.

IRM. (2014). *Cyber risk and cyber risk management.* Retrieved September 1, 2014, from The Institute of Risk Management: http://www.theirm.org/knowledge-and-resources/thought-leadership/cyber-risk/.

Kontzer, T. (2014, August 29). *Are C-Level execs disparaging CISOs?* Retrieved September 2, 2014, from BaseLine: http://www.baselinemag.com/careers/slideshows/are-c-level-execs-disparaging-cisos.html?kc=BLBLBEMNL09022014STR1&dni=162284743&rni=24846762.

Machina. (2014, March 27). *New ranking from Machina Research reveals the top global connected car manufacturers.* Retrieved August 2014, from Machina Research: https://machinaresearch.com/news/press-release-new-ranking-from-machina-research-reveals-the-top-global-connected-car-manufacturers/.

MSU. (2014). *Supply chain management.* Retrieved August 30, 2014, from Michigan State University, Broad College of Business, Department of Supply Chain Management: http://supplychain.broad.msu.edu/msscm/definition/.

Muller, J. (2013, June 26). *Connected cars: 10 tough problems automakers must solve.* Retrieved August 8, 2014, from Forbes: http://www.forbes.com/sites/

joannmuller/2013/06/26/connected-cars-10-tough-problems-automakers-must-solve/.

OECD. (2010, May). *Imports: improving productivity and competitiveness.* Retrieved June 22, 2014, from Organisation for Cooperation and Economic Competitiveness: http://www.oecd.org/trade/importsimprovi ngproductivityandcompetitiveness.htm.

Pagliery, J. (2014, June 2). *Your car is a giant computer—and it can be hacked.* Retrieved August 8, 2014, from CNN Money: http://money.cnn.com/2014/06/01/technology/security/car-hack/.

Perlroth, N. (2011, December 21). Hacked Chamber of Commerce opposed cybersecurity law. *New York Times.* Retrieved August 31, 2014, from http://bits.blogs.nytimes.com/2011/12/21/hacked-chamber-of-commerce-opposed-cybersecurity-law/?_php=true&_type=blogs&_r=0.

Protalinski, E. (2012, July 10). *NSA: Cybercrime is 'the greatest transfer of wealth in history.'* Retrieved May 23, 2014, from ZD Net: http://www.zdnet.com/nsa-cybercrime-is-the-greatest-transfer-of-wealth-in-history-7000000598/.

Risk Based Security. (2014). *Data breach quickview: Data breach trends in the first quarter of 2014.* Risk Based Security. Retrieved June 12, 2014, from https://www.riskbasedsecurity.com/2014/05/first-quarter-2014-exposes-176-million-records-troubling-trend-of-larger-more-severe-data-breaches-continues/.

Rosenblatt, S. (2013, August 2). *Car hacking code released at Defcon.* Retrieved August 8, 2014, from C|Net: http://www.cnet.com/news/car-hacking-code-released-at-defcon/.

SAFEGUARDING UNCLASSIFIED CONTROLLED TECHNICAL INFORMATION. (n.d.). *DFARS.* Retrieved August 12, 2014.

Simchi-Levi, D., Kyratzoglou, I., & Vassiliadis, C. (2013). *Supply chain and risk management.* MIT. Retrieved September 1, 2014.

Supply Chain. (n.d.). Retrieved August 30, 2014, from Wikipedia: http://en.wikipedia.org/wiki/Supply_chain.

Symantec. (2013). *Symantec Intelligence Report.* Symantec. Retrieved September 2, 2014.

Womack, J. P., Jones, D. T., & Roos, D. (1990). *The machine that changed the world.* New York: The Free Press, Simon & Schuster, Inc.

Yadron, D., Ziobro, P., & Levinson, C. (2014, January 29). Target hackers used stolen vendor credentials. *Wall Street Journal.* Retrieved July 25, 2014, from http://online.wsj.com/news/articles/SB100014240527023039 73704579350722480135220.

Chapter 2

Cybersecurity and the Internet of Things

JUSTIN ZEEFE

No [battle] plan survives contact with the enemy.

—Helmuth Karl Bernhard Graf von Moltke

Introduction

War has historically been waged for a common list of reasons—land, resources, theology—but among the lesser discussed reasons are wars over standards. A prime example of a standards war was the Video-tape Format War (1971–1988), which ended when VCR vanquished Betamax. Although no blood was spilt, it was nevertheless a war rife with pitched and strategic efforts by enemies seeking to capture the marketplace at the expense of the other. Ultimately, the market decided that the two-hour recording time that VHS offered was more important than the higher quality, yet shorter quantity, that Betamax cassettes held. The Betamax manufacturer's (Sony) plan to succeed with a superior quality product did not survive VHS's ability to deliver what the market really wanted, and by the time Sony adjusted their strategy, VHS had won the war (Owen, 1995).

As important as the spoils were—control over the rapidly growing home video market—this situation was ultimately a simple war
with few consequences beyond market control. A home could only
have so many video players and so the market had a theoretical cap;
there were only a handful of major industry players, and the issue
of security was absent from consideration. Expressing the concern
that videocassette players could be manipulated to wreak havoc upon
national critical infrastructure or to invade the privacy and security
of those who bought them would have been a stretch even for the
most dedicated conspiracy theorist.

If the battle for home video dominance was simple, at the other
end of the scale is the difficult and ongoing standards war of the
Internet of Things (IoT). The IoT, simply put, is the ad hoc network
created by the billions of 'smart' devices that communicate with one
another for myriad purposes. A particularly simple definition for IoT
is "the network of physical objects that contain embedded technology
to communicate and sense or interact with their internal states or
the external environment" (Biscotti & Skorupa, 2014). This network,
ranging from the simple (light bulbs controlled over the Internet) to
the sensitive (security systems or automobile command systems), is
rapidly expanding. Cisco Systems estimates that 50 billion [autono-
mous] devices and objects will be connected to the Internet by 2020
(Evans, 2011). The International Data Corporation (IDC) expects IoT
technology and services spending to generate global revenues of $4.8
trillion in 2012 and $8.9 trillion by 2020, growing at a compound
annual rate of 7.9% (International Data Corporation, 2014).

If that is the definition of the IoT, it is also important to define
'standard.' And in this context of IoT, standard has several meanings.
The first is the software/hardware system which controls the device;
some devices are programmed in Linux, others in HTTP, Android,
or one of a multitude of proprietary coding languages. The second
meaning for 'standard' is a uniform methodology applied to the soft-
ware/hardware combination to address security issues. There are generally accepted concepts for security standards in the Information
Technology space, but there is no agreement among the developers
of IoT-enabled devices, particularly those which are 'smart' variants

of previously 'dumb' technology (microwaves, toys, cars) for implementation or enforcement. This secondary type of standard (security) was not a factor in the video format war, and having both standards simultaneously in flux in a market of potentially billions of devices is what makes for a dangerous mix.

The war to dominate the IoT standard is as nuanced and critical as the war between VHS and Betamax was not—the only standard at issue in the earlier war was format; there were no security concerns. With IoT there are innumerable developers seeking to design/influence the programming standard, and there is virtually no limit to the type (or number) of machines that may be connected to the IoT. These products are often rushed to market with as expedient a programming language as can be placed into the device and without consideration to future vulnerabilities. The critical element of this battle to standardize the IoT is the issue of security, and the heart of security is the issue of vulnerability.

Increasing the number of connected devices proportionately increases the available attack surface for malicious actors, and the more competing programming standards there are, and the fewer agreed-upon security standards, the easier it is for an attacker to find and exploit vulnerabilities. Some of the devices coming together under the IoT banner are by themselves benign—few hackers are going to target your Internet-enabled Crock-Pot with the nefarious goal of ruining your stew. But some of the potential attacks are much less benign. When a lack of standards (programming and security) allows a hacker to leapfrog from your Internet-enabled refrigerator to your alarm system or from your mobile phone to your smart watch to your automobile's braking system, the level of potential damage grows significantly. It is not too far-fetched to imagine a hacker targeting an employee of a critical infrastructure, such as a power plant, by compromising the worker's home climate control system and using this to compromise his/her phone, which in turn will be programmed to attack any open node at the workplace.

Assuredly, as with all wars over standards, victors will emerge. It may be a patchwork alliance of interested parties who agree on standards rather than an industry leader, or a truce may ultimately be mandated or negotiated through legislation (possibly as a result of a series of significant attacks). Regardless of how the battles wage, it may take years before the fighting ends. In the intervening time, the nature and scope of the vulnerabilities will be dramatic.

But there are elements of IoT devices that, unlike traditional IT infrastructure and networks, cannot be addressed through logical (programming) and security standards regardless of how they are reached. In particular, there is no way to control physical access to these devices when by their very purpose they are in your pocket, on your wrist, or plugged into your wall. At present, it is not possible to eliminate hacking vulnerabilities on a device completely within the physical control of someone who means to do damage. Further, the sheer volume of data which these devices collect can also, in the aggregate, violate normally accepted standards of privacy (though admittedly, expectations of privacy are changing in our interconnected world).

This chapter explores several specific security challenges facing the IoT which are and will remain critical pressure points. In addition, it examines the safety issues from both logical and physical perspectives as well as outlining the current state of the effort to address this growing threat by addressing the lack of standards, as it is being addressed by manufacturers, industry groups, and regulatory bodies (including legislatures and international efforts).

Fundamental Issue Unique to the Internet of Things

Use of IoT-connected devices to launch attacks shifted from theory to reality in December 2013, when Proofpoint, a cybersecurity firm, detected what likely was the first exploit of an IoT-enabled 'smart' appliance. They discovered that between December 2013 and January 2014, hackers used the computing power of an online refrigerator along with approximately 100,000 other devices, to send 750,000 malicious e-mails (capable of enabling attacks through harmful links or other mechanisms) (Proofpoint, Inc., 2014). Proofpoint deduced that smart appliances (including televisions, entertainment systems, and home networking routers) were responsible for more than 25% of the malicious e-mails when they determined that the IP addresses belonged to appliances rather than traditional computers or devices. These 'smart' devices are expected to produce an increasing amount of malicious attacks, and it is only a matter of time before they are used as conduits for compromising additional devices connected via the IoT. Imagine, for example, a malicious actor hacking into your vehicle through its satellite radio or another Internet-enabled system, instructing it to identify its location and unlock/start, or worse—perhaps modifying the code to activate the vehicle's kill switch (or brakes, if it has any type of auto-braking capability) when it reaches 50 miles per hour.

Cybersecurity Threats that Challenge the Internet of Things

The aforementioned attack on a car's brake system might sound alarmist, but in 2013, the Defense Advanced Research Projects Agency (DARPA) spent $80,000 to fund a study to research just this sort of hack. Two researchers, Charlie Miller and Chris Valasek, positively demonstrated, in a highly technical 86-page report, the ability to hack the command and control of several modern-day vehicles in order to override the vehicle's brakes, steering, and acceleration (Miller & Valasek, 2012). Although most major car manufacturers are now aware of the threat and have hired technologists and programmers to address security flaws, it is a lopsided war in which the manufacturers cannot afford even one lost battle.

Another equally sobering threat vector is that of the rapidly increasing number of connected medical devices. While enabling doctors to remotely access insulin pumps and pacemakers increases medical community knowledge and provides a convenience to both doctor and patient, it creates an avenue for a particularly malicious attack. By way of example, an insulin pump has already been hacked in a laboratory environment; this led the FDA to issue a warning document outlining their concern and recommending steps to be taken by manufacturers (U.S. Food and Drug Administration, 2013).

Research intended to demonstrate the scary world of IoT frequently focuses on the safety threats. There have been a number of articles on hackers who have identified vulnerabilities in the U.S. Transportation and Safety Administration's (TSA) airport equipment, and in traffic control systems, as well as baby monitors, satellite ground terminals, and home security systems, to name a few (Greenberg, 2012; Hill, 2014; Lawrence, 2014). While it is true that these vectors are particularly concerning, they are not likely to comprise the bulk of the attacks facing the IoT. Most attacks are likely to be fashioned for financial gain, industrial espionage, or for malicious reasons with a design on causing financial, rather than physical, damage. In order to address vulnerabilities and probabilities of attack, however, it is not as important to understand the attacker's motivation as it is weaknesses in the system that allow malicious actors to open a channel for attack.

Failure to Patch

Users of Adobe or Java are well familiar with the regular, often weekly, prompts to update their software. Since Java 7 was released in 2011, there have been 67 updates; an average of slightly more than 22 a year (Oracle, 2014). These updates are normally patches (repairs) to recently discovered security vulnerabilities. Such vulnerabilities are found through a number of ways, including programmer-sponsored research and from a community of programmers who are encouraged to report vulnerability findings. Coding vulnerabilities are generally assigned a score according to the Common Vulnerability Scoring System (CVSS)—catalogued in the National Vulnerability Database and run by the National Institute of Standards and Technology (NIST, 2014). In fact, the market for identifying/reporting vulnerabilities is strong; there are entire secondary markets where programmers can sell their discoveries, which are then packaged and resold to the program's designer.

In contrast to dedicated software companies like Adobe (which have entire teams dedicated to patching or updating the software whenever a vulnerability is discovered or exploited), there is little incentive for the refrigerator manufacturer to monitor for exploits, hire a developer to repair the exploit, and push updates. This anticipated failure to update software to defeat bugs or vulnerabilities as they are uncovered—and there are always holes in the code—extends to most devices across the IoT landscape. Further, as most developers use either proprietary code or off-the-shelf freeware for programming their devices (diversity of programming standard), it will not be extraordinarily challenging for dedicated attackers, or even 'script kiddies' (amateur hackers following step-by-step guides found online) to find holes and cause damage (either by exploiting the vulnerability or by selling it to someone with malicious intent).

Even for those IoT-enabled devices which do on occasion push updates, a recent study revealed that 60% of those updates (and the software they replaced) were unencrypted during transmission from the provider as well as natively on the device (Hewlett-Packard, 2014). Practically speaking, this means that an interested party with a minimal level of technical experience could intercept, modify, and/or replace the software intended to operate an IoT-enabled device. This could be done to modify the controls of the device for which the software was modified, or, as discussed in the following section, it could enslave the device and use it to send malicious code or commands to other devices connected on the same network. In the already-mentioned case of a Crock-Pot, this is an annoyance—not a real threat. However, when applied to over-the-air updates to your automobile's command/control system, instructing it to identify its location and unlock/start or worse, modifying the code to activate the vehicle's kill switch (or brakes, if it has any type of auto-braking capability) is a serious matter.

Threat Vector Hopping

Regardless of the chosen attack vector, a compromised device can have a cascading effect in and on IT infrastructure. If, for example, our Crock-Pot is attacked because it represents a weak link, it may in turn be programmed to attack the device that monitors it (your phone perhaps) or to infiltrate the home router. Which type of frequency a device uses may also constitute a threat. For instance, an attack on Wi-Fi requires a different capability than an attack on Bluetooth—or what is now likely to be Bluetooth Low Energy (BLE)—but the practical effect is the same. It is not a one-to-one ratio of system surface to threat surface; as more devices become interconnected, the threat surface increases at a near-exponential rate.

The IoT is a system of conveniences, and so it makes sense that businesses will embrace many of the capabilities borne of the IoT; for example, automated monitoring/control of heating, ventilation, and air conditioning (HVAC) systems. Such a system opens an easy attack vector for an interested party to gain remote, and often persistent, access to systems of genuine interest to malicious actors. Security systems are also vulnerable; not only are the systems often Wi-Fi enabled, but the connection between the system and the means by which it contacts authorities can also be Voice Over IP (VoIP), and thus compromised. Although the capacity to remotely infect a system is real, as is the ability to cause system vulnerabilities to in turn affect other systems, there is often no need to find remote entry points into these systems when one maintains persistent or even periodic physical access, whether direct or indirect.

Data Privacy and Aggregation

Although this chapter does not focus on the positive impacts that the IoT has on society, there are many: saving electricity by intelligently monitoring utility usage, real-time monitoring of one's biometrics, and yes, the ability to control a Crock-Pot from across an ocean. But to efficiently perform many of these actions, a scaled IoT depends on a great deal of aggregated data from which to draw its calculations. The concept of data privacy, simply put, is the right of the originator of the information to control, to a reasonable degree, the dissemination of the collected data. Aggregation is the collection of those data into larger piles, stored on a known server somewhere, on a device, or somewhere in the nebulous cloud; a term often referred to as data warehousing (Chowdhery, 2013). Turning to our trusty crockpot, we discover that it records how many hours it has been used over periods of time and also when it was turned on/off. Because it can be controlled remotely, there is no need for the crockpot to store this usage data locally or if it is stored locally, it is also shared with the manufacturer. The same will be true of the more sensitive technologies and personal identity information (PII)—in addition to the question of who owns the aggregated data is the issue of its protection from dissemination or compromise (Liu, Gong, & Xing, 2014).

Here, the standard is not only one of how the data is collected, but also how it is transmitted (encrypted, sent together, or stripped of PII?), and how it is stored in the cloud (the most likely place it will be housed). Complicating this issue is the matter of privacy (Who owns the data?) and of course, the level of security (both logical and physical) applied to the servers on which the data reside (Huntington, 2009).

Physical Security

On a typical IT infrastructure, access to sensitive servers and other vulnerable equipment is protected not only through software features (logical security), but also through restricted physical access. More than a few studies have been written on the increasing need for both logical and physical security and the interaction between the two. It is the almost total lack of physical protection of the infrastructure that differentiates IoT (and the cloud in which the data are stored) from traditional IT. Even if operational security (OPSEC) standards were agreed upon, there is no way to control physical access to these devices when they are in a home or otherwise so easily accessible. Insecure programming, coupled with the inability to guard the access to the devices themselves, provide ample access and opportunity for someone with malicious intent to burrow their way into the system by finding and exploiting vulnerabilities; this includes physical manipulation or tampering of the system.

Even supposing that the problems of programming and security standards were addressed by the makers of IoT-enabled devices, the issue of physical access to the device cannot be solved through a system of standards. By their very nature, these devices are physically accessible to the end users with little-to-no means to prevent interference.

Simply put, a quasi-autonomous vehicle or smart thermostat (which are already on the market) is (in theory) much easier to take apart, study, and reprogram than is the command and control for a power plant. Theoretical solutions have been offered, the most secure of which is to provide end-to-end encryption built directly into the chips (as distinct from only traffic between the devices over the Internet) which cannot be modified (Bohan & Xu, 2013). Still, as the nascent IoT industry has not gathered around a set of standards, the threat of attack from a physical vector is real and is likely to remain so for the foreseeable future.

Laws and Policies Relevant to Standardization of the Internet of Things

Unlike the videocassette format war, the battle to dominate IoT standards has widespread ramifications, as previously discussed. It is no secret that the expanding surface area of the IoT presents increased opportunity for malicious exploits. In an effort to address the vulnerabilities caused by the lack of standardization, several international non-governmental groups have formed to address the issue. Efforts have also sprung up within the industry; as in a war with many factions, it is only natural that groups will band together to fight under a common banner. And finally, governments have recognized the threats posed by IoT and are (slowly) researching and taking first steps toward legislation of the issue and hardening vulnerable systems.

Non-governmental Organizational Standard Efforts

To that end, several concerned bodies have formed for the purpose of addressing the issues created by the disparate standards. Some of these efforts focus on security standardization (and the vulnerabilities created by a lack thereof) and others address the efforts from a need to create a programming standard. Of these efforts, three influential organizations bear mention.

1. The Open Web Application Security Project (OWASP), formed in 2001, describes itself as "an open community dedicated to enabling organizations to conceive, develop, acquire, operate, and maintain applications that can be trusted" (Open Web Application Security Project, 2014). One of their ongoing projects is to maintain a top-10 list of most pressing issues for a variety of important, timely subjects—including the IoT. Through their wiki-style website they maintain updated mitigation strategies to decrease attack surface and concepts for addressing what they have identified as the most pressing issues. As of September 2014, OWASP identified the following 10 issues as the most pressing:

   - Insecure Web Interface.

   - Insufficient Authentication/Authorization.

   - Insecure Network Services.

   - Lack of Transport Encryption.

   - Privacy Concerns.

   - Insecure Cloud Interface.

   - Insecure Mobile Interface.

   - Insufficient Security Configurability.

   - Insecure Software/Firmware.

   - Poor Physical Security.

   (Open Web Application Security Project, 2014)

   OWASP regularly sponsors hacking and security vulnerability ("Capture the Flag" style) contests, and is regularly considered a benchmark among IT professionals for issues to address within a corporate IT structure.

2. Perhaps the very definition of an international effort,
    the United Nations' International Telecommunications
    Union formed the Internet of Things Global Standards
    Initiative (GSI) with the purpose of "provide[ing]
    a visible single location for information on and
    development of IoT standards, these being the detailed
    standards necessary for IoT deployment and to give
    service providers the means to offer the wide range of
    services expected from the IoT. In collaboration with
    other bodies, IoT-GSI harmonizes different approaches
    to the IoT architecture worldwide" (United Nations
    International Telecommunications Union, 2013). As
    of late 2014, the GSI had held nine formal conferences
    to discuss the subject; their aim is not to set standards,
    but to suggest standards to existing organizations.

3. The International Organization for Standardization,
    populated by standards professionals from the various
    member states, provides codified standards for such
    things as food safety, quality management, and
    information technology (International Standards
    Organization, 2013). The ISO, in coordination
    with the Swiss-based International Electrotechnical
    Commission (IEC), created a set of International
    Information Security Standards (IISS). Of relevancy
    when it comes to the IoT is standard ISO/IISS/IEC
    27001:2013, which "specifies the requirements for
    establishing, implementing, maintaining and continually
    improving an information security management system
    within the context of the organization. It also includes
    requirements for the assessment and treatment of
    information security risks tailored to the needs of the
    organization" (International Standards Organization,
    2013).
         The ISO/IEC 27001:2013 specifies 114 controls
    in 14 groups:

- Information security policies.

- How information security is organized.

- Human resources security—controls that are applied before, during, or after employment.

- Asset management.

- Access controls and managing user access.

- Cryptographic technology.

- Physical security of the organization's sites and equipment.

- Operational security.

- Secure communications and data transfer.

- Secure acquisition, development, and support of information systems.

- Security for suppliers and third parties.

- Incident management.

- Business continuity/disaster recovery (to the extent that it affects information security).

- Compliance—with internal requirements, such as policies, and with external requirements, such as laws.

(International Standards Organization, 2013)

Meeting the ISO/IEC standard enables organizations to proclaim that their information security management system (ISMS) is ISO compliant, which fosters a level of transparency and predictability when conducting business or working to secure an ISMS.

Industry Standard Efforts

Google's decision to purchase Nest, an IoT-enabled thermostat, in early 2013 surprised some in the IT world in large part because Google paid $3.2 billion for the company. It was not long before industry analysts understood Google's game plan: their purchase was more about jump-starting a move to dominate the IoT than anything else. By purchasing one of the largest players in the game, Google acquired a massive amount of intellectual capital (in both proprietary data and personnel). It did not take long for Google to create the Thread Group, led by their Nest Labs (along with Samsung, Freescale Semiconductor, Silicon Labs, and others) with a goal of setting the industry standard and dominating the market—a skill not beyond Google's reach.

Many other Fortune 500 companies have begun taking the IoT standards issue seriously and quickly concluded that working together (on certain standards aspects) is in their collective interest. Groups such as the Open Interconnect Consortium (OIC), formed only in mid-2014, are led by (among others) Intel, Dell, Samsung, and Broadcom. OIC's focus is on security through common interfaces and languages. The members of the OIC have pledged to pool their intellectual capital to secure their vulnerabilities and dominate as much of the market as possible.

The Industrial Internet Consortium (IIC) is another of the major industry groups. Formed only in early 2014, IIC boasts more than 50 industry leaders, including AT&T, Intel, Cisco Systems, and IBM. The IIC seeks to "deliver best practices, reference architectures, case studies, and standards requirements to ease deployment of connected technologies" and to "Influence the global development standards process for Internet and industrial systems" (Industrial Internet Consortium, 2014).

Although some will argue strongly that industry can self-regulate, others will argue that their self-regulation may subjugate public good in lieu of profit. Further, and perhaps more critically, it may be necessary for government to be involved from a national security perspective.

United States Government Standard Efforts

Although government has a vested interest in encouraging economic growth (and thus encouraging standards to coalesce), the more
important issues that encourage either new legislation or application
of existing laws will be national security concerns (particularly critical infrastructure vulnerability) and the fundamental right to privacy.
While efforts to legislate this issue are still in their infancy, several
governments have recognized and addressed the issue, even if only to
acknowledge aloud that it must eventually be addressed.

The United States, the IoT as distinct from general cybersecurity concerns has not yet been specifically broached, but there have
been efforts to legislate cybersecurity. To understand how these efforts
affect the IoT it is helpful to explore the background of the effort.
The most well-known of these is the Cyber Intelligence Sharing and
Protection Act (CISPA), which has undergone several iterations in
both the U.S. House and Senate, first in 2011 and most recently in
2014 (when it failed to pass the Senate) (United States Congress,
2011–2014). The debate over the merits of the bill was, and continues
to be, heated; many privacy advocates argue that the law can too easily be used to violate individual freedoms, and industry largely prefers
to self-regulate. Thus far, however, this law has failed to materialize.

In part a result of frustration with congressional stalling on
cybersecurity law, in February 2013, President Obama issued Executive Order (EO) 13636, which establishes voluntary guidelines for
multiple areas of concern surrounding cybersecurity (Obama, 2013).
The EO covers cybersecurity information sharing (how industry and
government can share information to protect resources), privacy and
civil liberties protections, coordination of improvements to the critical
infrastructure cybersecurity, and most relevant to this chapter, the EO
designates the U.S. National Institute of Standards and Technology
(NIST) to develop a Cybersecurity Framework.

According to EO 13636, the goal of the framework is to provide a "prioritized, flexible, repeatable, performance-based, and cost-
effective approach" to help those organizations that deal with critical

infrastructure services to manage risk surrounding cybersecurity. Most critically, the EO mandates that the framework shall:

> [I]nclude a set of standards, methodologies, procedures, and processes that align policy, business, and technological approaches to address cyber risks. The Cybersecurity Framework shall incorporate voluntary consensus standards and industry best practices to the fullest extent possible. The Cybersecurity Framework shall be consistent with voluntary international standards when such international standards will advance the objectives of this order, and shall meet the requirements of the National Institute of Standards and Technology Act. (Executive Order 13636)

In October 2013, and prior to the 240 day deadline provided by EO 13636, NIST published its Preliminary Cybersecurity Framework. The framework lays out five 'cores': identify, protect, detect, respond, and recover. Each core has several subcomponents, which detail the effort an organization must undertake to affect sound cybersecurity policy. However, it is a tenuous claim that the framework addresses the problems of the IoT. Of the five cores, only the first two—identify and protect—are relevant to the IoT, and these two categories have thus far not driven any conversation about standards within the IoT.

That is not to say NIST is not aware of, or focused on, the issue of standards surrounding IoT. In August 2014, NIST sponsored the first in-person meeting of the Cyber-Physical Systems Public Working Group (CPS PWG). NIST defines Cyber-Physical Systems (CPS) as "smart systems, in which essential properties and functionalities emerge from the networked interaction of cyber technologies—both hardware and software—co-engineered with physical systems" (NIST CPS PWG, 2014). While several researchers distinguish between CPS and IoT (although they do not agree on the distinctions), it is almost certain that the working group's determinations will cover those devices commonly referred to as part of the IoT.

The CPS PWG has five subgroups—reference architecture, use cases, timing, cybersecurity, and data interoperability. Of particular interest in regard to standardization is data interoperability. The group's website explains that it will "address the simplification and streamlining of cross-domain data interactions by developing a sound underlying framework and standards base for CPS data interoperability, in part by developing an inventory of relevant existing practices and standards" (National Institute of Standards and Technology, 2014). It remains to be seen whether the CPS PWG's recommendations are in alignment with other organizations seeking to suggest standards, and despite NIST being a U.S. government organization, its recommendations could nevertheless conflict with the legislative (and executive) mandates previously discussed.

IoT Workforce Trends

With the number of devices and companies involved in IoT expected to swell to $8.9 trillion by 2020, the largest need in the workforce will likely be for developers and programmers. Although it is likely that most companies will rally around several interoperable standards, ideally with a similar security infrastructure, there are still not enough developers to meet current needs. A recent technical whitepaper estimates a need for 3.4 million IoT developers by 2020; a significant increase from the estimated 300,000 presently in the field (VisionMobile, 2014). Growth within the IT security sector must also grow to match the demand, and the wide open landscape is likely to be too inviting for malicious actors to ignore. Due to the relative infancy of the field, keeping abreast of IoT means networking and knowledge of new issues and capabilities. Diego Tamburini, a technology futurist with Autodesk, compared the IoT with running a triathlon; although it is considered a single event, there are multiple disciplines which tomorrow's programmer and security professional must understand (physical/logical security, programming, etc.) to function as an IoT professional (Platt, 2014). For the cybersecurity professional considering a future in IoT, the need is real, immediate, and only projected to grow larger.

Recommendations for Best Practices

The optic through which one views the advent of IoT will determine best practices, which are discipline-specific. For example, the hardware company seeking to drive the standard will be less focused on the security of their devices as regards their use to conduct man-in-the-middle attacks, and more focused on the ability of the products to interact with other products the intended user has or will likely want. Software programmers, however, will focus on learning as many of the program languages as possible so as to increase their employment opportunities, and organizations seeking to influence the standard (from a non-profit perspective) will focus on making recommendations which in the long-term will make the IoT more secure and adaptable for society-at-large.

The more interesting concerns belong to the cybersecurity expert whose opinion is sought on how to incorporate IoT devices into their workspace. Cybersecurity professionals will nevertheless be responsible for navigating the changing landscape of the IoT and its effects on security, regardless of the state of standardization. This professional must balance the need for security with the desire for convenience and expediency and maybe most of all, a lack of understanding by management who do not understand the general threat that unsecured systems present. Above all, security experts should remain abreast of developments in the field, from methodology to decrease the threat surface to discussions of particularly vulnerable systems and the contra-indications (to borrow an apt term from medicine) of pairing particular systems together. A smart thermostat in the office may seem like a good idea, but it only takes one enterprising hacker figuring out how to jump from an employee's personal system to the network, if for example this employee logged into the device from multiple systems.

Until, and even after, the eventual standardization across IoT devices has come to pass, cybersecurity professionals must remain vigilant and knowledgeable about developments in the field, through self-education and, unfortunately, also through negative examples set by others who suffer breaches—and add IoT to the ever-growing list of threat vectors which malicious actors will seek to exploit.

Conclusion

Eventually—and likely driven by the market more than by efforts to standardize—the IoT will pervade its way into society and daily life. There is no shortage of articles, research papers, or predictions for the rapidly growing IoT, on every subject from security to job opportunities to standardization efforts. From the explosive number of interconnected devices expected to come online before 2020, to the number of developers expected to work in the field, to the efforts of many international and not-for-profit organizations which seek to suggest standards, the IoT is undoubtedly a significant technological battlefield. As so often is the case with wars between multiple players, the standards war will likely see a multitude of strategies, continued efforts by non-combatants to set the rules, and formation of alliances before the dust settles. During this time, and hopefully to a diminished degree thereafter, there are likely to be serious security breaches resulting in significant costs, both financial and those less quantifiable (privacy, personal identity, etc.). These breaches will likely drive an increased urgency to repair the holes that caused the damage. Much like the standard Internet we all use today, the IoT will grow as it is cultured, but will remain a bit wild. The innovations and imaginations that create technologies and unpredicted innovations possible and the imaginations that find and exploit the holes do not necessarily intend to work together, but ultimately they often do.

Sources of Further Information

Although a number of books have been published on the IoT, which focus on many of the aforementioned subjects, the speed with which IoT standards, regulations, and controls develop demands that interested parties turn to the Internet as their primary source of current information. In fact, the subject is so nascent that even the websites claiming to compile resources for IoT subject matter are recently created and/or incomplete. Among the several worth noting are:

- Internet of Things Toolkit (http://postscapes.com/internet-of-things-resources/).

- Internet of Things (Europe) (http://www.internet-of-things.eu/resources).

- Internet of Things Architecture (http://www.iot-a.eu/public).

- Internet of Things Resources (http://www.internet-of-things.ws/).

- IoT World (http://www.iotworld.com/).

There are many other self-proclaimed guides to the IoT available as a result of a basic Internet search. Many of these guides are sponsored by companies pushing a specific agenda, so care must be taken and sources considered before using found information to inform decisions.

References

Biscotti, F., & Skorupa, J. (2014). *The impact of the internet of things on data centers.* Gartner Research. Retrieved September 18, 2014, from https://www.gartner.com/doc/2672920.

Bohan, Z., & Xu, W. (2013, August 23). Encryption node design in internet of things based on fingerprint features and CC2530. *2013 IEEE and Internet of Things,* pp. 1454–1457.

Chowdhery, A. (2013). *Privacy-preserving data-aggregation for internet-of-things in smart grid.* Stanford: Stanford University. Retrieved September 2014, from http://web.stanford.edu/class/ee392n/lecture/may6/MS_May6.pdf.

Evans, D. (2011). *The internet of things: How the next evolution of the internet is changing everything.* Cisco Internet Business Solutions Group. Retrieved September 20, 2014, from http://www.cisco.com/web/about/ac79/docs/innov/IoT_IBSG_0411FINAL.pdf.

Greenberg, A. (2012). *Next-gen air traffic control vulnerable to hackers spoofing planes out of thin air.* Forbes Magazine. Retrieved September 10, 2014, from http://www.forbes.com/sites/andygreenberg/2012/07/25/next-gen-air-traffic-control-vulnerable-to-hackers-spoofing-planes-out-of-thin-air/.

Hewlett-Packard. (2014). *HP study reveals 70 percent of internet of things devices vulnerable to attack.* Retrieved September 20, 2014, from http://www8. hp.com/us/en/hp-news/press-release.html?id=1744676.

Hill, K. (2014). *Baby monitor hacker still terrorizing babies and their parents.* Forbes Magazine. Retrieved September 19, 2014, from http://www. forbes.com/sites/kashmirhill/2014/04/29/baby-monitor-hacker-still-terrorizing-babies-and-their-parents/.

Huntington, G. (2009). *Integrating the two worlds of physical and logical security.* Huntington Ventures Ltd. Retrieved September 12, 2014, from http://www.authenticationworld.com/Papers/IntegratingtheTwoWorldsofPhysi calandLogical%20Security.pdf.

Industrial Internet Consortium. (2014, August). *Industrial Internet Consortium—Home.* Retrieved September 2014, from Industrial Internet Consortium: http://www.industrialinternetconsortium.org/.

International Data Corporation. (2014). *Worldwide internet of things spending by vertical market 2014–2017 forecast.* International Data Corporation. Retrieved September 16, 2014, from http://www.idc.com/getdoc. jsp?containerId=prUS24671614.

International Standards Organization. (2013). *ISO/IEC 27001.* International Standards Organization. Retrieved September 19, 2014, from http:// www.iso.org/iso/catalogue_detail?csnumber=54534.

Lawrence, D. (2014). *TSA checkpoints vulnerable to hacks through backdoors.* Bloomberg Businessweek. Retrieved September 10, 2014, from http://www.businessweek.com/articles/2014-08-07/tsa-checkpoints-vulnerable-to-hacks-through-backdoors.

Liu, Y., Gong, X., & Xing, C. (2014). A novel trust-based secure data aggregation. *The 9th International Conference on Computer Science & Education.* Vancouver.

Miller, D. C., & Valasek, C. (2012). *Adventures in automotive networks and control units.* Retrieved September 19, 2014, from http://illmatics.com/ car_hacking.pdf.

National Institute for Standards and Technology. (2014, September). *NVD common vulnerability scoring system.* Retrieved September 18, 2014, from NIST national vulnerability database: http://nvd.nist.gov/cvss.cfm.

National Institute of Standards and Technology. (2014). *CPS PWG: Data interoperability.* Retrieved September 2014, from National Institute of Standards and Technology: http://www.nist.gov/cps/cpspwg_datainterop. cfm.

NIST CPS PWG. (2014, August). *NIST CPS PWG homepage.* Retrieved September 2014, from National Institute for Standards and Technology: http://www.nist.gov/cps/cps-pwg-workshop.cfm.

Obama, B. H. (2013). Executive Order 13636—Improving critical infrastructure cybersecurity. *Federal Register, 78*(33).

Open Web Application Security Project. (2014, September). *OWASP internet of things top ten project.* Retrieved Sepetember 20, 2014, from OWASP: https://www.owasp.org/index.php/OWASP_Internet_of_Things_Top_ Ten_Project#tab=OWASP_Internet_of_Things_Top_10_for_2014.

Oracle. (2014, August 10). *Java 7 Releases.* Retrieved September 11, 2014, from Oracle—Java: http://www.java.com/en/download/faq/release_dates. xml.

Owen, D. (1995). *The Betamax vs VHS format war.* Retrieved September 10, 2014, from Media College: http://www.mediacollege.com/video/format/ compare/betamax-vhs.html.

Platt, J. R. (2014, April). The internet of things: The next big thing for technology careers. *Today's Engineer.* Retrieved September 2014, from http://www.todaysengineer.org/2014/Apr/career-focus.asp.

Proofpoint, Inc. (2014). *Proofpoint uncovers internet of things (IoT) cyberattack.* Sunnyvale: Proofpoint, Inc. Retrieved September 19, 2014, from http:// investors.proofpoint.com/releasedetail.cfm?ReleaseID=819799.

U.S. Food and Drug Administration. (2013). *Cybersecurity for medical devices and hospital networks: FDA Safety Communication.* Retrieved September 19, 2014, from http://www.fda.gov/MedicalDevices/Safety/ AlertsandNotices/ucm356423.htm.

United Nations International Telecommunications Union. (2013). *Terms of Reference (IoT-GSI).* New York: United Nations. Retrieved September 10, 2014, from http://www.itu.int/en/ITU-T/gsi/iot/Documents/tor-iot-gsi.pdf.

United States Congress. (2011–2014). Cyber Intelligence Sharing and Protection Act (CISPA H.R. 3523 (112th Congress), H.R. 624 (113th Congress)). Washington, DC: United States Congress.

VisionMobile. (2014). *IoT: Breaking free from internet and things.* London: VisionMobile. Retrieved September 11, 2014, from http://www. visionmobile.com/product/iot-breaking-free-internet-things/.

Chapter 3

Cybersecurity and Social Media

Ron Carpinella

Cybersecurity is more than securing a perimeter around your digital assets. It entails a comprehensive understanding of every element that might enable penetration, interaction, and/or compromise, and that can lead to catastrophic events.

Social media, an important element of the web, has seen amazing growth in the past decade, sending its grip into every element of our social, professional, and personal lives. This chapter will review elements of social media, how its use and misuse enables threats, and the ways we can address these threats while still enjoying the fruits of social media.

Introduction

Social media as defined by Merriam-Webster is a "*form(s) of electronic communication . . . through which users create online communities to share information, ideas, personal messages, and other content*" (2014). While experts might concur with the basic definition, most of us look at social media as the new telecom; essentially it has become the preferred way to communicate between and among friends, colleagues, and even adversaries. Social media in every form has become an indispensible element of our modern world.

The Birth of Social Media

The concept of social media and its utilization on the Internet is as old as the Internet itself. While many consider the birth of social media to be Tim O'Reilly's coining of the term "Web 2.0" at the O'Reilly Media Web Conference in 2004, its origins were clearly laid out years earlier (O'Reilly, 2005). Based on the definition of social media, one should consider the progenitor of what we call the Internet today—ARPANET—as the first social media.

ARPANET, a project of the Defense Advanced Research Projects Agency, was not developed (as commonly believed) as a network for resistance to nuclear attack. Rather, it was conceived to enable collaborative research, development, and computing between scientists (Herzfeld, n.d.). In essence, this was the first social media, enabling the sharing of resources and collaboration without all of the "stupid pet tricks" we see today.

As the ARPANET evolved into the commercial Internet, many new forms of communications and early social media developed including bulletin board services (BBS), Compuserve, and Delphi Forums. As a child of a PhD in electrical engineering, I was introduced at a young age to an early form of social media via the HeathUsers Group (HUG), a seemingly benign forum by today's standards. We would often dialup, interact, and (ahem) we would share software between users.

As technologies began to evolve, and the internet started to become a truly commercial tool, companies like AOL and GEOCITIES took root. Friendster, SixDegrees, and Classmates.com, what we now consider early social media, began leading the way. While slow to be adopted, they were important early path breakers that enabled MySpace, LinkedIn, and even Facebook to become what we are familiar with today.

Fast-forward to 2014 and it is clear that the "social" Internet is ubiquitous and pervasive. We interact through applications, websites, messengers, and even "ghost" apps that share information socially (and commercially) without any conscious control by users.

Fundamental Issues Unique to Social Media

> People have really gotten comfortable not only sharing more information and different kinds, but more openly and with more people.
>
> —Mark Zuckerberg

Social media is an amazing tool, it enables us to communicate, collaborate, and share in ways no one would have imagined a generation ago. The use of Facebook, in particular, demonstrates a simple and easy way to reconnect with old friends thought to have been lost. At the same time, it has opened society to the concept of celebrity on a personal scale in that many users try to reveal every element of their lives to the world, all with the prospect of being "famous" to their group of friends or even the world at large. How many times have we seen the stupid pet trick or some amazing party picture on a remote island? This is a clear indication of how social media has moved beyond the sharing of personal information among a circle of friends and into an effort to capture Andy Warhol's "15 minutes of fame."

Users of social media need to understand that with the use of a commercial social media platform, there is no privacy. Here is an interesting, and ironic concept to plant in the minds of social media users:

"A diamond is forever, but social media propagates perpetually."[1]

Once a post goes online, it will be there forever; it will continue to be stored in numerous databases essentially until the end of time.

While the old methods of communications such as a phone call or message passed between friends in the classroom were seemingly private, digital social media is far from private. If the goal is privacy, users should limit their use of social media and understand that the service is provided as a platform for commerce, not security. Such commercial interest benefits from individuals' data and its use for marketing purposes. That same data is also quite useful for illegitimate concerns if cybercriminals can get their hands on it.

Cybersecurity Threats that Challenge Social Media

As discussed earlier, in the first days of social media, the concept of security was not a priority. There was a general assumption that membership and access were invite only and that any user with access had to be vetted prior to receiving an invitation. These small social networks such as academia, research, professional, or even personal networks were controlled by a core administrator and could easily be policed. As the scale of these networks grew, the need for basic security controls emerged. User credentials (consisting of User IDs and passwords) were and still are the most common form of security into these networks. Unfortunately, as creatures of habit, humans tend to use the same User ID and password for these applications as they do for banking, e-mail, and work.

Social networks, recognizing the potential and real threats that develop from such an easy access formula have been developing methods to monitor for the most common hacks into the systems. Often they will tag a user's device, denoting whether it is trustworthy (usually by user approval) and monitor the IP address and geography of use to confirm if it is likely to be legitimate. Some social networks are offering multi-factor authentication as an added security tool, but adoption is still quite low due to the inconvenience. Last, if a password is too simple, it will be rejected and a more complex password will be encouraged. These are all good steps forward but are only a piece of the larger necessary security process.

Social media is a great tool for connecting and communicating, but it also possesses immense stores of information on users and those they know. While in the past (before modern social media), information had always been available on individuals, their behaviors, and a variety of valuable attributes, never before has it been so concentrated in one domain. Let us flash back a generation, when databases existed, but were only accessible to a particular entity. If users wanted information from a database they actually had to request it in person or sift through files to retrieve each attribute.

For example, public records such as property taxes, vital records (i.e., Marriage, Birth, or Death certificates), and legal proceedings were all available provided someone went to the appropriate jurisdiction and requested them. This process could be successful, but it was tedious and in some cases hard to locate. Flash forward to the late 90s and the dawn of electronic searches for vital records. Entrepreneurs and well-established companies saw opportunities to streamline government operations and create new revenue sources. These operations like vital-check.com (a service provided by LexisNexis Risk Solutions) would, for a fee, provide sensitive information. Today's social media with its access to personal data often provides enough information for bad actors to represent themselves as other individuals and infiltrate every element of victims' lives, if they so choose. This look "under the kimono" often seems benign, but in fact it is quite dangerous to our lives.

What are the potential impacts of the above mentioned vulnerability? We each have vital attributes tied to our identity that provide individuals and entities the ability to judge the integrity of an interaction or transaction. We almost all have a driver's license with Name, Address, Date of Birth (NADOB) and other features such as a photo, signature and ID#. While we do not see people posting their ID#'s on Facebook, we do see the name, address, date of birth, photo, and in many cases even more detailed info than an ID possesses. These attributes include: location of birth, high school, friends, current location, travel, and employer(s). What can a bad actor do with this type of information? The opportunities are much greater than most people think.

With core attributes such as "NADOB" we have the building blocks for identity theft (that is core identity theft). Add a little more detail, such as past addresses, employment, and education and what begins to emerge is a profile that can be used to apply for a car loan, a credit card, or even a mortgage. Even if they are missing an important element such as the Social Security Number (SSN), many experienced criminals can find a way to get a SSN or derive one that will satisfy their needs. How can this be done? First, is the fact that up until 2011, Social Security Numbers were issued on the basis of geography. The first three digits of the SSN (called an "Area Number") represented where the card was issued, most often the person's place of birth. If you were born in 1965 in New York, for instance, your area number would be in the range of 050-134 (ssa.gov, n.d.). After 1972, the area number was issued based on the zip code of the mailing address provided to the Social Security Administration; thus, the number would most likely be the first home address. The next digits are the "Group Number," simply a tool to manage processing operations. The last four digits are called the "Serial Number" and are supposed to be randomly assigned. In 2011, the Social Security Administration changed the issuance process to number randomization. This change was chosen in part due to a need to extend the longevity of the nine-digit SSN by eliminating state allocations, and in part due to increased concerns over security (SSA, n.d.).

This still does not fully explain how revealing place of birth might compromise one's SSN. The other relevant piece of this is the cleverness of the bad actors. With data analytics, processing power and lists of issued, known, and potential numbers, analytical software can create a list of probable numbers that can be quite rapidly tested across multiple sources to ascertain whether or not they could be legitimate. Once a cybercriminal has a SSN that seems viable, not only can one's credit be accessed, but there is also the potential of misrepresentation in many personal and business matters.

What are the other attributes of social media that can lead to identity theft? In today's digital world, we are exposed to greater immediacy and convenience through electronic means. Whether we are banking, shopping, or communicating, never before has humanity experienced such a rapid and easy transfer of goods and services, regardless of where they are located. At the same time, we depend more and more on these electronic services in assessing with whom to do business, why, and when. From the hiring process to the contracting process to the purchase process, we now exchange great volumes of information digitally; along with this comes new points of compromise. How do we enable security on common websites like our bank, Amazon, or even Gmail? Typically we "on-boarded" as new members, customers, or clients through an application of some type—electronic or otherwise. We would be issued a USERID and then we would create a Password. In the case of the bank (as well as other organizations) they have decided to ask personal security questions like:

"What was the make of your first car?"
"Where did you meet your spouse or significant other?"
"What street did you live on as a child?"

The idea behind these "personal knowledge" questions is that the information is intimate and most likely known only to the user (or those extremely close to the user). Additionally, they are self-asserted claims, in that any answer may be chosen, even one that is patently false, as long as the user can remember it. I'm sure we have all experimented with answers that are crazy; for example, dream cars, favorite cities, and even old college addresses. However, since most of us find it challenging to recall even a couple of passwords much less oddball answers, we often turn to the truth:

"Honda"
"Dallas"
"Main"

These answers probably represent at least a few hundred thousand people. And, by the way, some of these people actually have represented on their Facebook page a picture of their first car (a Honda Civic), the anniversary of their wedding day (Dallas, 1999), and their first home as a child (on Main St.). Sadly, these elements are very commonly posted to Facebook and to the professional, surprisingly easy to use.

The next important area that leads to personal vulnerability is e-commerce. We can start with a little quiz:

Question #1: What is the most common USERID in ecommerce?
Answer: An individual's e-mail address.

Question #2: What is the most common password in e-commerce?
Answer: An individual's e-mail password!

Question #3: Where can one get the e-mail address of most people?

Answer: Practically every social media platform . . . Facebook, LinkedIn, you name it.

The reply of most reasonable people to this would be: "but they don't have both my e-mail address and my password!"

Really? By now most hackers (and everyone else) do know the top common passwords; this is quite a good start to figuring out what one's password might be. As a matter of fact, below is the list of the 25 most common passwords, courtesy of SplashData (see Table 3.1):

Table 3.1. The 25 most common passwords (SplashData News, 2014)

1. 123456	10. adobe123	18. shadow
2. password	11. 123123	19. sunshine
3. 12345678	12. admin	20. 12345
4. qwerty	13. 1234567890	21. password1
5. abc123	14. letmein	22. princess
6. 123456789	15. photoshop	23. azerty
7. 111111	16. 1234	24. trustno1
8. 1234567	17. monkey	25. 000000
9. iloveyou		

Now, to add more fuel to the fire, readers will recall the "celebrity" iCloud hack in September, 2014 which revealed on the web some intimate photos of a number of well-known celebrities. This account compromise was a targeted attack, but it was enabled by a simple Python script (an open source programming language licensed by the Python Software Foundation) that was posted on Github (Forbes. com, 2014). Github is, ironically, another form of social media. The script would attempt access by using the 500 most common passwords and repeatedly testing the service for access. In this case, Apple fixed the problem with a quick patch, but often an event like this is less visible and random, making it harder to detect until it is too late. Unfortunately, by revealing e-mail accounts on social media, we open ourselves to potential hacks and anyone can have significantly more impact than they could have had just a few years ago with the move to cloud storage and computing.

The Arms Race

Much like the Cold War arms race where the development of a new weapon on one side of the Atlantic caused the development of a new, more capable weapon on the other side, the weapons of the cyber world continue to evolve, adapt and overcome the shields presented to thwart them. The first recognized computer virus "Elk Corner" attacked the Apple II operating system and was spread by floppy disk. Created originally as a prank by Rich Skrenta in 1982 (Jesdanun, 2007), "Elk Corner" devolved into a new tool to create chaos, while simultaneously creating two new industries: Anti-Virus Software and Malicious Code Crime. Then the Internet made this a bigger opportunity for both sides of the business. It became easier to spread code and criminals came to realize that the gave them a new way to steal. The cyber arms race stepped up and again the "good guys" created sensors and weapons to detect and clean malicious code, while the "bad guys" built weapons that worked around the good guys' code. Fast forward to 2014, we now have DDOS attacks, Trojan Horse, Man in the Middle (MITM), GameOver Zeus Botnet—all programs meant to hijack, steal, or support criminal elements. Today's criminals are creative; they crawl the web with sophisticated tools to obtain personal information. They scan search engines, they attempt to hack computers, and they crawl social media all with the goal of harvesting information that can enable them to steal from individuals and organizations with which they have relationships. Unfortunately, this arms race moves much faster than the Cold War did and the weapons actually "self-evolve" in many cases. The important concept here is that adversaries are looking to exploit information and that is the ammo that enables their weapon. If we disable their ability to "load" their weapons, we minimize their ability to cause harm, and in turn slow down the arms race.

Recall the fact that by revealing personal information (PII) on social media, individuals are not only sharing with their circle of friends but also with a large commercial enterprise whose business is to provide a platform for marketers to understand and communicate with the users of that social service. They gather everything provided and combine it with observed behaviors within their platform, and in some cases outside their platform. Just as this information is valuable to marketers, it is quite valuable to organizations with other intentions. This makes an attack on these large enterprises more appealing and at the same time more commonplace. The large social media giants have taken numerous steps to "secure" their services through a number of tools including the evaluation of threat vectors that include evaluating device ID, geography of access, IP address, behavior and the use of higher entropy models for passwords. In addition to these measures, we are now seeing the use of enterprise—like solutions for consumer applications. For example, "one-time passcode" or OTP, which is a multi-factor authentication solution that essentially creates a random number key to make it harder to hack in on an account. While it is a great tool, very few users enable it on their account because they do not want the burden of entering a passcode in addition to a USERID and Password. Also, OTP is not a panacea. Flashback to 2011 when RSA, which, via Microsoft and Netscape is the most commonly used encryption and authentication algorithm, had their well-regarded SecurID™ OTP token compromised (Zetter, 2011), causing a massive security concern for hundreds of millions of enterprise users. Many considered this tool as un-hackable; clearly it was not, but it and other OTP solutions do help. Similar to the legitimacy of car alarms, it is not that they stop thieves; they do, however, encourage them to go to an easier target. If they have a specific desired target, they will get in.

Social Media and Social Engineering

Most of us have experienced the "pleasure" of sitting on hold waiting for a customer service rep to answer and respond to a problem. Many times, when the human finally responds, they ask questions such as:

> "Can you confirm you mother's birthdate?"
> "What is your billing address?"
> "Where was your father born?"

These phrases, much like the knowledge questions a bank asks, are meant to determine the authenticity of the caller and whether they should provide access to the account. Interestingly, they are also attributes that social media often reveals to the world. The RSA hack mentioned above was a result of an organized attack that exploited social engineering to enter the RSA system. While not as easy as answering the customer service rep's questions, the same premise applies to how cybercriminals compromised RSA—through social engineering. The practice of social engineering is as old as humanity and is experienced in some way every day by someone using psychological manipulation techniques to encourage confidence and trust. This trust in turn enables people to drop their guard and reveal confidential information that can be used by perpetrators for their end objectives. In the case of the RSA breach, social engineering was enabled by exploiting information that was harvested when low-level employees enabled a Trojan horse app via e-mail. That application harvested credential information up the food chain in RSA until the hackers had their target (Kaplan, 2011).

Why is this relevant? The key ingredient is that a threat utilized data that was harvested from a network, in this case a relatively secure one. In social media, a threat does not have the same roadblocks and safeguards as was found in the RSA environment. Social media tends to provide data very publicly, and answers to questions like the ones presented earlier are commonly found in all of the major social media providers. Cunning threats understand that the weakest link in an enterprise's security system is humans. If a hacker can cull PII on an individual of interest, the hacker can use that information to present him/herself as that individual. This begins the process of compromise: accrual of logins, account info, personal info, passwords, and in the end, access. If readers believe this could not happen to them, they only need remember that in the fall of 2013, Target Corp. was hacked using credentials given to their HVAC contractor. This contractor was compromised by a targeted effort using e-mail malware that stole credentials from the contractor's system (Krebs, 2014). This attack was a form of social engineering called "spear phishing" that used customized e-mail messages based on content harvested from social media (i.e., LinkedIn, Facebook, et al). Once they convinced an employee to open the e-mail and malware, the hackers went about setting their trap and in the end obtained access to Target Corp's systems which wreaked havoc on its business and reputation.

If we still believe that the only target enabled from social media is an individual's identity and personal affairs, then we must consider that just as employee effectiveness at work impacts a company's success, so does personal digital integrity impact the digital integrity of one's employer.

Personal Security

We have discussed numerous concepts around social media and the adverse impact they can have on individuals and the entities with which they engage. It is also crucial to explore the final element that is as important as one's digital profiles and identity: that is, one's personal security. Many people think that digital life does not have a direct correlation to physical crimes such as larceny, extortion, assault, and kidnapping. However, there have been clear examples of such crimes being planned out and enabled through the use of social media. Below are a few examples and how they were enabled.

Many modern professionals like to stay linked with friends and colleagues throughout the world. When they travel for business (or pleasure), they often like to connect with friends near where they will be going. Often they send tweets or post on preferred social network stating that they are going to a conference, visiting a market for business, or simply hitting the beach. What we think is a great way to alert friends of our whereabouts is also a resource for the unscrupulous to stage a crime. Since many social media users do not set their privacy settings to the highest level, often plans are shared with everyone in the social network.

There have been examples of organized crime and gangs trolling social media to identify when targets are traveling and then capitalizing on the opportunity to rob their homes. One example was a gang that was caught breaking into homes in Nashua, New Hampshire, using Facebook to plan their heists (Mello, 2010). They identified targets, located them online, and waited for their future victim's Facebook updates indicating they were traveling or out of town. Add the fact that most social media apps can geo-tag locations and some apps, like Foursquare and Pinterest, are based on presence at a certain location, and one can see why criminals—petty or organized—can see opportunity with social media.

Recommendation for Social Media Cybersecurity Best Practices

We are all aware of the fact that social media is an amazing tool. It has become, in some ways indispensible in our modern lives and business affairs; from connecting us to lost friends and colleagues, to enabling connections to otherwise unrealized business opportunities. While we have discussed many of the pitfalls of social media and security, to suggest that we give up on it, lock it out, or even prevent all access to it would be silly and unproductive. Not only would the immense possibilities of extending business relationships and communications to larger market be lost, but people would be considered suspect for not even being present on social media. In essence, people would risk becoming pariahs if they were not involved in what many consider the necessary tools of modern society.

There are, however, steps to consider that can improve one's cybersecurity and engagement with social media. Some suggestions may seem quite simple and logical and some may already be in use. Vigilant execution of these steps is important to minimize potential threats and adverse actions.

Situational Awareness: "If it seems too good to be true it usually is." This well-known phrase can be of assistance in understanding the most basic of threat reduction techniques: situational awareness or "SA." The basic SA everyone should understand is that in social media, whether on a specific platform, through e-mail or even in bulletin boards, you should ask whether the e-mail message or offer seems logical. Many of us were taught that there is nothing free in life, so when we see some extraordinary offer, claim, or message, especially from an unfamiliar source, we should question it. Do not open e-mail attachments from strangers and always look at the links in any message received. A common tactic is sending a message from what appears to be a social media site to spoof the mark into revealing data via a redirect or fake website.

Privacy Features: In social media applications, it is best to use every privacy feature provided. Limit access to posts and information to only "friends" or "private circles." Remove from profile: birthday, mailing address, children's full names, and schools. Never post a current location or daily schedule online. If it is important for people to know current whereabouts, communicate privately with them. For those who like to brag about vacations, post it after returning home.

Permanency of the Web: Recognize that anything posted is permanent and will never go away. Items can be deleted from the visible timeline or webpage, but they are stored almost instantly by someone or something.

Two-factor/One-time Passcode/Multi-factor Authentications: Two-factor/one-time passcode/multi-factor authentication are now readily available and should be used as often as possible. Google and Facebook now offer these precautions to some users; those who are comfortable with it should use it. In addition, it is beneficial to use advanced passwords, and different password and user names for e-mail or bank addresses.

Cleaning of Timelines: It is good practice to clean e-mail, computer, smart phone, and social media timelines often. Most people do not look back more than a few posts on timelines. Cleaning up devices can minimize the potential of malicious code, apps, and hidden e-mail phishing attachments to become active. It is best practice to re-image computers at least quarterly and phones monthly.

Common Sense: Think before talking (posting). Understand that a minor piece of personal of data which by itself is benign can be immensely useful if harvested with other pieces of data from other sources.

Conclusion

In light of the above precautions, some of us might become frightened of social media. This will not, in the end, be productive. Rather than giving up on social media, recognize that just like any tool we have, there is a safe way and a dangerous way to use it. If those safe methods of use are practiced, social media will be a fruitful and fun resource for personal and professional enterprises.

Note

1. "A diamond is forever" is a registered trademark of DeBeers, Inc. and is not used to imply endorsement.

References

Forbes.com. (2014, September 2). ICloud data breach: Hacking and celebrity photos. 09/02/2014 Retrieved from http://www.forbes.com/sites/davelewis/2014/09/02/icloud-data-breach-hacking-and-nude-celebrity-photos/.

Herzfeld, C. (n.d.). Charles Herzfeld on ARPANet and computers. About.com. Retrieved on September 25, 2014 from http://inventors.about.com/library/inventors/bl_Charles_Herzfeld.htm.

Jesdanun, A. (2007, September 1). School prank starts 25 years of security woes. Associated Press. Retrieved from http://www.nbcnews.com/id/20534084/ns/technology_and_science-security/t/school-prank-starts-years-security-woes/#.VBH2Wi5dWBF.

Kaplan, D. (2011, April 1). Flash zero-day, social engineering enable RSA SecurID hack. SC Magazine. Retrieved from http://www.scmagazine.com/flash-zero-day-social-engineering-enable-rsa-securid-hack/article/199836/.

Krebs, B. (2011, February 14). Email attack on vendor set up breach at Target. KrebsonSecurity. Retrieved from http://krebsonsecurity.com/2014/02/email-attack-on-vendor-set-up-breach-at-target/.

Mello, J. P. Jr. (2010, September 10). Gang uses Facebook to rob houses. PCWorld. Retrieved from http://www.pcworld.com/article/205295/gang_uses_facebook_to_rob_houses.html.

Merriam-Webster. (2014). Retrieved from http://www.merriam-webster.com/dictionary/socialmedia.

O'Reilly, T. (2005, September 30). What is web 2.0: Design patterns and business models for the next generation of software. O'Reilly Media, Inc. Retrieved on September 30, 2014 from http://oreilly.com/pub/a/web2/archive/what-is-web-20.html?page=1.

Python Software Foundation. https://www.python.org/.

Social Security Administration. SSN number randomization. http://www.ssa.gov/policy/docs/ssb/v45n11/v45n11p29.pdf.

SplashData News. (2014, January 18). Worst Passwords 2013. January 18, 2014 http://splashdata.com/press/worstpasswords2013.htm.

Zetter, K. (2011, March 17). Hacker spies hit security firm RSA. Wired. Retrieved from http://www.wired.com/2011/03/rsa-hacked/.

Chapter 4

Cybersecurity and the Cloud

Diana L. Burley

Introduction

In 2011, 65% of U.S. companies moved some portion of their services to a cloud environment (Flood, 2013). In early 2014, RightScale reported that 94% of companies surveyed were using cloud services. Given this dramatic growth in usage, it is not surprising that estimates suggest spending on cloud services could top $180 billion by 2015 (Flood, 2013). The benefits of cloud computing are easily identifiable and include: rapid product and service development; improved access to applications and data; and reduced technology infrastructure costs.

However, along with this massive increase in usage comes a corresponding increase in security concerns. In fact, despite the high adoption rate, security concerns are a primary impediment for those organizations that have yet to migrate to the cloud environment. According to a recent Microsoft survey, 60% of small businesses not currently using cloud-based services cited security as a primary concern (Sanders & Praw, 2013). Yet, for those businesses that do migrate, 94% indicate security improvements. This difference in the perception of cloud security between adopters and non-adopters suggests that additional insight on fundamental issues of securing the cloud is needed. The purpose of this chapter is to provide just such an overview.

What is Cloud Computing?

The generally accepted definition of cloud computing comes from the National Institute of Standards and Technology:

> *Cloud computing is a model for enabling ubiquitous, convenient, on-demand network access to a shared pool of configurable computing resources (e.g., networks, servers, storage, applications, and services) that can be rapidly provisioned and released with minimal management effort or service provider interaction.*

(NIST 500-291, 2013)

Essential characteristics of cloud computing include on-demand self-service, broad network access, resource pooling, rapid elasticity, and measured service.

- On-demand self-service allows consumers to provision computing resources through automated interfaces and without human interaction;

- Broad network access ensures the availability of applications and data as needed through thick and thin clients such as web browsers, PDAs, and cell phones;

- Resource pooling means that the provider services multiple clients simultaneously with resources assigned dynamically based on user needs;

- Rapid elasticity allows resources to scale as necessary and based on demand; and

- Measured service supports usage driven billing.

In addition to these five characteristics, the Cloud Computing Alliance advocates for a sixth characteristic—multi-tenacity. Multi-tenacity is the ability to differentiate between consumers using the same technology (hardware and software) with regard to policy, governance, and billing. As will be discussed later in this chapter, multi-tenacity is particularly critical for ensuring data security in cloud environments.

Service Models

As shown in Figure 4.1, cloud service architectures are structured as three primary service models: Software as a Service, Platform as a Service, and Infrastructure as a Service.

Software as a Service—SaaS. Sometimes called 'software on demand' or 'hosted software,' SaaS is a software licensing and delivery model wherein software applications reside on a service provider's cloud infrastructure and are accessed by customers through a web interface. Customers use the applications while the service provider is responsible for software development, maintenance, updates, and support. Examples of

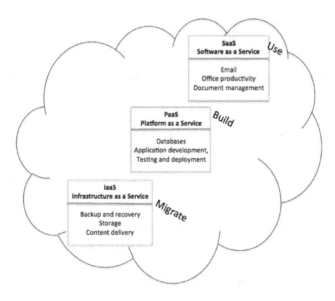

Figure 4.1. Three primary cloud service models. *Courtesy of the author.*

SaaS applications to use in the cloud include: e-mail, office productivity (e.g., word processing, spreadsheets), collaboration tools, document
management, and sales applications. With SaaS, instead of purchasing an individual copy of Microsoft Office for installation on a local
computer, a user would "rent" the software; accessing it as needed
through a web browser.

Platform as a Service—PaaS. With PaaS cloud providers deliver a
computing platform upon which customers can execute resources to
develop, test, and deploy applications. Examples of PaaS applications
to build in the cloud include: databases, application development, testing, and deployment. PaaS facilitates collaborative application development spanning multiple groups, large data integration projects, and
faster application deployments.

Infrastructure as a Service—IaaS. IaaS provides consumers with fundamental network infrastructure and computing resources to support
a virtual computing environment. IaaS can provide access to servers, load balancers, and virtual machines. Examples of IaaS tasks to
migrate to the cloud include: backup and recovery, content delivery
networks, and storage. With IaaS, users gain more control over managing runtime, operating systems, and applications. IaaS can support
quick and periodic increases in workload (e.g., holiday sales traffic,
tax return filings).

Deployment Models

Cloud service models are deployed throughone of four different models: private, public, community, or hybrid (see Figure 4.2).

Public Cloud. The public cloud infrastructure is available for use by
the general public. It is housed with the service provider and may be
owned or operated by government, business, academia, or any combination. Public cloud examples include Amazon web services, IBM
Blue Cloud, and Google AppEngine. Although convenient and cost
effective, public clouds may not provide the desired level of security
or configuration options needed by many organizations.

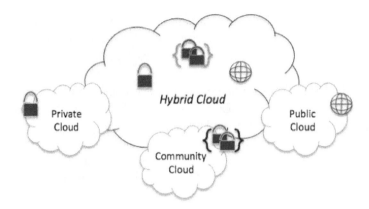

Figure 4.2. Cloud deployment models. *Courtesy of the author.*

Private Cloud. The private cloud infrastructure provides increased customization and security options. Private clouds are used by a single organization. Private clouds can be structured as either an internal service where the infrastructure is owned and operated by the organization using the cloud or an external service where the infrastructure is owned, managed or operated by a third party. With a private cloud, organizations are able to gain the benefits of cloud computing while maintaining some level of control over how the infrastructure is operated.

Community Cloud. The community cloud infrastructure is designed for use by a community (or group) of users. The organizations within the community typically share some set of policy or compliance requirements, mission, or common security concerns. The community cloud may be owned by members of the community (single or multiple), a third party, or some combination of the two. Although not widely used, community cloud groups are increasingly being established in the areas of health care, finance, and government. In health care, for example, the insurance provider UnitedHealthcare has established the Optima Health Cloud to provide a cloud computing environment that adheres to strict HIPPA regulations (Butler, 2012).

Hybrid Cloud. The hybrid cloud infrastructure consists of some combination of public, private, and or community cloud functions. The goal of the hybrid cloud is to create a unified, flexible cloud environment that leverages the benefits of the various models. For instance, a hybrid cloud could combine a public development platform with a private data center. This option would minimize costs associated with the development platform while providing enhanced data security. An increasingly popular hybrid cloud model includes dedicated connections between private and shared data centers; effectively extending the private infrastructure and the associated security benefits.

Fundamental Issues Unique to Securing the Cloud

Cloud computing environments are not immune to the basic security threats facing any system. Accidents, natural disasters, challenges to physical security, and malicious exploits can all be the source of potential security incidents. More specifically directed toward the cloud environment, the characteristics, service, and deployment models of cloud computing each have associated security risks that must be addressed. The number of variables associated with the different configurations of the computing environment complicates security and privacy concerns. Regardless of the configuration, however, three fundamental security areas should be addressed: the cloud provider; data classification and lifecycle management; data compliance and audit (Shackleford, 2011). These security concerns are detailed as nine specific security challenges. These challenges are briefly summarized below and are discussed in detail in the NIST Cloud Computing Standards Roadmap (NIST, 2013):

- Exploits that compromise data confidentiality and integrity whether in transit (i.e., during data processing) or at rest (i.e., within data storage environments).

- Abuses of cloud computing resources to rapidly scale attacks (e.g., by harnessing the processing power of multiple, networked servers) or to gain unauthorized access to another users data and resources (e.g., through stolen authentication credentials or the exploit of system vulnerabilities).

• Attacks that exploit vulnerabilities caused by the migration of legacy software and older virtual machines to the cloud environment. These applications and systems may never have been intended for use in a networked environment, or they may require new updates and/or patches.

• Data encryption procedures at rest and in a multi-tenant environment are limited.

• Application programming interface (API) standards are limited and constrain the secure movement of cloud consumers between service providers.

• Audit procedures with inadequate transparency requirements create vulnerabilities in the physical abstraction of cloud resources.

• Attacks based on vulnerabilities associated with inconsistent, overlapping, and sometimes conflicting policies, legal regulations, and geographically based requirements.

• Insider threat from the expanded set of insiders—which now includes staff members from the cloud service provider.

• Man-in-the-middle attacks that can disrupt data access and processing. NIST identifies this vulnerability as especially present when data is in transit from the supplier to the cloud service provider.

The Cloud Security Alliance (CSA) also provides a set of 12 cloud threat categories. Although similar to the NIST set of challenges, the CSA list provides a different perspective. While the NIST challenges are based on perceived vulnerabilities, the CSA list is based on actual cloud vulnerability incident data collected from published media reports. Although the lists are largely the same, the CSA reports threats by frequency of occurrence. Of the 12 threat categories enumerated by CSA, the most frequently reported incidents are insecure interfaces and APIs, data loss or leakage, and hardware failure. The full list of vulnerability incidents is available in the CSA incident report (Computer Security Alliance, 2013). CSA also published the *Notorious Nine*—top cloud security threats of 2013. Notably, the list includes the same general set of security threats as the other two lists, and, as such, are reflective of largely known vulnerabilities and are based in large part on shadow IT practices. Shadow IT practices occur when business users make IT decisions—entering into cloud computing arrangements without sufficient consideration or knowledge of the security implications of their decisions, for instance—without consulting or working with the actual IT department. Akin to signing a contract without review from the legal department, these lapses can expose the organization to considerable vulnerabilities.

Notorious Nine Cloud Threats

Data Breaches. Target—40 million credit cards stolen and $148 million in damages. Home Depot—more than 60 million credit cards stolen in the largest breach to date. These headlines tell the all too frequent story of the theft of thousands of customer data records— personally identifiable information, credit card accounts, and banking information. Data breaches, whether achieved through malware, social engineering, or other security vulnerabilities, represent a significant cloud computing threat.

Data Loss. Data loss is an equally serious occurrence. The Boston Computing Network estimates that 60% of companies that lose their data will close down operations within six months of the loss (BCN, 2013). However, unlike data breaches where data is stolen through purposeful and malicious activity, data loss can occur through technical malfunction, natural or manmade disasters, carelessness, or other purposeful or unintended actions. Data loss can result from insider behavior (e.g., circumventing data processing procedures for the sake of convenience) or outsider actions (e.g., hackers deleting user information).

Account or Service Hijacking. Account or service hijacking occurs when a bad actor takes control of a user account through stolen credentials or the exploitation of software vulnerabilities (e.g., buffer overflow attacks). With account access, the intruder can provide false data, manipulate transactions, eavesdrop, and do any number of damaging activities. CSA identified hijacking as the third greatest threat to cloud security. Proactive measures to avoid this vulnerability include two-factor authentication, and procedures that prohibit credential sharing among employees.

Insecure Interfaces and APIs. The application programming interface (API) specifies how software components should interact. Customers use the APIs of cloud service providers to manage and monitor cloud services (e.g., data access). Because the API provides direct access to software, cloud service security is dependent on the security of provider APIs. As the CSA report notes, APIs must be robust enough to protect users from both intended and unintended threats.

DDoS Attacks. A denial of service (DoS) or distributed denial of service (DDoS) attack prevents users from accessing the intended network resource. According to the Arbor Networks ninth annual Worldwide Infrastructure Security Report (Arbor Networks, 2014), DDoS attacks in the cloud computing environment are increasing. The report reveals that during the 12-month period between September 2013 and 2014: more than 70% of survey respondents acknowledged a DDoS attack; attacks over the 100Gbps mark were reported by multiple respondents; infrastructure attacks rose to be the top concern for users in 2014; and as seen in the previous survey period, customers remained a primary target of DDoS attacks.

Malicious Insiders. Insider threat is a persistent challenge in computing environments. Because the cloud computing environment can

blur the boundary between insiders and outsiders, this threat intensi-
fies. Are employees of the cloud service provider insiders or outsiders?
Depending on the cloud architecture, deployment model, and policy
agreement, these individuals could have equal or even greater access
to sensitive data than 'traditional' insiders.

Abuse of Cloud Computing Services. Not only must users broaden
their focus to examine the behavior of a larger set of "insiders," but
they must also consider that other service users may have unethical
and even criminal intentions. CSA presents this threat as more of a
concern for cloud service providers than for cloud users. However, it
does raise questions about the definition of ethical usage, and suggests
that users should be aware of usage guidelines as written in service
provider policies.

Inadequate Due Diligence. A cloud governance plan, as discussed
in more detail below, must include an assessment of the organization's readiness for cloud adoption. Inadequate preparation for the
implementation of cloud services can lead to many of the security
challenges discussed in this section and expose the organization to
extreme vulnerabilities.

Shared Technology. The multi-tenant environment demands that
users understand and agree to the technology-sharing protocols and
procedures within the cloud environment. Although the shared technology threat dropped from fourth in 2010 to ninth in the 2013 report,
82% of survey respondents list it as a significant threat.

Privacy Issues of the Cloud

While efficient and cost effective, the cloud computing environment
does pose risks to individual, government, and business consumer
privacy. In fact, the International Telecommunication Union asserts
that the "privacy disabling" potential of cloud computing is a widely
accepted major challenge faced by society (Guilloteau & Mauree,
2012). As discussed above, the number of service and deployment

model configurations, along with management and jurisdictional questions, complicates both security and privacy concerns. This complexity raises privacy questions related to personnel (e.g., Who will have access to the data while in storage? While in transit?), processes (e.g., How will data from different entities be secured and segmented in a multi-tenant environment?), and policies (e.g., How are regulations enforced and conflicting requirements resolved?). Within the context of this complexity, Subashini and Kavitha (2011) highlight several key privacy concerns:

- Personally identifiable information (PII), as well as business and government information, must be protected by cloud service providers. Provisions for the privacy of this data must be deliberately addressed in service contracts.

- The level of protection afforded to users varies widely based on differences in the privacy policies and terms of service of cloud service providers. These terms of service can contradict sector specific regulations. For example, a cloud data storage provider may have data handling procedures that are in accordance with basic security protocols but which are not in line with HIPPA regulations.

- User disclosures and storage decisions can change confidentiality obligations and impact legal protections. As decisions about delivery models change to meet business needs (a movement to shared vs. dedicated connections between data centers, for instance), the changes may also render particular protections null and void.

- Legal jurisdictions may overlap and cause confusion for law enforcement with regard to privacy and confidentiality standards and legal requirements. Legal concerns can be particularly acute when national borders are crossed. For example, many companies (and their home governments) based outside of the United States have serious concerns with the broad powers afforded to the U.S. government to access private data under the auspices of the U.S. Patriot Act.

Accordingly, data confidentiality and privacy are primary issues to be addressed by cloud providers in public, private, community, and hybrid cloud environments. For those implementing a cloud computing architecture, privacy advocates recommend using the Privacy by Design (PbD) principle to guide development and implementation activities (Guilloteau & Mauree, 2012). In its simplest form, PbD argues that legislation and policies alone cannot drive privacy. Rather, the principles of PbD: proactive, default, embedded, positive sum, lifecycle, transparency, and respect should be included within the software development process (http://www.privacybydesign.ca/). Since its development in the 1990s by Dr. Ann Cavoukian of the Information and Privacy Commissioner of Ontario, Canada, PbD has been translated into more than 35 languages and is positioned as an international standard for integrating privacy into the technology development process.

Governance, Legal, and Compliance Issues of the Cloud

In order to address security and privacy threats, a cloud governance plan should be included as a component in any cloud implementation strategy. The plan should address governance and risk, legal requirements, compliance and audit.

Governance and Risk

Governance questions should assess the organizational readiness for cloud computing and the relationship between the benefits of cloud computing and the mission of the enterprise. According to ISACA (2014), the governance plan should address:

- How risks and value will be measured. Have objective measures of ROI been established? How will baselines or industry standards be used to determine value?

- Existing investments in non-cloud architecture. Is the current architecture sufficient to meet current and short-term future business needs? Has a large software purchase been recently made?

- Strategic and mission alignment. Is a movement toward cloud data storage, for example, called for in strategic planning documents or is it critical to achieving mission objectives? Or, on the other hand, are data access and security requirements in conflict with the chosen deployment model?

- The readiness of organizational processes, policies and procedures, structures, and the culture, behavior, and skill sets of employees. Have existing data handling procedures been reviewed and adjusted to meet the new cloud environment? Have the acquisition professionals, for instance, received training on the different contractual requirements? Do the IT managers understand how to manage a cloud vendor contract?

Data Compliance and Audit

Compliance and audit standards do not shift simply because data is stored in a cloud environment. Awareness and adherence to existing and updated regulatory requirements must be maintained by the consumers and communicated to the cloud provider. This is especially true with public cloud environments where protocols may not be set to meet the demands of any one sector. In addition, organizations need to ensure that they are aware of data segmentation and security protocols guiding access to and security of co-located virtual resources (Shackleford, 2010).

Legal Requirements

Legal requirements can become complicated quickly in the cloud computing environment. Because data and services are often stored and/or provided from different physical locations, multiple jurisdictions may govern any single transaction. Location, however, is only one of many legal considerations to be managed with cloud providers. Steve McDonald, General Counsel at the Rhode Island School of Design, has compiled a comprehensive list of legal and quasi-legal issues to be considered when executing cloud computing contracts. These issues include: privacy and confidentiality; data ownership; access and security; service parameters; emergency services; location and jurisdiction. The full set of legal issues, along with a brief discussion of each, can be accessed at http://net.educause.edu/section_params/conf/ccw10/issues.pdf.

Securing the Cloud Requires Changes in the IT Workforce

The trend toward greater implementation of cloud-based services has significant implications for the IT workforce. The cloud-computing environment requires new skill sets and the need for 'cloud ready' IT professionals will see an annual growth rate of 26% through the year 2015 (Anderson & Gantz, 2012). In real numbers, this growth rate translates to a 'cloud ready' workforce shortage that will increase from 1.7 million unfilled cloud computing-related positions in 2012 to an estimated 7 million positions by 2015 (Anderson & Gantz, 2012). The IDC Cloud Skills Gap Survey identifies deficiencies in training, experience, and certification as drivers of the workforce shortage.

The 2013 (ISC)2 Global Information Security Workforce Study (Suby, 2013) helps to unbundle the skills' gap and provides a listing of the skills IT security professionals need in order to manage cloud security risks. Of the skills required, respondents assert that understanding how security applies to the cloud environment as well as understanding the basics of cloud security are the most critical. IDC survey respondents also identified the ability to understand and manage risk, along with a general understanding of the implications of cloud computing decisions on the overall IT infrastructure, as critical skills.

The level and type of understanding required will depend on the specific role(s) of the cloud computing workforce role. For instance, cloud project managers need to understand the implications of different configurations on enterprise security and business functioning. These individuals need to ask questions such as: Do the terms of the cloud service provider contract meet the business needs for data access, data storage, backup, and recovery? Cloud network architects, on the other hand, need to understand complex network architectures that integrate multiple systems across different platforms. Along with these roles, the IDC survey (Anderson & Gantz, 2013) provides a detailed discussion of the implications of cloud computing for several key IT roles including: business analysis, help desk and end user support, web management, and IT operations staff.

According to survey results, 89% of respondents highlighted the need for IT professionals to understand how security applies to the cloud, 78% of respondents point to the need for a basic understanding of cloud security, and 62% suggest a general need for enhanced technical skill sets. Managerial skills were deemed no less important with respondents pointing to the need for knowledge of compliance issues—71%; and contractual security requirements—61%. The more nuanced finding of the survey suggests that the need for enhanced understanding in both technical and managerial issues is also driven by the complex governance structures and unclear legal jurisdictions at play in the cloud computing environment.

Recommendations for Cloud Cybersecurity Best Practices

Based on cybersecurity threats, both suggested and actual, NIST identifies several cloud security objectives for anyone implementing a cloud computing environment. Not surprisingly, the NIST Cloud Computing Standards Roadmap (NIST, 2013) identifies the two primary cloud security objectives as the protection of consumer data and cloud infrastructure. Consumer data should be protected from the variety of threats discussed earlier in this chapter. Data should be secured in transit and in rest, from internal and external threats, and privacy requirements should be maintained. Moreover, cloud security should impede unauthorized use of cloud infrastructure and resources. Preventing cloud resource abuse should be a basic component of any cloud security plan.

Cloud computing architectures allow for several deployment models. As such, another cloud security objective should be to align deployment and threat models. Security should not be implemented without consideration for business needs. Users and user behaviors should also be incorporated into the security objectives. In particular, according to the Cloud Computing Standards Roadmap, the objectives should incorporate features to mitigate end-user vulnerabilities that may be exploited through Internet browsers. API standardization will reduce vulnerabilities associated with portability and interoperability. Finally, the security objectives should be articulated and well-defined in a management plan that identifies clear boundaries and responsibilities for cloud service providers and consumers. Ideally this plan will call for an independent assessment of all security features (e.g., access controls, intrusion detection, loss prevention) to verify functionality.

Future Trends in Cloud Cybersecurity

As cost savings grow, the cloud computing environment will continue to expand. Predictions of future trends in cloud computing are plentiful. Several of the major themes are highlighted below.

Sharing. The economies of scale gained through the pooling of resources makes community and hybrid models appealing. As such, the trend toward increased adoption of community clouds will heighten as regulatory requirements become more complex and security and privacy concerns become more acute. Sharing data across private clouds also will enable richer data analysis, particularly within corporate settings. Another key trend to watch for in the near future is an increase in the number of service providers that develop strategic partnerships with clients (Baig, 2014). This trend is driven by the increasingly complex regulatory environment, the demand for integrated services, and heightened security and privacy concerns. Technology sharing has significant security concerns and it ranks at number nine on the CSA Notorious Nine list of cloud security threats. However, as technical security methods and the sophistication of IT managers advance, it is likely that the significance of this threat will decrease over time. While 82% of CSA survey respondents list technology sharing as a relevant threat, its ranking fell from number four in the 2010 CSA list to number nine in 2013.

Standardization. Increased sharing requires enhanced standardization across platforms. The confidentiality, integrity, and availability (i.e., security) of data, integrated services, data analytics, and information sharing will be facilitated by enhanced standards. Cloud consumers are too often required to use proprietary services that do not support application or data portability. The lack of standardization increases security breakdowns, unreliable service delivery, and the potential for privacy breaches. Efforts to address standardization in cloud computing are plentiful. Through the Federal Risk and Authorization Management Program (FedRAMP), the U.S. federal government is working to certify cloud service providers as meeting a standard set of requirements, including security assessments, authorization, and continuous monitoring. The goal of this program is to require all cloud service providers to be FedRAMP certified before contracting with any federal agency. In addition to the U.S. federal government, institutions such as the Cloud Security Alliance and the ISO are working to develop cloud security standards.

Innovation. The ubiquity of cloud services provides the foundation for entrepreneurship and business innovation. The 2014 North Bridge Future of Cloud Computing Survey revealed that 49% of those surveyed are using the cloud for product development and revenue generating activities (Skok, 2014). For some, the true value of cloud-based services may lie in its ability to support open innovation—innovation based on the blending of ideas within and external to a single organization (Chlohessy & Acton, 2013). The cloud environment can facilitate open innovation but it also can expose vulnerabilities associated with data sharing—risks discussed throughout the chapter.

Mobility, Big Data, and Social Networking. The cloud computing environment provides the infrastructure for user mobility driven by smart phones, tablets, and the constellation of devices included in the so-called Internet of Things. Location-based applications transmit data on shopping, socializing, dating, and general activities. Business and personal users are able to access data and applications seemingly from anywhere and expectations for ease of use and on-demand processing will continue to expand. In addition to data access, users also produce an increasing volume of data through these devices to be stored, mined, and manipulated.

The security implications of mobility and big data are significant and touch on many of the threats discussed throughout this chapter. Consider, for example, the privacy implications of personal health data captured through wearable technology and posted to a public cloud for monitoring by personal trainers, wellness coaches, or other training partners. Consider too, how unauthorized access to this data might impact employment or insurance decisions. As the use of mobile devices and leverage cloud-based computing resources continues to grow, so too will the attention of privacy and security advocates.

Conclusion

By 2016, cloud computing usage in North America is estimated to top 1.1 Zb (a Zb is Zettabytes equivalent to 1 billion terabytes). At that same time, cloud computing use in the Asia-Pacific region is expected to top this number and reach 1.5 Zb (Eves, 2014). The broad set of configurations for cloud service provision, driven by environmental characteristics, service models, and deployment models, creates a complicated security environment. However, cloud users seeking security guidance can review the cloud security threats outlined in this chapter. These threats, which can be categorized as issues related to cloud provider management, data classification and lifecycle management, and data compliance and audit, provide a starting point for the development of a comprehensive security management plan.

Sources of Further Information

The following list of cloud computing associations and industry groups provides additional resources, including statistics, trends, incident updates, white papers, and case studies.

- Cloud Security Alliance: https://cloudsecurityalliance. org.

  The Cloud Security Alliance (CSA) is a not-for-profit organization with a mission to promote the use of best practices for providing security assurance within Cloud Computing, and to provide education on the uses of Cloud Computing to help secure all other forms of computing.

- Cloud Computing Association: www.cloudcomputingassn. org/.

  The Cloud Computing Association (CCA) is an independent membership organization dedicated to building a community of end users and service providers of cloud-based solutions and products.

- Cloud Industry Forum: http://cloudindustryforum.org/ about-us.

  The Cloud Industry Forum (CIF) is a not-for-profit company limited by guarantee, and is an industry body that champions and advocates the adoption and use of cloud-based services by businesses and individuals.

- Global Intercloud Technology Forum: http://www.gictf. jp/index_e.html.

The Global Intercloud Technology Forum promotes the standardization of network protocols and the interfaces through which cloud systems interwork with each other, and enables the provision of more reliable cloud services than those available today.

- Cloudbook: http://www.cloudbook.net/.

Cloudbook was founded to help accelerate the adoption of cloud computing by providing a comprehensive and educational resource community. Cloudbook brings together top leaders, experts, and specialists to share their insights and experiences with the broader public.

References

Anderson, C., & Gantz, J. (2012). Climate change: Cloud's impact on IT organizations and staffing. IDC White paper. Framingham, MA. Retrieved from http://news.microsoft.com/download/presskits/learning/docs/IDC.pdf.

Arbor Networks. (2014). Arbor special report: Ninth annual worldwide infrastructure security report. Arbor Networks.

Baig, A. (2014). 2014 Cloud trends outlook—Future of cloud services. Talkin' Cloud. Retrieved from http://talkincloud.com/cloud-computing/032114/2014-cloud-trends-outlook-future-cloud-services.

Boston Computing Network. (2013). Data loss statistics. Retrieved from http://www.bostoncomputing.net/consultation/databackup/statistics/.

Bulter, B. (2012). Are community cloud services the next hot thing? NetworkWorld. Retrieved from http://www.networkworld.com/article/2186444/cloud-computing/are-community-cloud-services-the-next-hot-thing-.html.

Chlohessy, T., & Acton, T. (2013). Open innovation as a route to value in cloud computing. BLED 2013 Proceedings. Paper 5. Retrieved from http://aisel.aisnet.org/bled2013/5.

Cloud Security Alliance. (2013). The notorious nine: Cloud computing top threats in 2013. Cloud Security Alliance. Retrieved from http://www.cloudsecurityalliance.org/topthreats.

Cloud Vulnerabilities Working Group. (2013). Cloud computing vulnerability incidents: A statistical overview. Cloud Security Alliance. August 23, 2012; revised March 13, 2013.

Eves, D. (2014). The explosive growth of cloud computing [infographic]. Cloudtech. Retrieved from http://www.cloudcomputing-news.net/news/2014/apr/23/explosive-growth-cloud-computing-infographic/.

Fang, L., Tong, J., Mao, J., Bohn, R., Messina, J., Badger, L., & Leaf, D. (2013). NIST cloud computing reference architecture. National Institutes of Standards and Technology. Special publication 500-292. Gaithersburg, MD.

Flood, G. (2013). Gartner tells outsourcers: Embrace cloud or die. Information Week. Retrieved from http://www.informationweek.com/cloud/infrastructure-as-a-service/gartner-tells-outsourcers-embrace-cloud-or-die/d/d-id/1110991.

Guilloteau, S., & Mauree, V. (2012). Privacy in cloud computing. ITU-T Technical Watch Report, France. March 2012.

ISACA. (2013). Cloud governance: Questions boards of directors need to ask. ISACA. Rolling Meadows, IL. http://www.isaca.org/Knowledge-Center/Research/Documents/Cloud-Governance_whp_Eng_0413.pdf?regnum=224558.

McDonald, S. (n.d.). Legal and quasi-legal issues in cloud computing contracts. Retrieved from http://net.educause.edu/section_params/conf/ccw10/issues.pdf.

Mell, P., & Grance, T. (2011). The NIST definition of cloud computing: recommendations of the National Institute of Standards and Technology. Special publication 800-145. National Institute of Standards and Technology, U.S. Department of Commerce. Gaithersburg, MD.

Mervat, A., & Sarfraz, N. (2011). Seven deadly threats and vulnerabilities in cloud computing. *International Journal of Advances in Engineering Science and Technology*, pp. 87–90.

NIST Cloud Computing Standards Roadmap Working Group. (2013). NIST cloud computing standards roadmap. National Institutes of Standards and Technology. Special publication 500-291, Version 2.

RightScale. (2014). 2014 State of the cloud report: See the latest trends on cloud adoption. RightScale.

Saunders, R., & Praw, J. (2013, June). Small and midsize businesses cloud trust study: U.S. study results. Microsoft Trustworthy Computing.

Shackleford, D. (2010). Cloud security and compliance: A primer. SANS Institute.

Skok, M. (2014). 2014 Future of cloud computing—4th annual survey results. North Bridge Venture Partners.

Subashini, S., & Kavitha, V. (2011). A survey on security issues in service delivery models of cloud computing. *Journal of Network and Computer Applications*, 34, 1–11.

Suby, M. (2013). The 2013 (ISC)2global information security workforce study. Frost and Sullivan/Booz Allen Hamilton. Retrieved from https://www.isc2.org/GISWSRSA2013/.

Chapter 5

Cybersecurity and Mobile Devices

THOMAS MALATESTA AND JAMES SWANSON

Introduction

Smartphones and mobile technology are a phenomenon-driven juggernaut that is forming consumer behaviors and human interactions and changing lives 24 hours a day, 7 days a week. The mobile revolution has been rapid and it is hard for many people to realize that the landline phone is disappearing. According to the Department of Health and Human Services' National Center for Health Statistics, approximately 39% of all adults in the United States (about 93 million) live in households with only wireless telephones (National Center for Health Statistics, 2013). Mobile phones play a central role in today's societal relationships satisfying critical consumer and commercial demands.

Fundamental Issues Unique to Mobile Devices

In analyzing mobile security today it is significant that we are looking at a commoditized technology where people have to manage their devices as well as all the apps that are downloaded. Managing human behavior is a much more complex task. There are so many apps on

95

mobile phones that the capability of the device is truly overwhelming. The great thing about emerging technology is the opportunity it brings to the user. At the same time, all of the new technologies make more avenues available to miscreants, and the threat vectors increase exponentially. While mobile capability is driving business transformation, the number of applications downloaded from app stores makes key stakeholders vulnerable to the numerous strategies and capabilities of hackers and other parties who want to steal information. The benefits are obvious: smarter, faster decision making; better interactions with peers, friends, and family; and theoretically better use of time and energy. The downside of this is the insecurity of the data and voice communications entering and leaving the mobile phone. Add to this government regulatory and compliance issues and the challenge for secure communications becomes a daunting task.

Mobile security strategies for a multitude of personal devices will impact productivity at home and in the workplace. Companies and users have to be confident that these devices and networks are trustworthy and the information stored on them is not compromised. The threat landscape overwhelmingly consists of criminals, but also includes espionage and terrorism. Attackers have discovered new methods to attack vulnerabilities in wireless networks. The core of the threat revolves around individual behavior because users consistently choose not to focus on security tools and controls. When given the chance most people will avoid taking the time to effectively utilize resources available to thwart persistent threats against their devices. Risk management takes time and commitment; it also requires continuing education concerning threats and their impact on users, particularly when users are hacked and their personal information is stolen.

There is no shortage of security challenges in the mobile space. Application threats and network threats abound. According to Verizon's 2014 Data Breach Investigations Report (DBIR) in 2013, there were 1,367 confirmed data breaches and 63,437 security incidents reported (DBIR, 2014). Modern malware is effective at attacking new platforms and there is rapid growth of malware targeting mobile devices. While malware for Android was just a lab example a few years ago, it has become a serious and growing threat (Sophos Security Threat Report, 2013).

Protecting information and sensitive data requires understanding of the risk matrix and the underlying infrastructure as it relates to mobile activity. Risk management for the user has to be easily managed and understood, particularly the interaction between users. Innovative thinking to educate users on disparate systems and communities means huge challenges ahead and the demand for better security tools will be boundless.

Cybersecurity Threats that Challenge Mobile Devices

Google's Android operating system averaged 5,768 malware attacks daily over a six-month period, according to CYREN's Security Yearbook 2013 in Review and Outlook for 2014 (CYREN, 2014). An overwhelming percentage of malware is designed for the Android platform. According to INFOSEC Institute, Android platforms are attacked mainly due to the fact that the Android applications market provides an open platform and that over 50 mobile phone companies manufacture Smartphones with the Android operating system (Krasas, 2014).

It is unwise to assume that iOS for Apple is immune to the threat as some users declare privately and in public. In the current environment of "BYOD" thinking mobile devices are the new frontier for attacking and infiltrating networks. An infected mobile phone is candy for the malware purveyor to exploit vulnerabilities by sugar coating the malware to get unsuspecting users to click on the malicious code.

According to the Mobile Security (mSecurity) Bible: 2014–2020, mobile networks around the globe are responsible for more than 86 exabytes of traffic annually (Report Buyer, 2014). Mobile malware, SMS spam, unlawful eavesdropping, and social network scraping open individuals and businesses to data loss which, when penetrated, are expensive and painful experiences for the user. An efficient attacker does not even need to physically access a device to pocket the data. If an adversary gains control of a device, all information gets stolen and the ability to actively target and penetrate other systems, both personal and business, is a cake walk. According to CISCO's Annual Security Report "many actors of the so-called 'shadow economy' also now send surveillance malware to collect information about an environment, including what security technology is deployed, so they can target their attacks" (CISCO, 2014). Human behaviors enable criminals. So does human ignorance. Users appear to have significantly lax views toward security of their devices and information. According to CISCO, "the exploitation of trust is a common mode of operation for online attackers and other malicious actors. They take advantage of users' trust in systems, applications, the people, and the businesses they interact with on a regular basis" (CISCO, 2014).

Clicking unrecognized links is a sure way to aggravation and potential harm. Tried and true exploits revolve around phishing and ransom ware to make the reader of a communication believe it is authentic and from a trusted source. Ransomware is the generic term for any malicious software that demands a payment be made before the mobile phone and its data are released. These viruses are delivered in the form of e-mails, texting, instant messaging, and ever increasing social network communications. According to Javelin's ninth annual "Identity Fraud Report," despite warnings consumers are still sharing on social websites a significant amount of personal information frequently used to authenticate a consumer's identity (Javelin Strategy and Research, 2012).

Then there is the phenomenon of downloading apps from myriad locations on the Net. In the rush to have the newest or the coolest app, or for that matter any app, users just click away in a trusting haze rarely checking for suspicious content let alone thinking about what they may be clicking on. Users should know by now that they should never open an attachment unless they know who it is from and why they are receiving it. Downloading software without knowing its content sits close to the top of the list of things not to do.

The most prevalent mobile threats are spam, poisoned links on social networking sites, and rogue apps. Human behavior is the weak link in the security chain because of the lack of understanding of the actual nature of the threat. Public Wi-Fi networks enable mobile malware Trojans which seize large amounts of data from the network.

According to the 2014 Mobile Malware Report by Blue Coat Systems, there are 1.5 billion new ways to steal data, passwords, or money (Blue Coat Systems, 2014). Mass market malware is a robust, highly functioning black market economy. The Dark Nets are prospering! Malicious apps from porn sites abound and the growth in rogue Android antivirus products increases users' chances of downloading something "nasty." As a result, fake anti-spy scams are more than common. Socially engineered, bogus mobile advertisements prompt the user to download the polluted file allowing the malware to do its thing. Understanding how users behave on their mobile devices is critical for identifying how and why they are at risk. Social networking has, for the most part, aggressively shifted to mobile devices where one in every five users is directed to mobile malware through web ads.

The interaction between effective security use and consumer behavior does not yet appear to be very successful. Over and over stories are told about the lack of education or interest among mobile users who remain unconcerned about threats or ignorant of security and the fact that their device requires constant updating. According to Symantec in 2013, 57% of adults were unaware that security solutions existed for their mobile devices—a rather stunning statistic. Smartphone users own feature-rich devices, but the average user is unaware that his/her phone must have security capabilities installed or it will not be able to keep up with the malware onslaught. Mobile phones are the new frontier for accessing all digital functions from banking to dating. While this access enhances the quality of life of each user, it is also a profitable gold mine for cyber hackers. If users receive unsolicited e-mail or warning messages telling them to download anything, they should hit the delete button immediately. If a stranger solicits information, for any reason, users should be very suspicious. Common sense is a great ally in the war against hackers.

The point to keep in mind is that the organized professional hacker is looking at mobile connectivity as the new frontier to penetrate both individuals' stored information as well as the information warehoused on the enterprise. When the hackers control a mobile device they will use that device and information to maliciously attack every system on the network and every contact of the individual user. It is that simple. Mobility is pervasive in contemporary society. Mobile e-mail contains sensitive information and individuals regularly access their information in public-domain Wi-Fi settings and rapidly share those sensitive files and documents. Mobile payments for online transactions are growing at an incredible rate. Consumers are starting to understand the benefits of routing payments through their mobile devices and sellers are tapping into the purchasing power of today's digital society. That is precisely why strong authentication, password management, and PIN usage are successful and effective tools to use in hindering hackers. Outdated software is rampant among mobile users. Older software retains the numerous vulnerabilities that have been corrected in successive versions. Technologies are constantly evolving, as are the creativity of attacks. Unless one plans to purchase a new phone every six months, fixes need to be constantly monitored and installed. If users do not upgrade to the carriers' latest version of the platform the odds of hacker penetration greatly increases.

One of the emerging mobile security risks is the usage of public Wi-Fi connections. Because wireless communications broadcast over radio waves, passive listeners can easily pick up unencrypted messages. Free access is now provided at coffee shops, airports, movie theaters, hotels, restaurants, cafés, trade shows, sporting events, and is now debuting on airlines in-flight. Users continue to click away and in many instances are not even aware of what they are clicking. Spoofing, hoaxing, tricking, and deceiving—whatever description you choose—is rampant on public Wi-Fi connections. The ability to hide one's entire identity while appearing to be a "for real" network is commonplace. Dedicated connections and encrypted protocols will enable secure communications over these public networks.

The wave of the future is large screen Smartphones with incredible computing power because consumers want more screen size choices than ever. While the overall market is still interested in tablets, many consumers are anxious to replace their existing tablets with the latest and greatest Smartphone, be it Android or iOS. It is a reality that cyber attack vectors will continue to expand exponentially day after day, 365 days a year. So why don't most Smartphone users take their security more seriously?

There are a number of surveys from such organizations as ADT/McAffee, Kaspersky, and *Consumer Reports* indicating that way less than half of users protect their connections. A majority of users, when queried, state they do not even take the primary step of having a passcode lock. Talk about apathy. It would seem Smartphone users are at the top of the list. Users who do not take any measures to protect their mobile devices are inviting an inevitable collision with an extremely educated adversary—the professional hacker.

This is even more critical when we take into account that these same users do not think about security when they hook up with public Wi-Fi offerings. The only conclusion that can be reached is that people do not really give a damn about security basics and privacy. Privacy is supposedly important to a vast majority of Americans and mobile device users. In reality few actually practice what they preach and most do not take steps to ensure their devices and the information stored in them are secure. Privacy apps abound, as do software programs to secure mobile phones with passcodes. However, the lazy practices of Smartphone users creates a broad range of risks for those who still view the actual device as a telephone rather than a "computer" used for a variety of activities. Modern mobile applications run on devices that have the functionality of a desktop or laptop. Personal details, payment information, health and pharmacy data—you name it—most of it is now stored on the Smartphone. So the insidious pesky reality of cybercrime abounds. Add to this the fact that companies and other entities allow their employees to use their Smartphones for work and the reader can begin to see how costly it may be to "Bring Your Own Device" ("BYOD") to work. Consequently, companies are just waking up to the reality that "BYOD" policies with growing mobile device work forces are fraught with threat matrixes that demand a much larger amount of support from the IT department than originally anticipated. "BYOD" will always be with us, but the changing regulatory environment will force individuals and companies to do a far better job of managing the devices and the risks associated with them.

Consumers who carry Smartphones must realize that they are never alone, particularly when they are connected to a wireless network, which is basically all of the time. There are no shortages of technologies that can "sniff" the airways. The professional hacker will see the names of Wi-Fi networks in airports, hotels, homes, planes,

trains, and just about everywhere else. With the ability to follow people on the move through their cell phone usage comes the realization
that there is a tremendous amount of information "out there" that is
interesting to miscreant personalities.

Many individuals are not aware that they are now tracked as
they move around stores, shopping malls, and even the streets. Today
almost all mobile applications interact with a server to send or retrieve
data. Google, Facebook, Yahoo, as well as banks and department and
grocery stores all want to know what the consumer is up to. According
to the 2014 Consumer and Mobile Financial Services Report by the
Board of Governors of the Federal Reserve System, "Smartphones are
changing the way people shop and make financial decisions. Fifty-one
percent of Smartphone owners have used mobile banking in the past
12 months" (Board of Governors). Businesses want to understand their
customers and their buying habits. Consumers who shop online notice
ads that recommend purchases based on what they purchased the last
time they were on the site. Stores can do the same thing. This fact is
just now making it into the press and it will be interesting to see how
consumers and mobile phone users react to these tracking systems. If
people reject the concept, it may well impact how they view privacy
and security issues with their mobile devices.

Cybersecurity Laws and Policies
Relevant to Mobile Devices

Compliance and public policy issues are being discussed in every corner of the earth by federal, state, and local governments. Great attention is being paid to the "BYOD" category. For example, the State of
California has recently passed a "kill switch" law to remotely disable
phones if they are stolen or lost. Many people view the California laws
as a big step forward, but the reality is that Smartphones for business
remain seriously exposed to data theft.

The Second Appellate District Court in California recently ruled
that employers need to reimburse employees when they use their cell
phones for work-related activity (Court of Appeals, 2014). The deploy-

ment of mobile devices without adequate policies, procedures, and internal controls poses significant risks to financial services firms and health-related entities. Rapidly changing technology and an increasingly mobile work force, plus the desire of individuals to use their own mobile devices, demands myriad mobile device policies and eventual oversight. Failing to have a strong program puts all firms at risk of regulatory enforcement.

There is no shortage of regulatory interest in the subject, be it the Financial Industry Regulatory Authority ("FINRA"), USDA, FDA, FCC, FTC, or the Consumer Affairs offices of all 50 states. Heightened security measures driven by tragedy and regulatory oversight will eventually encourage mobile device users to pay more attention to securing their personal devices. They will begin to realize that all cellular communications around the globe are targets of opportunity.

Status of Cybersecurity Skills Regarding Mobile Devices

Exploiting Device Safety

Mobile devices are part of everyday life and as such shopping on mobile devices is the fifth most popular activity. Add to this, new opportunities such as targeted coupons and the universe for cybercriminal activity expands quickly. More and more ads mean more and more "malvertising." The top four activities on mobile devices are: search engine and portal activity; content servers; social networking; web ads and analytics.

Companies are even more at risk from these behaviors. According to a study by the security firm Symantec, more than half of Internet website publishers have suffered a malware attack through a malicious advertisement (Thye, 2013). According to Holger Schulze, founder of the Information Security Community on LinkedIn, the loss of company or client data, followed by unauthorized access to company data and systems were survey respondents' biggest security concerns in the 2014 BYOD and Mobile Security Spotlight Report (Schulze, 2014).

Additionally, the study revealed that respondents' next biggest security concerns were "users bringing downloaded apps or content with embedded security exploits into their organization (47%), followed by malware infections (45%)" (Schulze, 2014). The survey results further shows that when it comes to sensitive data and intellectual property being accessed over "BYOD," respondents were most concerned with protecting business data (74%), customer/employee data (69%), and documents (66%) (Schulze, 2014).

Although consumers are becoming increasingly vigilant about safeguarding the information they share on the Internet, many are less informed about the plethora of information created about them by online companies as they travel the Internet (U.S. Senate, 2014). An apps-behavior on a mobile device most often lacks transparency, thereby setting up users for greater privacy risks. Consumers risk exposure to malware through everyday activity. A user can incur malware attacks without having taken any action other than visiting a mainstream website. Malvertising has overtaken porn as the leading mobile threat vector. Online advertising is not only annoying, but increasingly malicious. In February 2014, web ads represented the single biggest threat vector for mobile users: one in every five times that a user is directed to malware is through web ads. Some estimates state that malvertising increased over 200% in 2013 to over 209,000 incidents generating over 12.4 billion malicious ad impressions (U.S. Senate, 2014).

According to the report of the Senate Subcommittee on Investigations, visits to mainstream websites can expose consumers to hundreds of unknown, or potentially dangerous, third parties (U.S. Senate, 2014). Analysis of several popular websites found that visiting even a mainstream website exposes consumers to hundreds of third parties capable of collecting information on the consumer and, in extreme scenarios, is a potential source of malware.

The malware threats targeting mobile devices are still fairly basic—largely confined to potentially unwanted applications and premium SMS scams. The objective is to track human behavior and share personal information. Targets are User-Agent strings, which identify the mobile operating system (its version), the type of browser (its version), and perhaps even the mobile app the user is running at that time. It is also possible HTTP activity may reveal the user's habits, interests, or searches.

A big "no-no" is downloading apps from third-party sites or downloading apps that arrive by e-mail. Forty-six percent of infected apps recently tested by Trend Micro were sourced directly from Google Play (Ferguson, 2013). The precise problem with all these apps is that there is presently no clear requirement to explicitly identify what data they access, log, store, and share. Therefore, risk-based decisions about mobile phone usage are difficult to comprehend, let alone make. Malicious mobile apps tend to have longer lives, therefore, it is a best practice to only purchase or download apps for which one can check the legitimacy. Blue Coat Systems suggests that the makers of mobile phone operating systems would be well advised to help users better manage how, when, and with whom to safely communicate (Blue Coat Systems, 2014).

One sure way for users to enhance the security of their devices is by not clicking on ads while on their mobile devices! There are several tests that can easily be conducted to check whether or not a phone has been compromised. The most obvious is to regularly check the cellular bill and see if there are any odd charges. If there are, this would be an indication that there is a problem. Very often free app downloads are compromised and they can infect the phone with malware. By late January 2014, Kaspersky Lab had accumulated about 200,000 unique samples of mobile malware, up 34% from November 2013 when over 148,000 samples had been recorded. As of January 2014, the number of malicious Android apps topped the 10 million mark (Savitsky, 2014).

Checking the phone for unusual data access patterns shows how the device is sending and receiving data. If there is a big discrepancy between how much data the device is using and how much the apps are using, there is a problem. Another potential indicator of a problem is rapid battery life failure. Exhibiting caution with unknown sites is desirable. If suspicious, users should take the time to investigate the app in its entirety. Maintaining physical control over one's phone is also highly recommended. This will ensure that no one can install spyware on it. If a user decides to jailbreak the phone it is critical that users know what they are doing. Jailbreaking means bypassing the restrictions Apple puts on the operating system and taking full control of the device. Jailbroken phones and malware are a disastrous combination. Finally, make sure there is an anti-virus program running on the device. The powers of observation do not work without an antivirus program.

Recommendations for Mobile Device Best Practices

The digital revolution—while we may embrace it, we must also be educated on the threat matrix. There are great advantages to mobility, and the flexibility of communication via mobile devices is wonderful. The down side of having great advantages in communication is the security conundrum of flexibility vs. being a target for cyber attack. The frequency of cyber attacks will never let up. Every day there are reports of multiple breaches somewhere on the globe. Undiscovered threats are as rampant as existing threats. The number of devices that will connect to the Internet by 2020, according to Gartner, Inc., is in the area of 26 billion addressable devices—all on corporate networks (Gartner, Inc., 2013). This will create thousands of unsecured endpoints that will in turn produce multiple attack vectors, all in an effort to steal sensitive information. This valuable information can be monetized in the black economy.

Every new IT innovation requires adaption by its users. New problems stretch existing security practices, and security policies will have to be revised in perpetuity. Wireless connectivity is very popular among consumers and will continue to be so for decades if not longer. This means that mobile devices will constantly create points of exploitation. Existing anti-spam, anti-virus, and anti-malware infrastructure most likely will be inadequate in protecting against the threat matrix posed by the billions of insecure new endpoints in the mobile revolution.

Organizations and individuals need to figure out how "BYOD" fits into their personal and business lives. Individuals and corporations require mobile device policies and a sense of responsibility for the day-to-day interaction of mobile IT. Some products and providers deliver better security than others. The user, therefore, has to do some homework on what preemptive capabilities are best for keeping attackers at a distance so that their critical information is protected. Individuals and corporations (at least most of them) fail to implement and manage strategies that provide continuity of process in the security dialogue. If consumers are educated users on all matters of security, they will be very aware of the products, services, and technologies available for mobile security. If not, training is an invaluable tool. Educated consumers are least likely to do something that will result in a hack of their device.

Businesses must continually educate their employees, thus balancing risk, usability, and costs. Enforced mobile security policies reduce the potential threats. In a perfect world, individuals and businesses would take the time to educate themselves and their employees. Criminals pursue the easy targets. If they fail, they move on to the next window of opportunity. When they see a security weakness exhibited in the target they aggressively move to exploit that individual or business.

In general, apps pose a serious widespread security threat. According to the security firm Metaintel, 92% of the top Android apps carry either a security or privacy risk. iOS, Android, SMS are major platform targets globally and the hardware on these platforms is a huge security concern (Business Wire, 2014).

A quick peek at the tool kit available to users of mobile devices to enhance their security perimeter will show several reasonably easy rules to follow:

- Easiest one. Stronger passwords and rotation of those passwords on a frequent basis. Yes, it takes time and is a pain, but it remains a simple and effective tool for protecting the device and the information stored in it. Take the time.

- Lock down the device.

- Update versions of apps.

- Do not download software from untrusted sites. Do not store information on a device that is not fully known or is unauthorized in one's business life.

- Use mobile device management "MDM" software that helps in wise decision making when using the phone.

- Perform regular automatic back-ups of the device plus all relevant updates of the hardware and operating system. If the system is not up to date there is no chance it will defeat the onslaught of new malware spawning over the network.

It is crucial to protect information when on Wi-Fi. It is a good rule of thumb not to conduct transactions if sensitive data must be revealed on an open network. Along with this, we would suggest no transmission of sensitive information via text. There can be too many eyes on the transmission. Finally, be cautious when on information-sharing sites. They pose a high threat matrix and it is a proven fact that these sites are constantly under aggressive attack by hackers.

User Awareness/Mobile Use in the Workforce

Gartner defines "Consumerization" as the specific impact that consumer-oriented technology can have on the enterprise (Gartner Inc., 2013). It reflects how enterprises will be affected by, and can take advantage of, new technologies and models that originate and develop in the consumer space, rather than in the enterprise IT sector. "Consumerization" is not a strategy or something to be "adopted." "Consumerization" can be embraced and it must be dealt with, but it cannot be stopped. That is precisely the description of "BYOD" because "BYOD" has reshaped the way IT is purchased, managed, delivered, and secured. "Consumerization" of IT not only refers to the use of personal devices at work (Smartphones and Apple devices, etc.) but also online services, including e-mail, social media, and data storage.

Users are fully embracing the power to access data from anywhere. The "BYOD" phenomenon is a rapidly evolving trend (threat vector) and it is being driven by employees who purchase their own devices, use their personal online accounts, download their own apps, and then connect to a corporate network with that same device. Over and over this action is taken without the knowledge or approval of the corporate entity. This, in turn, opens new vectors of attack and clouds the limits of business and private use. For the last several years companies and governments, and everything in between, thought that the "BYOD" movement could save money and improve employee productivity. While these benefits may not prove to be the case, "BYOD" will never go away.

From basic tasks such as allowing individuals to access corporate e-mail on their personal Smartphone to the purchase and distribution of company owned devices, "BYOD" has significant challenges. Data on devices, company owned or not, has to be secured and protected. New policies have to be developed as well as procedures for procurement and app deployment. So the question becomes: Can sensitive information and work product be protected for end user activities on all devices?

Forrester Research says that 12% of enterprises saw an increase in productivity when implementing "BYOD" policies (Forrester, 2012). Unfortunately, many enterprises are inadequately prepared to meet the security challenges of "BYOD" implementation strategies. At the same time, the intenseness around protecting information flow increased dramatically because of diverse hacker activity against mobile devices. Enterprises have begun to realize that to protect themselves and their information they need to secure both individuals and devices.

Empowering employees is a worthwhile business objective for any entity. Giving them productivity tools to help them do a better job is in the interest of all parties. Mitigating the risk, however, becomes a daunting task: One that is never-ending and costly to obtain. Accepting the fact that employees will actively access company networks with portable devices, enterprises must have solutions ready to protect against data loss. The key to all of this is defense in depth. Protect the information anywhere, anytime, and on any device. Awareness of the threat is critical to both individuals and enterprise systems. Users must comprehend the reality that mobile devices are an extension of self as well as the business environment of which they are a part. As device use and demand increases, risk increases. As previously noted, the human factor is the major cause of security breaches. One cannot fix ignorance or inattention. According to a 2013 Consumers Report, 34% of users took no security actions of any kind to protect their phones (Consumer Reports, 2013).

So how to get users to practice secure habits? Employees and non-employees alike need to know how to keep mobile devices and their content safe. Better methods of informing users on security require creative and customized efforts so that users can actually relate to and retain the information they are being given. It can be argued that in many cases security designs may be flawed, but for the most part, it is human behavior that needs to be the focus of the security dialogue. Even with improved security designs the human factor remains. Keeping corporate and personal mobile devices secure is the #1 objective.

So what is security awareness and is it the same as security training? Many believe there is a distinct difference between "security awareness" and "security training." Focusing on programs that build a security culture within an organization is a smart play. It is best to get the culture of the organization invested in the importance of security measures. Changing human behavior is key and continuously reaching out and engaging users is a must for any organization. IT managers have control over company-issued devices. But policing an employee's personal phone connected to the enterprise network presents a new test entirely. Compliance-driven activity allows entities to check a box but in reality it may not do much against aggressive phishing programs. Driving security best practices for mobile devices will improve knowledge and awareness of the persistent and debilitating threat matrix. Some suggestions are:

- Engage people; do not bore them to the point of ignoring the topic. Let them know why certain practices are very important;

- Be careful of, and perhaps avoid all together, unsecured Wi-Fi hotspots;

- Disable Bluetooth and Wi-Fi when not in use;

- Be very careful about downloading anything to a mobile phone, particularly apps;

- Make sure all security features are enabled and encourage users to think about what they are doing before they do it.

Future Trends in Mobile Devices

The global connection of mobile devices has given rise to the global mobile ecosystem. These devices are ever increasing in sophistication and the ability to connect more and more of them expands and enables the mobile ecosystem. The mobile ecosystem is an enormously complex, vibrant system consisting of over a billion and a half users and an evolving diversity of hardware and software. It is dominated by a small number of platforms. The operating system for a large percentage of these devices globally is the Android platform. iOS is a factor in North America.

Logging in to devices and sharing content is the essence of the mobile ecosystem. This content or data can be accessed from anywhere on any connected device. Wireless connectivity allows the sharing of information and makes the global reach of the connectivity instantaneous. Videos, photos, music, e-mail, files, documents, power points, whatever can be shared instantaneously. The individual ecosystem theoretically should make the user's digital connected life easier and seamless across the device universe. In a personal ecosystem all that is needed is two devices that connect in the cloud. These devices are usually a mobile phone, a tablet, or a laptop. As with all things tech, personal preference drives the ecosystem. The drivers in this universe are Google, Microsoft, Apple, and Blackberry. Apple's hardware works seamlessly, while Google has the open source ecosystem. Blackberry is still very efficient, particularly for businesses. There is always an element of risk when accessing and storing data on any platform and now we have the emphasis on the cloud. Utilizing "BYOD" devices and cloud computing now makes it easier to access data and information behind firewalls and outside of secure data systems.

Sharing information between devices and platforms is what mobile and wireless is all about. It is immediate and users can reap many benefits. Smart TV is on the way and other dynamic properties such as Google Glass are not far behind. The ecosystem will keep on expanding just like the universe and galaxies we live in.

The evolution of the connected society in 2014 has mobility as its cornerstone. The demand for mobile communication is growing dramatically every day and users of mobile devices cannot assume anything when it comes to protecting their devices. Increasing demand from users calls for more efficient and better online security and privacy capabilities to protect digital assets, personal information, and identities. There is no digital privacy without the corresponding cybersecurity. Monitoring the threat landscape is not enough. The wireless ecosystem is indeed complex. Mobile security represents the technology and practices that determine what works best for the user. Securing the wireless ecosystem demands the best efforts of Mobile Network Operators, manufacturers of hardware, application developers, operating system vendors, network service providers, and software vendors, among others.

Consumers and end users need constant education on everything from configuring devices to how to check permissions. Anti-malware, anti-spam, authentication, and secure connectivity are critical touch points in the process of securing the device. Consumers should be more demanding of the networks they use and fully understand their policies for privacy and protection of data. Mobile Device Management (MDM) helps enforce security policies and protect the information. At the basic level, authentication is enormously important. It identifies and protects the user.

Security policies and risk management protocols abound. Users should be sure they understand the capabilities of both. Stay on top of security technology, standards, and trends. Use technologies that stop problems before they occur. Try to stay ahead of threats by being educated to their existence. The changing threat environment means the solutions that work today may not, and probably will not, work tomorrow.

No discussion about mobile security would be complete without drilling down on mobile apps. Portio Research estimates 1.2 billion people worldwide were using mobile apps at the end of 2012. Predictions are for 4.4 billion users by 2017. According to Mobithinking the total number of apps worldwide is hard to come by, but the Apple App Store and Google Play are believed to be the largest stores with over 800,000 apps apiece (Mobithinking, 2014). The other resources of note are Amazon App Store, App Store, Blackberry World, Nokia Store, Windows Phone Store, Windows Store, and Samsung Apps Store. Again Mobithinking estimates the download of apps in 2013 ranges from 56 to 82 billion, and in 2017 there could be 200 billion downloads. The top apps in the United States were led by Facebook, You Tube, Google Play, Google Search, Pandora, Google Maps, Gmail, and Instagram.

Numerous users are lax when it comes to security scrutiny of downloaded apps. According to Kaspersky Lab, it has now logged some 10 million dubious apps, as cybercriminals also use legitimate Android software to carry malicious code. Developers of apps are not necessarily focused on security and apps are fraught with security challenges. Apps very often store user names, e-mail addresses, and passwords in clear text. That means that anyone with access to the phone can see all the same information. When this information is stolen, unauthorized individuals can log in, employ the same user name and password across the system, and compromise user accounts. Data collection is a popular function of all apps and weak server side controls means all API's should be verified and proper security methods employed to ensure only authorized personnel have access. Marketers, and just about everyone else, covet the kind of personal information some mobile apps retain. Not too long ago the NSA was accused of tapping popular Smartphone apps like Angry Birds to gather huge amounts of personal data, including age, location, gender, and more. Consumer apps, health care apps, banking apps, dating apps, whatever, they all have the potential to leak information. It is a best practice to never have any analytic app on the device. When a third party is watching the what, how, and when of data movement, that is the mother lode for bad actors. Poor key management is another issue to watch. Broken cryptography is not uncommon and when this happens security is easily compromised. Mobile apps are like digital sponges and attackers are constantly looking for ways to bypass security. We should not make it easy for them. Watch out for unintended consequences from apps because when data is at risk someone will be "out there" looking to exploit the information.

It is clear that consumers have embraced the digital revolution in North America and much of the civilized world. Cyber attacks are on the increase and will continue in their complexity and frequency. More and more wireless devices will make their way into the business world, all seeking to deliver flexible and easy-to-use capabilities. Soon everyone will own a mobile phone. The blending of personal and work life is creating serious risk. Unfortunately, convenience beats security. There are presently 1.08 billion Smartphones on the globe. As of this year more people will access a search engine on a mobile device than on a computer.

Last year, in 2013, one million small businesses built a mobile website. Devices will continue to become faster and more intelligent. So what does the future of mobile engagement look like and what is the future of mobile security that will keep up with the mobile threat explosion? The focus will continue to be on data protection and mobile application management. By 2017, Cisco predicts that Smartphones will account for over 67% of all global mobile data traffic and will be responsible for 90 Exabyte's of data traffic. By comparison the total mobile traffic from all devices in 2012 was 11 Exabyte's (Cox, 2013).

Improvements in mobile antivirus capabilities are a given. In addition, mobile content management tools for secure access to file storage, file sharing, and identity management will proliferate. Cloud security capabilities will expand and there is much conversation about protecting data instead of the device, as well as moving the security dynamics into the hardware per the Samsung Knox effect. Mobile device management has to get better for both company-owned and user-owned devices. All of these will be surrounded by stricter enforcement of security policies for the mobile workforce.

The ubiquity of mobile phones is changing the way consumers are accessing financial services. According to the Federal Reserve

Board of Governors, 51% of Smartphone owners have used mobile banking in the past 12 months, up from 48% a year earlier (2014). One of the critical growth areas in mobile devices will be mobile payments. According to the Federal Reserve, 17% of mobile phone owners have made a mobile payment in the past 12 months (Board of Governors, 2014).

More merchants are accepting mobile payments and the mobile payment market space is on the verge of exploding. As soon as the mobile payment market becomes clearer between merchant and customer, look for consumers to climb on the band wagon very quickly. Mobile shopping has been embraced by all ages and the concern will be, again, protecting both personal and financial data. Bitcoin, Bluetooth Low Energy, Amazon, Mobile Wallet, and all retail banks will compete aggressively for both mobile and online audiences. We will see more Point of Sale Payments (stores will accept this instead of credit cards); direct mobile billing will expand; Smartphone credit card payments will abound; Peer-to-Peer mobile payments will increase and payment by text message will be seen in more environments, such as restaurants. In order to make payments by mobile phones easier requires enhanced security, increased trust, and increasing consumer familiarity with mobile payment methods, all contributing to continued growth in the mobile payment space.

Conclusion

The new frontiers part of the mobile security dialogue will include safeguarding technologies such as voice biometrics and device fingerprinting (phone printing). Biometric security including eye scanners, fingerprint scanners, and facial recognition will continue to be actively tested in the marketplace. Securing e-mail content in the age of NSA and regulations (The Snowden Experience) will be on everyone's mind for quite a while. The real challenge, however, is Internet privacy in general and privacy in the cloud. We need greater legal regulation and clearer privacy policies. There is absolutely no stopping the astounding growth for malware on mobile devices. The scope of the problem becomes even more evident when consideration is given to how many items have varied computer technologies in their core makeup. Automobiles, Smart TV's, Smart Homes, Smart Toilets, Smart Lighting Systems, ID Cameras, Refrigerators, Digital Locks, and the Android platform run game consoles, clocks, and home appliances just to mention a few. Security has to improve and increase its capabilities as there will be no shortage of entrepreneurs—the good and the bad—to lead the way.

References

Business Wire. (2014, January 22). MetaI ntell identifies enterprise security risks, privacy risks and data leakage in 92% of Top 500 Android mobile applications. Retrieved from http://www.businesswire.com/news/home/ 20140122006295/en/MetaIntell-Identifies-Enterprise-Security-Risks- Privacy-Risks#.VDwygPldXwY. Accessed 10/13/2014.

Blue Coat Systems. (2014). Mobile malware report: A new look at old threats, 2014. Retrieved from file:///C:/Users/Samsung/Downloads/report-mobile malware-fn.pdf. Accessed 10/13/2014.

Board of Governors Federal Reserve System. Consumers and Mobile Financial Services. (2014, March). Retrieved from http://www.federalreserve.gov/ econresdata/consumers-and-mobile-financial-services-report-201403. pdf(page 1).

CISCO. (2014). CISCO Annual Security Report. Retrieved from http:// www.cisco.com/web/offer/gist_ty2_asset/Cisco_2014_ASR.pdf. Accessed 08/28/2014.

Consumer Reports. (2014, May 28). Smart phone thefts rose to 3.1 million last year, Consumer Reports finds. Retrieved from http://www. consumerreports.org/cro/news/2014/04/smart-phone-thefts-rose-to-3-1- million-last-year/index.htm. Accessed 08/29/2014.

Court of Appeal of the State of California, Second Appellate District, Division Two. (2014, August 12). Case B247160, Colin Cochran versus Schwan's Home Service, Inc. Retrieved from http://www.courts.ca.gov/opinions/ documents/B247160.PDF. Accessed 10/14/2014.

Cox, J. (2013, February 7). Mobile data growth accelerating worldwide, led by smartphone users. NetworkWorld | February 7, 2013 9:33 AM PT. Retrieved from http://www.networkworld.com/article/2163348/smartphones/mobile- data-growth-accelerating-worldwide--led-by-smartphone-users.html. Accessed 8/29/2014.

Cyren. (2013). Security Yearbook, 2013 in Review and Outlook for 2014. Retrieved from http://www.cyren.com/tl_files/downloads/CYREN_

Security_Yearbook_EN.pdf?mkt_tok=3RkMMJWWfF9wsRokvq3IZKX onjHpfsX57%2BUkW6e2lMI%2F0ER3fOvrPUfGjI4ASspnI%2BSLDw EYGJlv6SgFQ7TBMbBn1bgNXBc%3D. Accessed 10/13/2014.

Ferguson, R. (2013, October 15). The bugs don't work, apparently! Retrieved from http://countermeasures.trendmicro.eu/the-bugs-dont-work-apparently/. Accessed 10/13/2014.

Forrester. (2012, May). Key strategies to capture and measure the value of consumerization of IT enterprises achieve a wide range of benefits by deploying Bring-Your-Own-Device programs. Retrieved from http://www.trendmicro.com/cloud-content/us/pdfs/business/white-papers/wp_forrester_measure-value-of-consumerization.pdf. Accessed 10/14/2014.

Gartner, Inc. (2013, December 12). Gartner says the Internet of Things installed base will grow to 26 billion units by 2020. Retrieved from http://www.gartner.com/newsroom/id/2636073. Accessed 10/13/2014.

Gartner, Inc. (2013). Gartner IT glossary. Retrieved from http://www.gartner.com/it-glossary/consumerization. Accessed 10/14/2014.

Krasas, N. (2014, January). Android malware analysis. Infosecinstitute. Retrieved from http://resources.infosecinstitute.com/android-malware-analysis/. Accessed 10/14/2014.

Javelin Strategy and Research. (2012). *Identity fraud industry report: Social media and mobile forming the new fraud frontier.* Retrieved from https://www.javelinstrategy.com/brochure/239.

Kaspersky Labs. (2014). Digital consumer's online trends and risks. Retrieved from http://www.kaspersky.com/downloads/pdf/kaspersky_lab_consumer_survey_report_eng_final.Pdf. Accessed 10/14/2014.

McAffee for Business. (2014, January). ADT and McAfee study shows strong tie between physical and digital security risks: More than half of respondents have had both their online and/or physical security compromised. Retrieved from http://www.mcaf.com.

Mobithinking. (2014, June 13). Global mobile statistics 2014 home: all the latest stats on mobile Web, apps, marketing, advertising, subscribers, and trends. http://mobiforge.com/research-analysis/global-mobile-statistics-2014-home-all-latest-stats-mobile-web-apps-marketing-advertising-subscriber?mT. Accessed 10/13/2014.

National Center for Health Statistics. (2014, July). Wireless substitution: Early release of estimates from the National Health Interview Survey, July-December 2013. Department of Health and Human Services, National Center for Health Statistics, July 2014. Retrieved from http://www.cdc.gov/nchs/data/nhis/earlyrelease/wireless201407.pdf.

Report Buyer. (2014, April). The Mobile Security (mSecurity) Bible: 2014–2020—Device Security, Infrastructure Security & Security Services, April 2014. Retrieved from https://www.reportbuyer.com/product/2092772/the-mobile-security-msecurity-bible-2014-2020-device-security-infrastructure-security-and-security-services.html. Accessed 10/13/2014.

Sophos Security Threat Report. (2013). Retrieved from http://www.sophos. com/en-us/medialibrary/PDFs/other/sophossecuritythreatreport2013.pdf. Accessed 08/29/2014.

Spiezle, C. D. (2014, May 15). Written Testimony before the Senate Committee on Homeland Security & Government Affairs Permanent Subcommittee on Investigations, May 15, 2014. Online advertising and hidden hazards to consumer security and data privacy, Majority and Minority Staff Report Permanent Subcommittee on Investigations United States Senate. Released in conjunction with the Permanente Subcommittee on Investigations May 12, 2014 Hearing.

Savitsky, A. (2014, February 6). Number of the Week: 10 Million Malicious Android Apps. Retrieved from http://blog.kaspersky.com/number-of-the-week-10-million-malicious-android-apps/. Accessed 10/14/2014.

Schulze, Holger. (2104). Group Founder, Information Security Committee, "BYOD and Mobile Security" Spotlight Report, 2014 Edition. Retrieved from http://www.slideshare.net/informationsecurity/byod-mobile-security-report. Accessed 10/14/2014.

Symantec. (2014). 2013 Norton Report. Symantec. Retrieved from http://www. symantec.com/about/news/resources/press_kits/detail.jsp?pkid=norton-report-2013. Accessed 10/14/2014.

Thye, L. (2013, January 17). Danger: Malware ahead!—Please, not my site. SYMANTEC (January 17, 2013). Retrieved from http://www.symantec. com/connect/blogs/danger-malware-ahead-please-not-my-site.

Online advertising and hidden hazards to consumer security and data privacy. Majority and Minority Staff Report Permanent Subcommittee on Investigations United States Senate. Released in conjunction with the Permanent Subcommittee on Investigations May 12, 2014 Hearing.

U.S. Senate. (2014, May 15). Online advertising and hidden hazards to consumer security and data privacy. Majority and Minority Staff Report Permanent Subcommittee on Investigations United States Senate. Released in conjunction with the Permanente Subcommittee on Investigations May 12, 2014 Hearing.

Verizon. (2014). Verizon's Data Breach Investigations Report DBIR 2014. Retrieved from file:///C:/Users/Samsung/Downloads/rp_Verizon-DBIR-2014_en_xg.pdf. Accessed 8/29/2014.

Virus News. (2014, February 6). Number of the week: List of malicious Android apps hits 10 million. Retrieved from http://www.kaspersky.com/about/news/virus/2014/Number-of-the-week-list-of-malicious-Android-apps-hits-10-million. Accessed 8/29/2014.

Chapter 6

Cybersecurity and the Legal Profession

Andrew A. Proia and Drew Simshaw

Introduction

The relationship between the law and cybersecurity continues to grow in significance and complexity every day. According to a report by the Congressional Research Service, more than 40 federal laws contain provisions addressing cybersecurity (Fischer, 2013), a number that is likely to increase in the coming years. Recent large-scale data breaches have spawned numerous class-action lawsuits against some of the country's largest companies, with many of the plaintiffs arguing that it was these companies' legally insufficient information security measures that allowed the breaches to occur. Federal regulators and state attorneys general have also begun utilizing their legal authority to investigate information security incidents, and ensuring that companies have implemented reasonable security measures when handling sensitive data.

As governments, industries, and individuals become more reliant on increasingly complex and vulnerable technologies, professionals skilled in applying, enforcing, and interpreting the law will play an increasingly important role in cybersecurity. Lawyers, paralegals, and

119

other legal professionals are becoming keenly aware of the demands cybersecurity brings to the profession. While great attention is rightfully paid to the need for technical expertise, an effective cybersecurity workforce also depends, in part, on a legal profession that fully understands and embraces the importance of cybersecurity. Overall, "[a] large number of professionals—with not only technical skills, but also an understanding of cyber policy, law, and other disciplines— will be needed to ensure the continued success of the U.S. economy, government, and society in the 21st-century information age" (Kay, Pudas, & Young, 2012).

A need for specialized legal services is created by the numerous statutes, regulations, legal doctrines, and policies related to the protection of information and information systems from unauthorized access, use, disclosure, disruption, modification, or destruction. "Cybersecurity," "data protection," and "data security" law and policy practice areas are taking shape in some of the country's largest and most prestigious law firms. Typical among these practice areas are legal services for complying with domestic and global data security and privacy laws, developing security plans and managing information security risks, drafting contracts with vendors that require certain security protections, and supporting organizational responses to data breaches.

At the same time, the legal profession itself faces a number of cybersecurity challenges and is beginning to recognize the importance of protecting its own assets and information systems. In some ways, legal professionals are better suited to handle these challenges than members of other professions; confidentiality is already ingrained into the culture of legal practice and the top-down power structure of law firms enables partners to efficiently and effectively enforce priorities, including proper information security plans. However, other aspects of the legal profession present unique hurdles to achieving effective cybersecurity. Law firms and lawyers are often averse to discussing the topic before a breach—which takes time away from providing direct legal services—and after a breach—when such news can cause embarrassment to the lawyer, the law firm, and its clients. Basic cybersecurity measures (like keeping up to date on security-relevant software updates) are sometimes seen as inhibitors to efficiency and convenience, both of which are highly valued in the fast-paced world of law.

This chapter will examine the unique role of cybersecurity within the legal profession as both an innovative practice area and an ethical requirement for those practicing law. First, this chapter will examine the individuals that make up the legal profession and the unique ethical obligations imposed on practicing lawyers and their staff to implement reasonable cybersecurity measures. Second, this chapter highlights the threats facing the profession, and why lawyers and law firms are prime targets for cyber attacks. Third, this chapter reviews some of the skills necessary for members of the legal profession, and how these skills shape the cybersecurity law and policy landscape. Finally, this chapter provides recommendations for the legal cybersecurity workforce and additional resources for the curious reader.

This discussion does not intend to provide an exhaustive review of the many components that make up the legal profession's role in cybersecurity. Instead, the chapter highlights some of the unique ways in which legal professionals are developing cybersecurity law and policy as a growing practice area, while also examining some of the challenges the profession still faces as emerging technology continues to play a critical role in providing the public with sound—and con-fidential—legal services. Nothing contained in this chapter is to be considered as the rendering of legal advice, and readers should consult legal counsel with any questions or issues they may have.

The Legal Profession's Unique Cybersecurity Roles and Obligations

The Legal Profession

Legal professionals are among the most educated members of the American workforce, and should be well suited to understand the complexities of the cybersecurity challenges that face most organizations and the country. The core professionals within the legal profession are lawyers, or the men and women who are licensed to practice law. Typically, a lawyer will have received a bachelor's degree from an accredited college or university, and will have received a law degree, known as a "juris doctorate" or "doctor of jurisprudence," from a law school accredited by the American Bar Association (ABA). The practice of law is primarily a self-regulated profession, in which licensing and practice requirements are governed, for the most part, by state bar associations. In order to receive a license to practice law in a given state, applicants must be successfully admitted into a state's bar. While state requirements vary, bar admission generally requires a law degree, a rigorous character and fitness examination by the state's board of bar examiners, and a satisfactory score on both the Multistate Professional Responsibility Exam and the state-issued bar examination of the state in which the applicant wishes to practice (National Conference of Bar Examiners, 2014).

Licensed attorneys, however, represent only one of the many occupations that make up the legal profession. Non-lawyer legal professionals serve an important function in the enforcement, administration, and interpretation of law. Paralegals, for instance, are individuals trained to conduct substantive legal work and assist lawyers in their day-to-day operations. While not allowed to provide legal advice or otherwise engage in the practice of law, paralegals work across all legal practice areas and can gain qualifications through education, training, or work experience (National Federation of Paralegal Associations, 2011). Other positions within the legal profession include court clerks, who help administer trial proceedings and run many of the day-to-day operations of the judiciary; and mediators, who help resolve disagreements, such as contract disputes, outside of the formal legal process (American Bar Association, 2010).

As cybersecurity continues to become more heavily regulated in the public and private sectors, non-lawyer legal professionals will become an even greater asset within cybersecurity programs. Specifically, these individuals will be tasked with understanding relevant cybersecurity laws and policies, and making sure that an organization's implemented security and privacy controls are in compliance with applicable requirements. Although still an area of growth and likely to be found only in organizations with more comprehensive cybersecurity programs, these non-lawyer legal and compliance positions will continue to increase in value and importance, even though they do not involve providing legal advice.

Cybersecurity and the Rules of Professional Conduct

The standards of professional conduct imposed upon lawyers are some of the most unique of any profession. Each state has varying ethical standards required of lawyers practicing within that state. For most states, ethical standards are based upon the ABA's Model Rules of Professional Conduct (2013). These model rules are divided into eight sections, and include rules that govern the establishment of an attorney–client relationship, the responsibilities of a lawyer in maintaining an attorney–client relationship, and the responsibilities of a lawyer as an advocate, counselor, and public servant. Although this discussion uses the ABA Model Rules as a guide, the particular ethical rules in a given state may vary.

Increasingly, these ethics rules impose duties and obligations upon lawyers to practice reasonable cybersecurity—and to make sure that their employees and business partners do the same. Many of these ethical obligations, such as the duty of competency and the duty of confidentiality, ensure for clients that the lawyers with whom they are consulting will have sufficient knowledge of the laws and policies affecting cybersecurity, and will keep all attorney–client communications confidential. In addition, these ethical obligations require lawyers, more so than many other professions, to implement proper safeguards to protect their clients' information. Ensuring that sensitive, confidential, and privileged data are kept secure is no longer just good business practice—it is a requirement, and violations are punishable by a state bar's ethics body (Rhodes & Polley, 2014). This section reviews some of the relevant ethical obligations related to cybersecurity.

Duty of Confidentiality

First, a lawyer has a duty of confidentiality. With very limited exceptions, ABA Model Rule 1.6 states that "[a] lawyer shall not reveal information relating to the representation of a client unless the client gives informed consent" (ABA Rule 1.6, 2013). In light of technological advancements and the ethics rules already being practiced in jurisdictions across the country, the ABA recently approved several changes to the Model Rules. A recent addition to Rule 1.6, *Confidentiality of Information*, was language stating that "[a] lawyer shall make reasonable efforts to prevent the inadvertent or unauthorized disclosure of, or unauthorized access to, information relating to the representation of a client." The comments to the amended rule now provide a non-exhaustive list of "[f]actors to be considered in determining the reasonableness of the lawyer's efforts," including:

- the sensitivity of the information;

- the likelihood of disclosure if additional safeguards are not employed;

- the cost of employing additional safeguards;

- the difficulty of implementing the safeguards; and

- the extent to which the safeguards adversely affect the lawyer's ability to represent clients (e.g., by making a device or important piece of software excessively difficult to use).

(ABA Rule 1.6, comm. 18, 2013)

The comments to Rule 1.6 also note that "[w]hen transmitting a communication that includes information relating to the representation of a client, the lawyer must take reasonable precautions to prevent the information from coming into the hands of unintended recipients" (ABA Rule 1.6, comm. 19, 2013). However, no special security measures are required if the communication method affords a "reasonable expectation of privacy," unless there are special circumstances. In determining "the reasonableness of the lawyer's expectation of confidentiality," factors to be considered include "the sensitivity of the information and the extent to which the privacy of the communication is protected by law or by a confidentiality agreement" (ABA Rule 1.6, comm. 19, 2013).

Finally, the comments to Rule 1.6 state that "[a] client may require the lawyer to implement special security measures not required by this Rule or may give informed consent to the use of a means of communication that would otherwise be prohibited by this Rule" (ABA Rule 1.6, comm. 19, 2013). It should be noted that cyber threats to confidential information do not cease to exist once a client's legal needs have been resolved and formal representation ends, and ABA Model Rule 1.9(c) explains that a lawyer's obligation of confidentiality applies to former clients, as well.

Although the ABA's Model Rules use general terms and factors to guide ethical practices regarding confidential information in light of cyber threats, several states have offered specific examples of how to properly secure a client's electronically stored information in various contexts. For example, in 2009, the State Bar of Arizona determined that, "[i]n satisfying the duty to take reasonable security precautions, lawyers should consider firewalls, password protection schemes, encryption, anti-virus measures," and other related measures (State Bar of Arizona, 2009). Lawyers should be mindful of specific precautionary requirements within their jurisdiction, but should also realize that compliance with minimum standards of any kind—including those delineated in ethics rules—should only be a starting point for effective cybersecurity practices. Lawyers should consider ways in which extra security measures can be employed where appropriate and feasible. The ABA Cybersecurity Handbook eloquently summarizes that, "[i]n short, a lawyer cannot take the 'ostrich' approach of hiding his head in the sand and hoping that his office or firm will not suffer a data breach that compromises client information." Instead, "[l]awyers must implement administrative, technical, and physical safeguards to meet their obligation to make reasonable efforts to protect client information" (Rhodes & Polley, 2014).

Duty of Competence

In addition to the duty of confidentiality, lawyers are also ethically required to provide competent representation. Under ABA Rule 1.1, lawyers are required to provide "the legal knowledge, skill, thoroughness and preparation reasonably necessary for the representation" (ABA Rule 1.1, 2013). The ABA recently added language to the rule's commentary stating, "[t]o maintain the requisite knowledge and skill, a lawyer should keep abreast of changes in the law and its practice, including the benefits and risks associated with relevant technology" (ABA Rule 1.5 comm. 8, 2013). The new language reflects the dual role lawyers play in cybersecurity: First, part of a lawyer's competence includes understanding technology well enough to protect confidential client information; second, this language means that a lawyer must understand technology and the law well enough to properly advise clients on how to satisfy legal requirements and protect information and information systems.

Competence from a cybersecurity perspective requires lawyers to understand the types of legal problems that may arise from a client's cybersecurity incidents and how to properly respond to them. The importance of this aspect of competence was apparent in the aftermath of the 2013 data breach of major retail store Target. During the 2013 holiday season, Target suffered a major data breach of customer information. According to a report by the U.S. Senate Committee on Commerce, Science, and Transportation, malware on Target's point of sale terminals resulted in the exposure of account data linked to an estimated 40 million credit and debit cards (2014). Since the discovery of the Target breach, dozens of lawsuits have been filed arguing a wide variety of legal theories, all of which Target's legal representatives need to understand. Many Target consumers, for instance, filed together in what is known as a class-action lawsuit, alleging numerous theories of liability, including negligence and breach of contract. In addition, Target's shareholders filed a lawsuit against the company's leadership, claiming that Target directors' and officers' failure to take reasonable steps to safeguard consumer information, and their delay in disclosing the breach to shareholders, breached their legal obligations to act in the best interest of their shareholders—commonly known as a breach of fiduciary duties. Banks, too, claimed that Target's lax cybersecurity measures entitled the banks to compensation for credit card reimbursement made to affected customers as a result of the breach. Umpqua Holdings Corporation, an Oregon-based commercial bank, even made the "cleaver and novel" argument, according to cybersecurity attorney Joseph Burton, that Target, a Minneapolis-based company, breached Minnesota's Plastic Card Security Act (Kitten, 2014). The Target incident is just one example of how a massive cybersecurity incident can implicate numerous laws and legal doctrines. As cybersecurity law and policy continue to develop, lawyers and other legal professionals will need to become especially well versed in the laws specifically addressing the security of information and information systems. At the same time, lawyers must also be knowledgeable of the more traditional legal doctrines, and how technology may affect the interpretation of these doctrines in new and innovative ways.

Supervising Third Parties

In order to comply with ethical requirements, lawyers must also properly supervise those who work for them. The ABA Model Rules contain two rules that apply to a law firm partner, as well as "a lawyer who individually or together with other lawyers possesses comparable managerial authority in a law firm." The Rules state that those lawyers "shall make reasonable efforts to ensure that the firm has in effect measures giving reasonable assurance that," under Rule 5.1, "all lawyers in the firm conform to the Rules of Professional Conduct" (ABA Rule 5.1, 2013), and under Rule 5.3, that the conduct of a non-lawyer employed by, retained by, or associated with the lawyer, "is compatible with the professional obligations of the lawyer" (ABA Rule 5.3, 2013).

Under these rules, it is essential that all members of the legal profession, not just lawyers, understand cybersecurity and the unique ethical obligations associated with protecting client information. A law office's cybersecurity is only as strong as its weakest link. Subordinate attorneys, legal interns, paralegals, case managers, administrative assistants, and business partners must all understand their critical cybersecurity role in the legal profession, including the need to conform their conduct to the ethics standards of lawyers in their jurisdiction.

Cybersecurity Threats to the Legal Profession

Cybersecurity has been and continues to be a growing concern for lawyers and the legal profession as a whole. A 2014 study of nearly 500 directors and general counsels ranked data security as one of the top concerns for both groups. In addition, IT/cyber risk "was chosen by . . . 33% of general counsel as an issue they spend significant time on" (FTI Consulting, 2014). This concern is for good reason. Law firms are increasingly becoming a target of attacks. Recognizing this vulnerability, large organizational clients are asking their law firms to increase their cybersecurity efforts as FBI officials and security experts warn that "law firms remain a weak link when it comes to online security" (Goldstein, 2014).

Law firms of all sizes are seen as attractive targets for hackers for two compounding reasons. First, the law firm represents a treasure trove of valuable information. By breaching one firm, a hacker can gain access to the information of all of that firm's clients—a far more efficient hack than going after the clients individually. In addition, lawyers are usually involved in only their client's most important business matters, meaning hackers may not need to sift through extraneous data to find the more valuable information. Having successfully completed a breach, malicious actors will have access to all sorts of sensitive information, including a client's intellectual property, business strategies, transaction information, and financial records. Second, not only are law firms viewed by hackers as valuable targets, they are also seen as easy ones. Law firms are perceived to have fewer security resources than their clients, with less understanding of and appreciation for cyber risks.

In order to confront this harsh reality and adopt effective cybersecurity measures, the legal profession must understand the actors behind these attacks, including their motives and methods. At one time, a law firm's biggest worry may have been that its known vulnerabilities and weaknesses were being exploited. Indeed, firms must always be wary of malicious insiders hoping to cause embarrassment to the firm or advance their own pecuniary interest. However, outside social engineering is becoming especially popular and effective, especially targeted phishing attacks that compromise a firm's network by installing malicious software and backdoors. Finally, law firms are increasingly finding themselves targeted by more sophisticated state-sponsored attackers capable of executing advanced persistent threats or distributed denial of service attacks against even well-secured systems. These actors' motives are wide ranging, from economic espionage to advancing political or ideological interests.

The consequences of successful targeted attacks against law offices are great, beyond the obvious destruction of attorney–client privilege. Clients and third parties may find themselves victims of fraud, identity theft, and bankruptcy, not to mention negative publicity and tarnished business reputation. Depending on the circumstances and severity of the attack, these parties could face civil actions from other harmed individuals or organizations, administrative proceedings from state or federal agencies, or even criminal charges.

Consequences of attacks for law firms can also be dire. If a firm failed to employ reasonable security measures, lawyers could find themselves facing ethics violations, threatening their ability to continue the practice of law. Attorneys can also face serious discipline from courts that may have imposed protective orders on certain sensitive information pertaining to a case. In addition, law offices could face government investigations, fines, and private law suits. Clients, whether directly affected by the breach or not, would likely claim malpractice and find other legal representation. But perhaps most damaging could be the irreparable harm done to the reputation of the practice and its members. The trust of clients, judges, the legal community, and the public are essential to any member of the legal profession. The embarrassment, negative publicity, and reputational harm resulting from a cyber attack could not only threaten the viability of a particular practice, but could also jeopardize the ability of its members to remain in the field.

Important Skills Needed by Legal Professionals

The ABA offers a number of important skills and values that provide a solid foundation for lawyers, and for those interested in entering the legal profession. These skills and values include:

- Problem Solving

- Critical Reading

- Writing and Editing

- Oral Communication and Listening

- Research

- Organization and Management

- Public Service and Promotion of Justice

- Relationship Building and Collaboration

- Background Knowledge of the Law and the Profession

- Exposure to the Law

(ABA Section of Legal Education and
Admission to the Bar, 2014)

While these skills and values are critical to the profession in general, they are especially important to addressing cybersecurity law and policy. To elaborate upon these and other skills in a cybersecurity context, this section examines two roles served by lawyers: (1) the lawyer-as-counselor, and (2) the lawyer-as-advocate.

Counseling the Client on the Law and Cybersecurity

Lawyers are often sought to provide clients with candid and straightforward advice. In representing clients, lawyers are ethically required to exercise independent professional judgment, referring not only to the law, "but to other considerations such as moral, economic, social and political factors, that may be relevant to the client's situation" (ABA Rule 2.1, 2013). As one Virginia attorney astutely recognized, legal advice is rarely limited to only legal considerations: "Good legal advice means the lawyer must listen closely in order to appreciate and understand the client's particular concerns and values," and "requires the lawyer to draw on personal experience, skill, and knowledge to formulate the strategies and solutions that will help achieve the client's goals" (Burtch, 2013). In some contexts, including cybersecurity, a lawyer's advice could be of a technical nature, as long as the lawyer maintains the requisite knowledge to provide competent advice on the subject matter.

Utilizing technological knowledge in order to help clients navigate the myriad of cybersecurity laws and regulations is an essential part of the legal profession's role in providing effective cybersecurity advice. Fulfilling this role requires lawyers to be skilled in understanding how to appropriately identify clients' information assets, while also properly assessing potential risks to those assets. For instance, determining the type of data a client maintains, where it is stored, and precisely how it is handled will help lawyers ascertain the scope of relevant regulations, all the while realizing that a change in client behavior may trigger the application of additional regulations. In the same way that a client's data practices might change, so too may the regulations themselves. Whenever a new cybersecurity regulation is issued, or an existing one is amended or reinterpreted, a lawyer must not only be aware of such changes, but must understand how the change will affect each client. Finally, all this information is critical so that lawyers can properly advise clients before and after they experience a cyber incident, with particular attention paid to mitigating internal and external damages and complying with industry standards and federal and state requirements.

Counseling clients on the intricate web of breach notification laws provides a good example. According to the National Conference of State Legislatures, 47 states, the District of Columbia, Guam, Puerto Rico, and the Virgin Islands have enacted security breach notification legislation—laws which require "private or government entities to notify individuals of security breaches of information involving personally identifiable information" (National Conference of State Legislatures, 2014). Each state law, however, varies in what is required of organizations who have suffered a security breach. For example, states vary on what type of personal information would trigger the statute, and what needs to happen in order for any particular incident to constitute a "breach." In responding to a breach, states differ as to what information must be included in the subsequently required notice, who must receive the notice, and the amount of time an organization has to provide notice after the breach is discovered. Some states even provide for an exception when the breached information meets certain encryption standards. Whether assisting clients in developing a breach response plan or in responding to a potential breach, lawyers need to be aware of these distinct breach notification requirements and ask the right questions in order to properly advise clients on their particular situation.

Cybersecurity, however, should not just be a concern of lawyers who practice "cybersecurity law," or who represent large technology corporations—it must be a concern of all members of the legal profession. As the ABA Cybersecurity Handbook explains, "the profusion of digital technologies has added cybersecurity to every client's primary interests, whether or not the client knows it, thereby drawing cybersecurity into the field of view that counsel must watch over if it is to provide competent representation of a client" (Rhodes & Polley, 2014).

Advocating for the Client and the Public Interest

A lawyer's role as a client advocate is one of the profession's most well-known responsibilities. While this includes skills such as oral advocacy in front of a jury or tribunal, the lawyer-as-advocate includes so much more. Persuasive motions, briefs, and other written documents filed with a court on behalf of a client are also a critical component of arguing a legal position. A successful advocate must have strong critical reading, writing, editing, and oral communication skills. "Language is the most important tool of a lawyer," according to the ABA, "and lawyers must learn to express themselves clearly and concisely" (ABA Section of Legal Education and Admission to the Bar, 2014). Lawyers are taught early and often in their education how important legal research and writing is to the practice of law. Skilled and effective advocates can help protect the rights of a client, enforce or change the law, and "make sure that the legal system works as it was intended to work" (Oates, Enquist, & Krontz, 2008). The important role of lawyers-as-advocates is outlined in the Preamble and Scope of the ABA Model Rules of Professional Conduct, stating that, as an advocate, a lawyer "zealously asserts the client's position under the rules of the adversary system" (2013).

Because laws and policies surrounding cybersecurity are still being formed, persuasive advocacy is especially important. The laws and regulations surrounding cybersecurity lack the maturity of other areas of the law. This means that legal disputes on cybersecurity issues will frequently be questions of first impression. What does it mean to require "reasonable" or "appropriate" security safeguards when protecting consumer data, as some laws currently mandate? Can a company be liable for a breach of consumer information, even if the only "harm" that results is an increased risk of harm, such as the increased risk of identity theft? Can federal agencies regulate cybersecurity related issues, even without explicit authority to do so? If so, what specifically do they have the authority to regulate? It is very likely that many of these questions will need to be answered in the court room, with lawyers arguing to a judge how the text and the intent of a particular law should be interpreted.

Legal advocacy, however, is not limited to court rooms or to individual clients, particularly when it comes to cybersecurity. Many public interest organizations, some employing dozens of lawyers and policy analysts specializing in cybersecurity law and policy, advocate on behalf of the public-at-large to ensure that the growing body of law addressing cybersecurity will properly respect the constitutional rights and civil liberties of all. These organizations may issue public letters and formal comments to policymakers and executive agencies advocating for a particular action or approach to cybersecurity-related issues, speak at congressional hearings or other fora to advocate their opinions and concerns, or even file "friend of the court," or "amicus curiae," briefs in court cases to assist the judiciary in understanding perspectives of a legal issue that may not otherwise be considered.

A number of public interest organizations have specifically focused their advocacy efforts on issues related to cybersecurity. The Center for Democracy and Technology (CDT), a Washington, D.C.-based non-profit organization working to keep the Internet open, innovative, and free, has a number of public interest attorneys and policy analysts working on cybersecurity-related issues. CDT advocates for cybersecurity policies "based on the principles of openness, collaboration, and a respect for human rights" (Center for Democracy and Technology, 2014). The Electronic Frontier Foundation (EFF), a San Francisco-based non-profit, has been a leading advocate of the protection of civil liberties and free expressions in the digital age since 1990. EFF's work includes issues related to free speech, fair use, innovation, privacy, transparency, and a number of other national and international issues (Electronic Frontier Foundation, 2014).

Advocates working in these public interest organizations can have a tremendous effect on cybersecurity law and policy. For instance, many public interest organizations have been fighting recent cyber threat information-sharing legislation, advocating for more comprehensive cybersecurity laws that better protect individual privacy and civil liberties. In 2014, for example, dozens of public interest organizations (including EFF and CDT) urged President Obama to pledge to veto the proposed Senate Bill 2588, the Cybersecurity Information Sharing Act of 2014. "Legislation that focuses exclusively on facilitation of information sharing," the letter to President Obama stated, "jeopardizes the foundation of cybersecurity by improperly pitting human rights against security" (Access et al., 2014). As laws like these continue to be proposed and implemented, lawyers working at public interest organizations, utilizing their strong advocacy skill sets, will continue to play an active role in shaping the way the country approaches cybersecurity.

Recommendations Going Forward

Embracing the Role of the Law and the Legal Profession

Efforts to "professionalize" the cybersecurity workforce must continue to recognize the important role the law plays in cybersecurity. While technical expertise is still an important skill for cybersecurity professionals, effective cybersecurity programs require a multi-disciplinary approach. Greater effort is needed to develop cybersecurity professionals that have knowledge beyond their technical training. According to a recent report issued by the Pell Center for International Relations and Public Policy, "few American universities and colleges offer courses or degree programs that combine cybersecurity technology, policy, business and other disciplines, and even fewer encourage collaboration among departments to optimize their efforts and insights available from cross-fertilization" (Spidalieri & Kern, 2014). The report correctly urges cybersecurity programs to expand and integrate into other relevant university programs, both technical and non-technical. Overall, more can be done to educate cybersecurity professionals of the vast and often complex legal and regulatory cybersecurity requirements that exist.

Some efforts do exist, however, that utilize a broad, interdisciplinary approach to developing the cybersecurity workforce. The National Initiative for Cybersecurity Education's (NICE) National Cybersecurity Workforce Framework recommends that certain cybersecurity positions maintain a sufficient level of knowledge regarding relevant cybersecurity laws. Additionally, the NICE Framework's position taxonomy includes "Legal Advice and Advocacy" workers who "[p]rovide legally sound advice and recommendations to leadership and staff on a variety of relevant topics within the pertinent subject domain" (National Initiative for Cybersecurity Education, 2014). Efforts to include legal professionals within the cybersecurity profession, such as the NICE Framework, should be encouraged, and discussions on how to standardize cybersecurity education and training would be wise to include a greater focus on cybersecurity law and policy.

Educating Lawyers

Greater efforts should also be made to encourage lawyers to invest in cybersecurity. Despite cybersecurity becoming a growing legal practice area, lawyers still lack the technological savvy to secure their own information and devices. The *Wall Street Journal* has reported that, in the eyes of security experts and technology directors, "the weakest links at law firms of any size are often their own employees, including lawyers" (Smith, 2012). Licensed attorneys should attend conferences and mandatory continuing legal education courses in order to better understand technology jargon. In addition, lawyers should keep up to date with industry cybersecurity standards and what constitutes "reasonable" data security measures, so that they may understand both the obligations and best practices of their office, and so they can properly advise clients. The call for a legal response to the current threats to information and information systems has created an opportunity for the legal profession to play a significant role in cybersecurity. However, in order to credibly and competently contribute to this field, the profession must start by ensuring that all lawyers and law firms are properly educated.

Educating Non-Lawyer Legal Professionals

In addition to increasing the cybersecurity knowledge of lawyers, programs should be providing paralegals, case managers, administrative assistants, and other non-lawyer legal professionals with cybersecurity awareness and training. As discussed earlier, lawyers are responsible for their staff—their ethical violations are the lawyer's ethical violations. Law firm employees and contractors should undergo frequent cybersecurity training. Lawyers should also advise their clients to do the same for their own employees, as many laws and industry standards require internal data security policies that apply to all personnel within an organization. The importance of cybersecurity, and the role of individuals in an organization-wide cybersecurity program, should be stressed early and often, beyond what is required for mere legal compliance. Orientations of new staff should include cybersecurity, and specific responsibilities and policies should be reiterated during frequent and regular training courses. Relevant laws, specific legal requirements, ethical obligations, and consequences of noncompliance or—far worse—a breach, are not just things that should be "left to the lawyers"; they are imperative components of any educated, cyber-aware workforce.

Conclusion

This chapter has provided an overview of some of the cybersecurity issues within the legal profession. The legal profession's ethical obligations are unlike those of any other, and impose certain cybersecurity requirements that pertain to the profession's continued utilization of new and innovative technologies. In addition, the confidential nature of legal work, and the highly sensitive information entrusted to lawyers by their clients, creates a great incentive for malicious actors to target lawyers and law firms. As the nation's reliance on technology continues to advance, and as threats become more sophisticated and prevalent, the legal profession will continue to play a critical role in the ever-growing cybersecurity landscape. By taking the recommendations of this chapter into consideration, the growing role of the legal profession within cybersecurity can be a prosperous one.

Sources of Further Information

- *The ABA Cybersecurity Handbook: A Resource for Attorneys, Law Firms, and Business Professionals*, referenced throughout this chapter and greatly admired by the authors, provides a practical guide to a number of cybersecurity challenges facing lawyers. In addition, the American Bar Association's Cybersecurity Legal Task Force, comprised of ABA members tasked with compiling cybersecurity resources, maintains a very informative website with podcasts, books, and ABA policy initiatives related to cybersecurity. At the time of this writing, the website can be found at: www.americanbar.org/groups/leadership/office_of_the_president/cybersecurity.

- The National Conference of State Legislatures maintains a website with all state breach notification laws, as well as additional materials. At the time of this writing, the page was last updated in April of 2014,

and can be found at: http://www.ncsl.org/research/
telecommunications-and-information-technology/
security-breach-notification-laws.

- The Congressional Research Services (CRS) is a non-
  partisan legislative branch agency tasked with providing
  policy and legal analysis to members of Congress. The
  agency's recently updated report, *Cybersecurity: Authoritative Reports and Resources, by Topic*, provides a thorough
  review of "analytical reports on cybersecurity from CRS,
  other government agencies, trade associations, and interest groups." In addition to listing the numerous reports
  issued by CRS dealing specifically with cybersecurity, the
  report lists dozens of authoritative documents on a range
  of cybersecurity issues.

- For a global perspective, the international law firm DLA
  Piper has released its handbook, *Data Protection Laws
  of the World*. In addition to the handbook's overview
  of the world's data privacy and security laws, the law
  firm has provided users with an interactive online map
  that contains a snapshot of each country's laws, and
  the ability to compare countries side-by-side. At the
  time of this writing, the interactive online map can be
  found at: http://dlapiperdataprotection.com/#handbook/
  world-map-section.

References

Access et al. (2014). Letter to President Barack Obama. *Electronic Frontier Foundation*. https://www.eff.org/files/2014/07/15/coalition-ltr-cisa-20140715.pdf.

American Bar Association Center for Professional Responsibility. (2013). Model rules of professional conduct. *Preamble and Scope*. Retrieved from http://www.americanbar.org/groups/professional_responsibility/publications/model_rules_of_professional_conduct/model_rules_of_professional_conduct_preamble_scope.html. Accessed September 1, 2014.

American Bar Association Center for Professional Responsibility. (2013). Model rules of professional conduct. *Rule 1.1 Competence*. Retrieved from http:// www.americanbar.org/groups/professional_responsibility/publications/ model_rules_of_professional_conduct/rule_1_1_competence.html. Accessed September 1, 2014.

American Bar Association Center for Professional Responsibility. (2013). Model rules of professional conduct. *Rule 1.1 Competence—Comment*. Accessed September 1, 2014. Retrieved from http://www.americanbar. org/groups/professional_responsibility/publications/model_rules_of_ professional_conduct/rule_1_1_competence/comment_on_rule_1_1. html.

American Bar Association Center for Professional Responsibility. (2013). Model rules of professional conduct. *Rule 1.6 Confidentiality of Information*. Retrieved from http://www.americanbar.org/groups/professional_ responsibility/publications/model_rules_of_professional_conduct/ rule_1_6_confidentiality_of_information.html. Accessed September 1, 2014.

American Bar Association Center for Professional Responsibility. (2013). Model rules of professional conduct. *Rule 1.6 Confidentiality of Information—Comment*. Retrieved from http://www.americanbar.org/ groups/professional_responsibility/publications/model_rules_of_ professional_conduct/rule_1_6_confidentiality_of_information/ comment_on_rule_1_6.html. Accessed September 1, 2014.

American Bar Association Center for Professional Responsibility. (2013). Model rules of professional conduct. *Rule 2.1 Advisor*. Retrieved from http:// www.americanbar.org/groups/professional_responsibility/publications/ model_rules_of_professional_conduct/rule_2_1_advisor.html. Accessed September 1, 2014.

American Bar Association Center for Professional Responsibility. (2013). Model rules of professional conduct. *Rule 5.1 Responsibilities of a Partner or Supervisory Lawyer*. Retrieved from http://www.americanbar.org/groups/ professional_responsibility/publications/model_rules_of_professional_ conduct/rule_5_1_responsibilities_of_a_partner_or_supervisory_lawyer. html. Accessed September 1, 2014.

American Bar Association Center for Professional Responsibility. (2013). Model rules of professional conduct. *Rule 5.3 Responsibilities Regarding Nonlawyer Assistance*. Retrieved from http://www.americanbar.org/groups/ professional_responsibility/publications/model_rules_of_professional_ conduct/rule_5_3_responsibilities_regarding_nonlawyer_assistant.html. Accessed September 1, 2014.

ABA Section of Legal Education and Admission to the Bar. (2014). Pre-law: Preparing for law school. *American Bar Association*. Retrieved from

http://www.americanbar.org/groups/legal_education/resources/pre_law.
html. Accessed September 1, 2014.

Burtch Jr., J. W. (2010). The lawyer as counselor. *Virginia Lawyer*, April.
http://www.vsb.org/docs/valawyermagazine/vl0410_counselor.pdf.

Center for Democracy and Technology. (2014). Cybersecurity. Retrieved
from https://cdt.org/issue/global-internet-policy/cybersecurity. Accessed
September 1, 2014.

Electronic Frontier Foundation. (2014). Our work. Retrieved from https://
www.eff.org/issues. Accessed September 1, 2014.

Fischer, E. A. (2013). Federal laws relating to cybersecurity: Overview and
discussion of proposed revisions. *Congressional Research Service*. http://
fas.org/sgp/crs/natsec/R42114.pdf.

FTI Consulting, and NYSE Governance Services. (2014). Law in the
boardroom in 2014. http://www.fticonsulting.com/global2/critical-
thinking/reports/law-in-the-boardroom-in-2014.aspx.

Goldstein, M. (2014). Law firms are pressed on security for data. *New
York Times*, March 27. Retrieved from http://dealbook.nytimes.
com/2014/03/26/law-firms-scrutinized-as-hacking-increases/. Accessed
September 1, 2014.

Kay, D. J., Pudas, T. J., and Young, B. (2012, August 1). Preparing the
pipeline: The U.S. cyber workforce for the future. *Defense Horizons*.
Washington, DC: Institute for National Strategic Studies.

Kitten, T. (2014. March 17). Bank files unique suit against Target.
BankInfoSecurity. Retrieved from http://www.bankinfosecurity.com/
bank-files-unique-suit-against-target-a-6639. Accessed September 1,
2014.

Lamm, C. B., Rodriguez, E. R., and McKinney-Browning, M. C. (2010).
"A Life in the Law." American Bar Association. Chicago, IL: ABA
Division for Public Education.

National Conference of Bar Examiners, and American Bar Association Section
of Legal Education and Admission to the Bar. (2014). Comprehensive
guide to bar admission requirements 2014. Retrieved from http://www.
ncbex.org/assets/media_files/Comp-Guide/CompGuide.pdf.

National Conference of State Legislatures. (2014). Security breach notification
laws. Retrieved from http://www.ncsl.org/research/telecommunications-
and-information-technology/security-breach-notification-laws.aspx.
Accessed September 1, 2014.

National Federation of Paralegal Associations. (2011). Paralegal responsibilities.
Retrieved from http://www.paralegals.org/associations/2270/files/paralegal_
responsibilities.pdf.

National Initiative for Cybersecurity Education. (2014). The National
Cybersecurity Workforce framework. Retrieved from http://csrc.nist.
gov/nice/framework/. Accessed September 1, 2014.

Oates, L. C., Enquist, A., and Krontz, C. (2008). *Just briefs*. 2nd ed. New York: Aspen Publishers, Inc.

Rhodes, J. D., and Polley, V. I. (2014). *The ABA cybersecurity handbook: A resource for attorneys, law firms, and business professionals*. Chicago, IL: American Bar Association.

Spidalieri, F, and Kern, S. (2014). Professionalizing cybersecurity: A path to universal standards and status. *Pell Center for International Relations and Public Policy*. Retrieved from http://pellcenter.salvereginablogs.com/files/2014/07/Professionalization-of-Cybersecurity-7-28-14.pdf.

Smith, J. (2012, June 26). Lawyers get vigilant on cybersecurity. *Wall Street Journal*. Retrieved from http://online.wsj.com/news/articles/SB10001424052702304458604577486761101726748. Accessed September 1, 2014.

State Bar of Arizona. (2009, Sept. 4) Confidentiality; Maintaining client files; Electronic storage; Internet. Retrieved from http://www.azbar.org/Ethics/EthicsOpinions/ViewEthicsOpinion?id=704. Accessed September 1, 2014.

United States Senate Committee on Commerce, Science, and Transportation. (2014). A 'kill chain' analysis of the 2013 Target data breach: Majority staff report for Chairman Rockefeller. Retrieved from http://www.commerce.senate.gov/public/?a=Files.Serve&File_id=24d3c229-4f2f-405d-b8db-a3a67f183883.

Chapter 7

Cybersecurity in the World of Social Engineering

REG HARNISH

Introduction

Social engineering is one of the greatest threats facing businesses, individuals, and nations today. The human layer of cybersecurity has become increasingly targeted due to its inherent weaknesses in cognitive processing. The success of social engineering is irrefutable—evolution takes a long time and human beings simply have not kept pace with the threats that they face.

What is Social Engineering?

Social engineering is the act of human manipulation. It can be artful or clunky, sophisticated or simple. It can target groups or individuals. It can be performed in a pursuit of benign convenience or it can be deployed maliciously for nefarious purposes. It is possibly the greatest tool in the hacker's arsenal.

As defined by social-engineer.org, social engineering is "any act that influences a person to take an action that may or may not be in their best interest" (Social Engineering, Inc., 2014). While social engineering has its share of social stigma, it can be a powerful tool for educating workforces, promoting security awareness, and reducing risk. The percentage of security breaches, incidents, and other events that start with the failure of a human being is staggering. Nearly every recent, publicized breach has been enabled or directly caused by an employee clicking a malicious link, opening an infected attachment, or installing unauthorized software. In many instances, these incidents are enabled by downstream human failures, like the circumvention of a procedure, configuration errors, or flawed security design.

Categories of Social Engineers

Social engineering can be employed by various types of individuals, in differing roles with varying objectives. There are no restrictions on social engineering, and there are few if any prerequisites. While certain skills, experiences, and attitudes can make for better social engineers, anyone can attempt it.

The following is a sampling of common social engineers (whether or not they are aware of their participation and power):

Hackers—Social engineering is commonly employed by hackers due to the fact that human beings are the weakest security control in any organization. Hackers commonly devote significant resources to reconnaissance and collecting intelligence about their targets so that they can construct a perfectly crafted attack on an unsuspecting individual. Through social engineering maneuvers such as phishing, vishing, impersonation, and other techniques, hackers can gain personal information, credentials, account information, banking information, and sensitive patient data, among other things.

Penetration Testers—A penetration tester is a trained individual who tests the efficacy of an organization's security controls by simulating the same types of attacks conducted by cybercriminals. The benefit of this exercise is to measure how well an organization's controls will withstand a real attack. A penetration tester's ultimate goal is to gain unauthorized access to (and potentially exfiltrate) critical assets, such as bank accounts and money, credit card data, personally identifiable information (PII), and other assets that could be monetized if stolen. Penetration testing targets may also include physical assets, such as data centers, mobile devices, and laptops.

Identity Thieves—An identity thief is someone who uses another person's information such as a name, bank account, social security number, address, birth date, and other personal information without the victim's awareness. Identity thief incidents consist of various levels of severity as well as tactics, and as noted through studies, there is known to be a strong link between cyber breaches and identity theft (Finklea, 2014).

Disgruntled Employees—While there are many reasons an employee can become disgruntled, the results can be extremely negative and these situations should be taken seriously. Unhappy employees can damage the company reputation via social networks, theft of company property, and leakage of company secrets. While often employees already have privileged access to sensitive data, they can abuse these privileges and use the information against their companies.

Information Brokers—Information brokers collect data and provide services to various organizations including the FBI, credit monitoring services, and the DoD. While they are likely a prime target for hackers due to their high capacity of sensitive data, information brokers also use social engineering themselves through elicitation, pretexting, courting, and other methods.

Scam Artists—While the term "social engineering" may be a relatively new concept, scam artists have been around for centuries and continue to victimize individuals through fraud, scams, and manipulation. Many of the tactics used by scam artists can also be used by social engineers.

Recruiters—Executive recruiters, also known as "head hunters," use social engineering to solicit people for certain jobs with certain companies. They tend to gather information through various online sources to find out everything they can about individuals to attract and promise them their dream jobs.

Sales People—Sales people often use social engineering as a tactic for gaining business. Many times they uses competitive information gathering as well as elicitation to gain sensitive information or privileged access about an individual or a business in order to craft their selling technique to better serve their potential customers.

Governments—Governments tend to use social engineering methods to control or sway public opinion in order to gain support for things such as policy implementation. These tactics have been utilized for millennia, probably for as long as governments have existed.

Everyday Citizens—While social engineering can be utilized for various motives as well as by a diverse group of individuals within a variety of occupations, it is also commonly used among everyday citizens such as children, parents, customer service representatives, and so on. Whether through a pouting child, or a representative's cheerful manner, we have all been manipulated in some form or another.

All of Us—We should each ask ourselves when the last time was that we manipulated someone for our own benefit. It can be assumed that it was very recently.

Why Attackers Use Social Engineering

While there are many different reasons an attacker might use social engineering, it all comes down to the fact that humans are the greatest vulnerability in any organization, and there is really no easy way to apply a patch on human judgment. Social engineering is often "the path of least resistance," and subsequently it has become a frequent mode of attack. While trying to compromise a network by breaking technical controls may take countless hours, dressing up as the delivery person, dumpster diving, or phone call spoofing can produce sensitive information with limited time and effort. With social engineering on the rise and employee awareness limited, it creates the perfect environment for both sophisticated and simple attacks.

Social Engineering Scenarios

Customer Service—Customer service attacks are generally conducted over the phone, but it is not uncommon to see these types of attacks in e-mails. The attacker usually obtains the customer service phone number on the company website, provides a fake last name to the representative on the other end, and requests a password reset. Without the proper training and procedures in place, the representative may authorize the password reset without customer verification, thus giving the social engineer access to another individual's account.

Delivery Person—Delivery person impersonation is a common, yet risky, type of social engineering attack. Impersonation can be anyone from the U.S. mail carrier to the pizza and flower delivery person. One of the reasons this maneuver is utilized so often is the way uniforms are perceived in our culture. Uniforms generate a certain amount of automatic trust in an individual. If individuals look the part, they generally have no issues getting in the door and are many times left unsupervised, thus opening the door for the social engineer to gain access to classified and sensitive data.

Vishing—Another common social engineering tactic is Vishing, or Voice Phishing. Individuals can spoof the phone number that they are calling from and pose as a co-worker, technician, or other employee to obtain sensitive information. The attackers can also use voice changers to conceal their true identity. The caller will pose as a specific individual and try to obtain as much information from the person on the other end, including passwords, social security numbers, banking credentials, home address, and essentially any personal information that can potentially be used to successfully implement a more sophisticated attack further down the road.

Fundamental Issues Unique to Social Engineering

The threats posed by social engineering are misunderstood, primarily because they are issues of psychology, not security. This fundamental difference has made social engineering easy to exploit and difficult to fix. Firewalls operate in binary and respond only to 1s and 0s. They do exactly what we tell them to do, each and every time. They do not have bad days, emotions, or ulterior motives. They do not get tired, change their mind, or hate their boss. They are fallible, but predictably and consistently so.

Human beings are far more complicated than firewalls. They are unpredictable, inconsistent, and motivated by fear, ego, and survival. They can be lazy, angry, or sleepy. They can make decisions for themselves, and worse yet, for others. They are independent, cynical, and excitable. They are inherently bad at assessing risk, and their brain works against them. They are the greatest challenge to cybersecurity.

Humans are also resistant to change (Heathfield, 2014). This secondary issue has allowed the social engineering threat to continue virtually unabated. Technology has come a long way—we can do more with access controls, backup, and intrusion detection than ever before. Unfortunately, human beings are still utilizing the same brain and cognitive biases that they were given thousands of years ago. We are basically cave people when it comes to cybersecurity. Just as cave people were drawn to fire, water, and the opposite sex, so are people today drawn to winning the lottery, pictures of naked celebrities, and unexpected packages from FedEx. We simply cannot help ourselves— we absolutely, positively need to open that e-mail attachment named "2015 Layoff Plans."

Changing our collective ability to identify, resist, and report social engineering attacks requires evolution in our thinking. It also requires evolution in our training for employees. Cybersecurity training needs to be presented in a way that feels relevant to employees, and it needs to be short and engaging. It should also be interactive, fun, and delivered regularly if we expect it to be successful. In short, it needs to be effective (Cimons, 2012). And yet, effective training does not and will not guarantee success in defeating social engineering attacks. Susceptibility is inevitable; we can only hope to reduce the frequency and impact of the events.

To most, cybersecurity is inconvenient, irrelevant, and misunderstood. There is no cheese at the end of the maze, just as exercise may never produce weight loss. There is no finish line in this race. These conditions add to our inability to secure human beings.

Cybersecurity Threats that Challenge Social Engineering

With technology changing so rapidly, one of the biggest threats to social engineering is keeping up. While some say social engineering revolves around humans more so than technology, improvements in technology can challenge and make the task of a penetration tester much more difficult. Along with improvements and increased complexity in technology, increased employee awareness, while extremely positive, can also have a major threat to social engineering. Previously, when cybersecurity was not given much attention, employee immaturity made it much easier for social engineers to gain access to sensitive data. Currently, with cybersecurity being such a relevant threat, it has gained much more responsiveness worldwide, and companies are beginning to invest more time and money in cybersecurity defenses, one of the most important being security awareness training (Goldman, 2014). Employees are now being provided with better training and implementing efficient and effective protocols to detect and be made aware of social engineering maneuvers.

As noted, the key cybersecurity risk areas in social engineering are any sort of sensitive, personal, or classified data that can be used against an individual or a company at large. Personal information— name, address, financial information, workplace, hobbies, or essentially anything pertaining to an individual—can be used against people in a social engineering attack. The same threats apply to a company and can include client lists, trade secrets, banking information, and numerous amounts of other data. While it is virtually impossible to protect every single asset within a company, it is important to recognize the "crown jewels" within an organization, as they will most likely be the targets of an attack and potentially have the most devastating impact on the organization if compromised.

Cybersecurity Laws/Policies Relevant to Social Engineering

We are in the earliest stages of the cybercriminal revolution. This immaturity has left little legal recourse for victimized organizations. Hacking is legal in most countries, and some governments even subsidize these activities. The United States has historically been on the leading edge of anti-hacking legislation. As you might expect, this legislation is usually too little too late, non-prescriptive, and in the worst cases, an anchor for the very organizations that it intends to protect.

The Telephone Records and Privacy Protection Act of 2006 is a great example of this. The law as defined by government, as well as the sanctions for violations:

> *Amends the federal criminal code to prohibit the obtaining, in interstate or foreign commerce, of confidential phone records information from a telecommunications carrier or IP-enabled voice service provider (covered entity) by: (1) making false or fraudulent statements to an employee of a covered entity or to a customer of a covered entity; (2) providing false or fraudulent documents to a covered entity; or (3) accessing customer accounts of a covered entity through the Internet or by fraudulent computer-related activities without prior authorization.*

> *Imposes a fine and/or imprisonment of up to 10 years.*

> *Prohibits the unauthorized sale or transfer, in interstate or foreign commerce, of confidential phone records information by any person or the purchase or receipt of such information with knowledge that it was fraudulently obtained or obtained without prior authorization.*

> *Imposes a fine and/or imprisonment of up to 10 years.*

Exempts covered entities from such restrictions to the extent authorized by the Communications Act of 1934 (e.g., for billing, protection of property rights, or for emergency purposes).

Doubles fines and imposes an additional five-year prison term for violations occurring in a 12-month period involving more than $100,000 or more than 50 customers of a covered entity.

Imposes an additional five-year prison term for violations involving the use of confidential phone records information to commit crimes of violence, crimes of domestic violence, and crimes against law enforcement officials and the administration of justice.

Grants extraterritorial jurisdiction over crimes defined by this Act.

Exempts lawfully authorized federal or state investigative, protective, or intelligence activities from the prohibitions of this Act.

Directs the U.S. Sentencing Commission to review and amend, if appropriate, federal sentencing guidelines and policy statements for crimes defined by this Act.

(H.R. 4709, 2006)

Clearly, the legislation is antiquated. The government has made an attempt to govern an activity that is effectively undetectable, and very often unreported.

Title 18 U.S. Code sec. 912 also limits social engineering, as it states that impersonating a government worker or officer is illegal (Title 18 U.S. Code sec. 912, 1948). The law prohibits impersonation, but does little to define it:

Whoever falsely assumes or pretends to be an officer or employee acting under the authority of the United States or any department, agency or officer thereof, and acts as such, or in such pretended character demands or obtains any money, paper, document, or thing of value, shall be fined under this title or imprisoned not more than three years, or both.

(Title 18 U.S. Code sec. 912, 1948)

In many regards, social engineers are criminals for all intents and purposes. They disregard our laws in pursuit of information, which, as defined by U.S. codes makes them criminals.

Cybersecurity Skills Necessary in the Social Engineering Workforce

Those of us fighting cybercrime are very aware of one simple fact—we are outnumbered.

There are far more people stealing money, credit card numbers, and intellectual property than there are people trying to stop them. The motivations in cybercrime are massive and growing. The impact of cyber theft is incalculable. The value of the assets stolen by cyber thieves is so large that it is difficult to put a number on it; some estimates put the loss at $500 billion annually (Eagan, 2013). This money is going directly into the pockets of cybercriminals. It is not hard for them to get rich in this business. Secondarily, the odds are not in our favor. We have to be right every time—the bad guys only need to be right once.

Organizations spend millions of dollars and many years building a cybersecurity program to protect their assets, only to be defeated by a few people working over a weekend. Yadron, notes that "Companies wrestle daily with the question of how much security is enough. Global cybersecurity spending by critical infrastructure industries was expected to hit $46 billion in 2013, up 10% from a year earlier, according to Allied Business Intelligence Inc." (2014).

Rarely does a football game end in a 0-0 tie. Offense is easier than defense. This condition can leave organizations despondent and demotivated, and perhaps most importantly, lacking cybersecurity resources. These resources come in the form of time, money, and energy. And nowhere are we feeling the pinch more than in the shortage of cybersecurity professionals and subject matter experts. The immaturity of the industry has left us with a serious shortage of talent. Only recently has cybersecurity become a common word, let alone a career path. Colleges and universities are only now recognizing this need and building cybersecurity programs. Cybersecurity certifications have been around for a long time, but only recently have they started specializing in specific arts.

The government has done little to assist in this effort. While the president uses the word "cyber" in speeches, the incentives do not match their political rhetoric. The cyber talent shortage has become a major issue that has been phrased as a possible "national crisis." With hackers on the rise and cybercrime growing exponentially, a lack of trained professionals to secure sensitive information is a major risk. While the lack of cybersecurity experts has become a serious issue, it has created massive opportunity for those willing to brave the field. Getting started in cybersecurity has become much easier, and there are a number of strategies that can be utilized.

The first strategy is education. As in any occupation, having a solid educational background can provide a solid foundation. While there is no one specific course or curriculum to become a social engineer, courses in human psychology and communications will help develop the skills required to combat social engineering and other attacks. There are a variety of specialized certifications that will help budding cybersecurity experts gain skills, including the Certified Ethical Hacker. Hacking certifications in particular focus on social engineering techniques and defensive measures. Organizations that offer these certifications, degrees, and courses are available below.

Another strategy to focus on is practice. As we all know, practice makes perfect, and in social engineering, the same rules apply. The art of social engineering revolves around communication and social engagement, so going out in public and practicing conversing with people, talking on the phone, and practicing on friends and family can be the best way to gain experience. Therefore, when the time comes for a real engagement, social engineers can stay calm, cool, and collected, especially under pressure.

Obtaining individual recognition would be another strategy in the right direction. Building a name for oneself (a positive one) can be one of the most valued credentials. Up and coming social engineers can: present at a cybersecurity conference; write a blog or an article for a security journal; and do some networking at DEFCON and BlackHat. Not only will these types of high-profile activities increase recognition, but credibility and expertise as well (Blackhat, 2014).

Another important step in this journey is staying up to date. Being aware of the latest attacks, trends, and technology in the industry is critical. The cybersecurity industry is growing at an exponential rate and to be relevant, practitioners need to keep up. Reading the latest journals such as the *International Journal of Cyber-Security and Digital Forensics (IJCSDF)*, or the *National Cybersecurity Institute Journal (NCIJ)*, attending conferences, and staying involved in the field will make candidates stand out from the competition.

The last component for entering the cybersecurity workforce is getting experience—somehow, some way. There is no better teacher than doing. While it can be difficult initially when one might not have much to offer, the best way to gain experience is to go out and get it. Working as an intern for companies that provide penetration testing as a service would be a great start. Having certifications and knowledge from a recognized educational institution, combined with real-world practice, provides the credentials to make one an ideal social engineering candidate.

Recommendations for Cybersecurity Best Practices in Social Engineering

Defending oneself and the organization from social engineering requires practicing the following:

Patience—Corporate culture will not change overnight, and expecting radical change will only lead to frustration. It is important that we continue to assess susceptibility and build our training and education programs around our goals, business strategy, and risk tolerance.

Pragmatism—People will always be susceptible, and no amount of training will change this. Setting realistic expectations will help avoid exaggerated reactions, especially when the accounting assistant continues to click links in the phishing tests. Remember that 100% is not the goal, risk reduction is. Matching training and education goals to the specific business is critical.

Psychology—Remember that we are dealing with organic, carbon-based organisms, not firewalls. Changing behaviors in employees means outthinking them and using their natural instincts against them. The same cognitive biases that make people susceptible to online links promising fortunes can be used to motivate them to protect themselves. They want their egos stroked. They want to feel like they are part of the solution. They want to be recognized. And they do not want to be the losers.

Here are a few things that can be done to reduce one's own susceptibility to social engineering:

Trust but Verify—Just because the stranger in the hallway shows up in a UPS uniform and announces that he is delivering a package, does not mean it is true. Do not be afraid to ask for identification.

When in Doubt, Throw It Out—Over 60% of all e-mail sent each day is spam, and much of it is malicious (Wagner, 2013). If the sender cannot be verified, if the e-mail has links or attachments, if it wants the recipient to do something urgently—throw it out. If it is a legitimate e-mail the sender will recognize that there has not been a response and will resend.

If It's Too Good to Be True—You did not win the African lottery. You do not have a rich uncle and he did not leave you a fortune. That pill will not make you younger. If it seems too good to be true, it probably is.

Remember That We Are All Vulnerable—No matter what precautions are taken, how much we know about security, or how paranoid we are, we will always be susceptible to social engineering. We have all been blessed with the same, human brain, and it is flawed. Keeping this in mind may just save the catastrophe waiting to happen in the form of that next malicious e-mail.

However, best practices are not limited to defending ourselves from the bad guys. Ethical hacking often (as it should) includes social engineering. Becoming an effective social engineer may help other organizations—perhaps our clients—better defend themselves from similar attacks. Due to the controversial nature of social engineering, it is very important to act within the boundaries of one's position. One of the first steps penetration testers should perform is due diligence. They should be aware of all the laws of the locality in which they are engaging in social engineering. For example, in some states, video or audio recording (common practice among social engineers) is illegal if only one party is aware of the act.

Threatening people, obtaining federal documents, and other actions, such as impersonation may be illegal in various states and countries. Thus, it is critical to be aware of any legal limitations prior to carrying out any social engineering attacks. While social engineering may require a bit of falsehood to get the job done, abiding by one's moral compass is advisable.

Social engineering tests should also simulate a real-world attack, not an exaggerated situation that is unlikely to occur. A company needs to be tested in an everyday work environment, not a theatrical scene from the latest action movie. The appropriate personal should always be notified well in advance of the test. While having documented authorization is required, making sure the appropriate people are notified is necessary not only to help ensure the success of the operation, but also to avoid winding up in an uncomfortable situation.

To successfully complete a social engineering attack, one of the most critical factors is extensive preparation and information gathering. There are multiple methods for gathering information, and no matter how insignificant the information may seem on its own, when combined with others it can create the perfect storm for social engineering. One form of information gathering common among social engineers is dumpster diving. Dumpster diving is sifting through "garbage" tossed out by companies or individuals. While you may come across a few banana peels, dumpster diving can result in a surplus of valuable materials including old financial statements, company documents, and even old technology such as computers and hardware. Dumpster diving is a popular form of information gathering in that it's effortless. While it can take hours upon hours digging up information needed for social engineering through various outlets, dumpster diving can provide material almost instantaneously. While it may be a simple way of gaining information, there are some legality issues that can interfere. While in the United States of America, items discarded in the trash are technically legal to take, if a dumpster is on private property of a residential or business, going through it can be illegal and considered trespassing.

A more conventional form of information gathering is research. Research in social engineering can pertain to many different tactics including using a phone, phishing, and tail gating. The phone, specifically Caller ID, can provide information such as the phone number, company, and the name of the individual. Another tactic is to send phishing e-mails. A phishing e-mail is a fake web address or site that attackers use to lure someone. The site often looks legitimate but is created and controlled by the social engineer. From the site, the social engineer can gain information such as potential login or password combinations used by the individual. Maneuvers known as "tail gating" are frequently exercised among social engineers as well. The social engineer will run up behind an actual employee and enter the building or a remote area and simply gain access by having the employee hold the door for them. Social media is also an excellent source for information gathering as it provides material many times without any security measures in place. Finally, "shoulder surfing" is a common tactic, and with a little bit of practice can be accomplished very easily. Peering over the shoulder of an employee or individual to see what their technological passwords belonging to their phone, tablet, computer or any other devices are is simple, especially if the password is not complex. The social engineer is then able to have free range access to all their devices. There are many different tactics used by social engineers, and each one is different and contains both its benefits and its challenges. Recognizing when to use certain procedures in certain situations is a skill set gained upon experience.

Future Trends in Cybersecurity Social Engineering

Social Media

One major trend that has become increasingly popular in social engineering is social media. In today's world, social media is everywhere. With billions of users on various social sites such as Facebook, Twitter, LinkedIn, Instagram, Pinterest, and so on, this is the perfect way to gather information about individuals. While some may think social media sites are not relevant to social engineering, hackers, penetration testers, and other trained individuals think otherwise. Social sites are excellent tools for social engineers primarily due to their purpose—sharing information. People post tons of personal information all over the web, and it is all free for the taking. Information that was once saved for in-person, face-to-face conversation is now free for the world to see. Details such as job title and company, hobbies, interests, and family and friends are all over the web and can be pulled and used by a social engineer to craft a personalized attack tailored to specific individuals. Phishing e-mails spoofed to look like colleagues, friends, or family can often contain accurate and convincing information. These e-mails can be crafted with nothing more than information found online. Virus-infected applications, links containing malware, and phony friend requests are typical tactics used by social engineers. Many times individuals do not have the necessary privacy measures in place on their personal social media sites, which makes them a prime target for social engineering.

Mobile Technology

Mobile devices are increasingly targeted by hackers and social engineers. With the Internet in the palm of our hand virtually at all times, it has become very easy for social engineers to attack via mobile devices such as Smartphones and tablets. Poorly secured applications filled with malware are a common attack in the mobile realm. Unsuspecting users try to download an app, unaware that it can actually be a virus. Engineers can design an app that looks virtually identical to the real app and upon downloading the malicious application, the attacker then has control of the mobile device. Infected barcodes are also common among users and can be very effective in social engineering engagements.

Technology is continuing to evolve and along with it so are tactics used by social engineers. Keeping up to date on the latest technology and social websites will improve skill sets as well as increase success rates when implementing a social engineering-based attack.

Sources of Further Information

- http://www.social-engineer.org—The Social Engineering Framework is a searchable information resource for people wishing to learn more about the psychological, physical, and historical aspects of social engineering.

- http://www.csoonline.com—This site offers the latest information related to cybersecurity issues.

- http://www.sans.org/—SANS Information Security Training is a trusted sources for cybersecurity training and research.

References

Armerding, T. (2014). The human OS: Overdue for a social engineering patch. Retrieved from the Internet on 10/23/2014 at http://www.csoonline. com/article/2824563/social-engineering/the-human-os-overdue-for-a-social-engineering-patch.html.

Blackhat USA 2014. (2014). Retrieved from the Internet on 10/22/2014 at https://www.blackhat.com/us-14/.

Cimons, M. (2012). Cybersecurity: Training students. Retrieved from the Internet on 10/25/2014 at http://www.usnews.com/science/articles/ 2012/05/29/cybersecurity--training-students.

Eagan, M. (2013). Report: Cyber crime costs global economy up to $500B a year. Retrieved from the Internet on 10/26/2014 at http://www. foxbusiness.com/technology/2013/07/22/report-cyber-crime-costs-global-economy-up-to-1-trillion-year/.

Finklea, K. (2014). Identity theft: Trends and issues. Retrieved from the Internet on 10/22/2014 at http://fas.org/sgp/crs/misc/R40599.pdf.

Ghandi, V. K. (2012). An overview study on cyber crimes in Internet. Retrieved from the Internet on 10/26/2014 at http://www.iiste.org/ Journals/index.php/JIEA/article/view/1201.

Goldman, J. (2014). No easy fix for point-of-sale security. Retrieved from the Internet on 10/24/2014 at http://www.esecurityplanet.com/malware/ no-easy-fix-for-point-of-sale-security.html.

Hadnagy, C. (2011). Social engineering: The art of human hacking. Indianapolis, IN: Wiley Publishing, Inc.

Heathfield, S. (2014). Resistance to change definition. Retrieved from the Internet on 10/24/2014 at http://humanresources.about.com/od/ glossaryr/g/Resistance-To-Change-Definition.htm.

H.R.4709—Telephone Records and Privacy Protection Act of 2006. (2006). Retrieved from the Internet on 10/25/2014 at https://www.congress.gov/ bill/109th-congress/house-bill/4709.

Social Engineering, Inc. (2014). The social engineering framework. Retrieved from the Internet on 10/23/2014 at http://www.social-engineer.org/ framework/general-discussion/social-engineering-defined/.

Title 18 U.S. Code 912- (1948, June 25). ch. 645, 62 Stat. 742; Pub. L. 103–322, title XXXIII, § 330016(1) (H), Sept. 13, 1994, 108 Stat. 2147.

Wagner, K. (2013). More than 70% of email is spam. Retrieved from the Internet on 10/20/2014 at http://mashable.com/2013/08/09/70-percent-email-is-spam/.

Yadron, D. (2014). Companies wrestle with the cost of cybersecurity. Retrieved from the Internet on 10/22/2014 at http://online.wsj.com/articles/SB100 01424052702304834704579403421539734550.

Chapter 8

Cybersecurity and Insider Threat

Derek Smith

Introduction

As a former federal agent responsible for investigating insider threats for over 18 years, this author came to realize that damage to organizations caused by authorized users, or insiders, is one of the toughest security challenges organizations face today. According to the 2014 "Verizon Data Breach Investigations Report," incidents caused by insider threats, increased by 10% between 2011 and 2012 (Verizon Enterprise Solutions, 2014). Hackers are well aware that attacks from the inside are more lucrative than their normal exploits. The Association of Certified Fraud Examiner's (ACFE) reported in its 2014 "Occupational Fraud and Abuse Report" that organizations lose 5% of their yearly revenue to fraudulent activity, amounting to roughly $3.7 trillion globally (Association of Certified Fraud Examiners, 2014). The report estimated the average organizational loss due to fraud at $145,000. In the 1,500 cases ACFE analyzed, more than one in five reported employees defrauding their companies for at least $1 million (Association of Certified Fraud Examiners, 2014).

The Intelligence and National Security Alliance Cyber Council reports even higher figures, stating that, "The average cost per incident is $412,000, and the average loss per industry is $15 million over ten years. In several instances, damages reached more than $1 billion" (Mazzafro, 2013). Because of the potential gain, hackers are inclined to attempt to obtain access from the inside; using authorized credentials and activities that make them appear as though they are conducting authorized work.

A PricewaterhouseCoopers survey stated that insider threats "typically fly under the media radar." The survey reported that "28% of respondents pointed the finger at insiders, which includes trusted parties such as current and former employees, service providers, and contractors. Almost one-third (32%) say insider crimes are more costly or damaging than incidents perpetrated by outsiders" (Mickelberg, Pollard, & Schive, 2014).

As demonstrated by these examples, insider threat is a major concern for organizations, and it is not a new one. Hackers have been infiltrating sensitive information systems since the 1990s. However, because of the proliferation of many high-profile and highly damaging security breaches, such as Target and Home Depot, focus and media attention on insider threat has rapidly increased. Much attention is paid when financial and physical damage across critical national and corporate infrastructures is perpetrated.

Insider Threat Defined

There are many definitions of insider threat. For our purposes the CERT Insider Threat Center definition correctly identifies the term. CERT defines insider threat as "a current or former employee, contractor, or other business partner who has or had authorized access to an organization's network, system, or data and intentionally exceeded or misused that access in a manner that negatively affected the confidentiality, integrity, or availability of the organization's information or information systems" (Overview, 2014).

There is not one "type" of insider threat, but it is important to note that in almost all cases the threat comes from a trusted individual with access to the organization's proprietary information. As a result, organizations must develop a keen awareness of the insider threat issue and focus a part of their cybersecurity efforts on effectively mitigating the risk of insider threat within the organization. Effectively handling insider threats takes understanding, support, and communication among all employees within the organization, including buy-in from top leaders to support the communications required throughout the organization to develop an effective insider threat mitigation strategy.

As this chapter will demonstrate, losses attributed to insider threat incidents can be very costly in many ways for an organization. The organization may suffer financial losses, serious impact to its operations, damage to the organization's reputation, and individuals can be harmed. These damages can range from a loss of a few staff hours to devastating financial losses that can force the organization to shut down. The consequences of insider incidents even go beyond the victim organization, disrupting operations or services critical to a specific sector or creating serious risks to public safety and national security (Cappelli, Moore, & Trzeciak, 2012).

Fundamental Issues Unique to Insider Threat

Insiders have a keen awareness of their organization's networks, policies, and procedures, providing them a tactical advantage, and cybersecurity professionals a tactical nightmare. Based on their intentions, and the degree of access, skill, and craftiness, insiders are able to overcome most of the preliminary obstacles they encounter while breaching the physical, cyber, and personnel perimeters of a targeted asset. This leaves insiders unencumbered to operate within the organization's network. Cybersecurity professionals face some major challenges to prevent, detect, and respond to these insider attacks. Most use technical approaches to attempt to mitigate this problem; however, based on current events, technical mitigation seems to offer little progress in reducing the numbers of insider incidents as well as their impacts. This lack of success can be attributed to three main causes:

1. Cybersecurity professionals do not really understand the complexities of collecting, correlating, and detecting the technical indicators of insider threat.

2. Because insider threat is not a traditional area of study for cybersecurity professionals, most do not understand the underlying human issues motivating insider threat.

3. Organizations are reluctant to expose attack data, making it difficult for cybersecurity professionals to learn the methods and means used to perpetrate insider attacks.

Thus, it is difficult for cybersecurity professionals to accurately estimate how often organizations are attacked by insiders. There is no silver bullet for combatting insider threats, and technology alone is not yet the most effective way to prevent and/or detect an incident perpetrated by a trusted insider.

Security is about safeguarding the organization, not just its IT infrastructure! A fundamental challenge is that insiders can accidentally or maliciously steal, erase, or expose sensitive data for a variety of reasons, causing great risk to their organizations. They have a great advantage due to their trusted positions within the organization, making them uniquely aware of the organization's vulnerabilities, which allow them to evade many of its established cyber defenses. This is difficult to mitigate because these insiders must be trusted with a certain level of access to conduct their daily employee activities. This level of access to, and knowledge of, the organization, its assets, and systems increases the consequences of an insider attack. This makes it critical that cybersecurity professionals understand the damaging effects of insider attacker and the motivations of those who perpetrate these attacks.

Organizations have realized that insider threats can be as complex and devastating as threats posed by malicious attackers. These threats may originate from disgruntled employees or even well-intentioned ones. However, attacks from the inside are much more dangerous than external attacks; this is due to employee access, especially super users such as system administrators, to the organization's most sensitive information and knowledge of how to get to it. Because hackers realize this, they often target employees who may end up unintentionally providing them access to important organizational data and networks. Then there are the unintentional actions by employees when they lose devices that contain sensitive data, like IPADS, phones, USB drives, or laptops. Some disgruntled employees may even voluntarily provide hackers with this access.

Insider data breaches seem to appear almost on a daily basis. Lions Gate Entertainment Corporation recently announced that at least 2.2 million people had downloaded from the Internet and watched a "complete and pristine" copy of "The Expendables 3" movie up to two weeks prior to its release (Fritz, 2014). The *Wall Street Journal* stated this was Hollywood's highest profile piracy leak since 2009, when an incomplete version of "X-Men Origins: Wolverine" found its way onto the Internet prior to the superhero movie's release (Fritz, 2014). With the average movie ticket costing $8, according to the Hollywood Reporter, that is a potential loss of over $17 million dollars to Lions Gate (McClintock, 2014).

In its 2014 Data Breach Investigations Report, Verizon named insider threat as one of the key attack categories with 11,698 incidents reported. The report found that 48% of data breaches are caused by insiders, and another 11% are caused by business partners. The report also found that 48% of all data breaches occur because of privilege misuse (Verizon Enterprise Solutions, 2014).

In June 2014, AT&T suffered a data breach, allegedly caused by a third-party vendor, which could potentially lead to serious implications for businesses. AT&T sent out a letter to its customers, which stated: "We recently determined that employees of one of our service providers violated our strict privacy and security guidelines by accessing your account without authorization between April 9 and 21, 2014, and, while doing so, would have been able to view your social security number and possibly your date of birth" (Bautista, 2014). The AT&T data breach is a combination of three serious security concerns: third-party vendors, insider attacks, and "bring your own devices," also known as BYOD.

In March 2009, Information Week Analytics released a report called "Understanding the Danger Within" that discussed the different types of insider threats and how enterprises are addressing them.

According to that report, 20% of insiders admitted to changing the security settings on their company-issued devices, and 35% admitted to violating corporate security policies in order to expedite their work or increase productivity (Wilson, 2009). We would hope that number has changed to be significantly lower in 2014.

Another study from the Ponemon Institute and Symantec Corporation found that two-thirds of employees who left their companies in 2013 took sensitive corporate data with them (Symantec Corporation, 2013). The survey reported that employees thought it was acceptable to transfer sensitive work documents to personal computers, tablets, Smartphones, or online file-sharing applications. Half of the 3,317 individuals surveyed admitted to regularly using personal accounts, like Gmail, to send corporate documents to their home computers (Symantec Corporation, 2013).

The CERT Insider Threat Center, which focuses research on insider breaches, determined that in more than 70% of the IP theft cases they collected, employees stole sensitive organization information within 30 days of announcing their resignation (Verizon Enterprise Solutions, 2014). Based on this data it is evident that employees often violate security policies and circumvent practices that were designed to protect an organization's IT systems. Whether these violations are meant to be malicious or if they are simply mistakes, they can lead to data leaks and expose sensitive corporate information.

The fundamental issue is that threats from insiders can be very dangerous since employees often know the organization's most sensitive secrets (or how to locate them), as well as the company's vulnerabilities. The 2014 Verizon Data Breach Investigations Report concluded that it costs more to repair damage caused by insider incidents than those caused by external attacks (Verizon Enterprise Solutions, 2014; Mickelberg, Pollard, & Schive, 2014).

According to CSO Magazine's 2012 CyberSecurity Watch Survey, organizations that had cyber incidences within the previous 12 months reported that 51% of violators disobeyed IT security policies and 19% were identified by managers for behavioral or performance issues (Kroll Advisory Solutions, 2013). Considering these percentages, the report deduced that organizations could prevent or quickly detect 70% of insider incidences by more closely monitoring employees who have demonstrated behavioral or performance non-conformity (Kroll Advisory Solutions, 2013).

Cybersecurity Threats Based on Insider Threats

A 2012 Insider Threat Study by Carnegie Mellon University's Software Engineering Institute examined fraud and illicit cyber activity in the U.S. financial services sector. Among other findings, the study concluded that an average of 32 months elapsed between the beginning of fraud activity and its detection by the victim organization (Cummings, Lewellen, McIntire, Moore, & Trzeciak, 2012). That is a significant amount of time for fraud to be operating in an organization. In order to create a plan to detect and mitigate insider threats, organizations must first understand the methods insiders use to attack their organizations as well as behaviors and motivations of insiders that might perpetrate such attacks. This is crucial to pinpointing which employees might attack the organization. Researching actual insider attack cases that have occurred in the United States, the CERT insider threat team studies the behavioral and technical aspects of insider incidences. Based on its finding, CERT separated malicious and intentional insider attacks into four broad categories:

1. IT sabotage

2. Fraud

3. Theft of intellectual property (IP)

4. National security espionage

(Software Engineering Institute, 2013)

IT Sabotage

IT Sabotage occurs when a malicious insider intentionally causes damage to the organization's network, system, or database. The perpetrators are usually former employees who are upset with the organization because they have been reprimanded, demoted, or fired. Some of these employees may likely have held technical positions that provided them with escalated privileges. These disgruntled former insiders often wait until they have left the organization before launching their attacks.

Fraud

Often non-technical or lower-level employees are the perpetrators of fraud attacks, but managers can be likely culprits as well. The employee often misappropriates funds from the organization for personal gain through such schemes as procurement fraud or by "cooking the books." Enron and WorldCom are classic examples of this type of malicious activity. According to a survey conducted by the Association for Certified Fraud Examiners, "73% of all frauds are committed by trusted employees in the executive management, procurement, sales, finance and accounting divisions of small, medium, large-sized companies" (Association of Certified Fraud Examiners, 2014).

Theft of Intellectual Property

Often intellectual property is stolen by the "brain trust" of the organization such as scientists, researchers, engineers, or programmers. They believe that because they created, or helped create, the intellectual property they are entitled to it. These insiders often take the stolen information with them to their new employers and freely share it, or they use it to create a business of their own. Studies show that they usually steal this information within 30 days of announcing their resignation from the organization (Blades, 2010).

National Security Espionage

This insider attack occurs when the "insider" leaks out confidential national information. The perpetrators of this type of insider threat have a different type of motivation than the typical insider threat. They cite their personal morals as their main motivations for leaking national information. A recent example is that of the Booz Allen employee and National Security Analyst, Edward Snowden. NSA Director Keith Alexander initially estimated that Snowden had copied anywhere from 50,000 to 200,000 NSA documents (Hosenball, 2013). Snowden was a trusted employee who seems to have had more access rights than was required for his job, which allowed him to access and leak such highly confidential information. Snowden himself stated, "When you're in positions of privileged access, like a systems administrator for the intelligence community agencies, you're exposed to a lot more information on a broader scale than the average employee" (Hill, 2013). He explained that the reason he leaked the data was due to his "concern about how easy it is to spy on people given the way we live today" (Hill, 2013).

The Unintentional Insider Attack

Another type of insider threat, not mentioned as a CERT category, is unintentional attacks from employees or trusted partners who do not have the intention for malicious attacks but are simply negligent, and those who violate corporate policy, allowing for unintentional data loss. These employees usually do not deliberately cause damage to the organization; however, their actions have given opportunity to those who want to attack the organization. To perform their job functions, employees come into contact with sensitive information every day, and some employees also send work documents home via e-mail so that they can continue working at home. While these employees are simply doing their jobs, the risk of transferring sensitive information via e-mail makes the data vulnerable during transmission. Others leave work carrying mobile devices, such as flash drives and laptops, which hold a large amount of sensitive information. Loss of such devices would again expose sensitive information to the public. There are many ways in which ordinary, "good employees" can turn into "bad employees" because of the absence of proper controls and policies in the organization to prevent corporate data from being vulnerable.

Common Motivations of a Malicious "Insider Threat"

There are a number of motivations for those who commit intentional malicious acts against their employers. There is an old saying that has long been accepted in fraud prevention circles called the 10-10-80 rule: 10% of people will never steal no matter what, 10% of people will steal at any opportunity, and the other 80% of employees will go either way depending on how they rationalize a particular opportunity (Schaefer, 2012).

Another widely accepted theory is Dr. Donald R. Cressey's "Fraud Triangle" theory. Dr. Cressey asserted that there are three factors—each a leg of a triangle—that, when combined, lead people to commit fraud. The first leg is an individual's financial problem or need that he or she perceives is non-sharable, such as a gambling debt. The second leg is this individual's perception that there exists in the organization an opportunity to resolve the financial problem without getting caught. The third leg is the individual's ability to rationalize or justify the intended illegal action. In other words, PRESSURE plus PERCEIVED OPPORTUNITY plus RATIONALIZATION equals FRAUD (Schaefer, 2012).

On the next page, in Table 8.1, are but a few examples of common motivators of insider threats (Raytheon, 2014).

Cybersecurity Laws/Policies Relevant to Insider Threat

Many laws address the different types of insider threats, including misuse, sabotage, or espionage. On October 7, 2011, the president signed Executive Order 13587, "Structural Reforms to Improve Security of Classified Networks and the Responsible Sharing and Safeguarding of Classified Information." Executive Order 13587 directs the heads of agencies that operate or access classified computer networks to have responsibility for appropriately sharing and safeguarding classified information (Office of the Press Secretary, 2007).

In November 2012, the White House issued National Insider Threat Policy and Minimum Standards for Executive Branch Insider Threat Programs (Office of the Press Secretary, 2012). These minimum standards provide the departments and agencies with the minimum elements necessary to establish effective insider threat programs. These elements include the designation of a senior official(s) and the capability to: gather, integrate, and centrally analyze and respond to

Table 8.1. Common motivators of insider threats

Motivation	Explanation
Anger/revenge	Many "insiders" are angry because they have been fired or laid off and commit malicious activities in order to "get back" at their employers.
Personal issues	Some "insiders" have personal problems such as drug or alcohol abuse, other addictions, or family problems that motivate them to commit these activities.
Greed/financial hardship	Some "insiders" commit fraud due to financial situations or just plain old greed. These insiders have discovered how easy it is to make money selling their organization's secrets to interested parties and take advantage of this situation.
Thrill-seeking	Some "insiders" are inspired by the spy activities they see on television or hear about in the papers and cannot help but seek an exciting clandestine spy adventure for themselves.
Disengagement	This insider motivation is closely related to the anger/revenge one. The "insider" feels unappreciated, unfulfilled, or resentful toward the organization. An alarming one-quarter of professionals worldwide are described as "actively disengaged" (Raytheon, 2014) the most extreme level of dissatisfaction.
Ideology	The "ideology insider" expresses allegiance to another person, organization, or nation.
Ego	This "insider" thinks he/she does not have to follow the organizational rules, or it can be the IT person who wants to prove what a hotshot she/he is.

key threat-related information; monitor employee use of classified networks; provide the workforce with insider-threat awareness training; and protect the civil liberties and privacy of all personnel (Office of the Press Secretary, 2012). For civilian government and IC members, these laws fall under Title 18 of the United States Code. The DoD and military members would be bound under the Uniform Code of Military Justice.

Governments and private organizations around the world have collaborated to develop regulations, standards, and guidelines to deploy physical, operational, and cybersecurity controls in and around the automated environment of critical control systems. A few important laws and policies are mentioned in Table 8.2 on the next page.

Recommended Best Practices to Thwart Insider Threat

Insider threats are influenced by a combination of technical, behavioral, and organizational issues and many organizations already have policies in place to address these threats accordingly. However, there is more needed. Best practices to mitigate insider threats must involve the synergistic combination of three components: people, processes, and technology. Decision makers across the organization must understand the overarching problem of the insider threat and communicate it to all employees. Then all of an organization's staff needs to work together to battle the insider threat.

People

Properly training employees about insider threat is one of the most powerful ways to increase security practices within an organization. Employees must undergo effective security awareness training, such as how to tell the difference between a real web address and a fake one and how to recognize fake phishing scams. Organizations might also secure and restrict the use of portable devices and teach employees how to properly secure them. Employees should be trained on what kinds of information they should never share and the risks of sharing

Table 8.2. Laws and policies pertaining to insider threats

Law or Policy	Description
Executive Order 13587	Directs U.S. Government executive branch departments and agencies to establish, implement, monitor, and report on the effectiveness of insider threat programs to protect classified national security information; requires the development of an executive branch program for the deterrence, detection, and mitigation of insider threats, including the safeguarding of classified information from exploitation, compromise, or other unauthorized disclosure.
Title 18 of the United States Code	Acts of Espionage, Sabotage, and Treason are defined under Sections 792–799, Chapter 37 of title 18.
Economic Espionage, Title 18 U.S.C., Section 1831	Economic espionage is whoever (1) knowingly performs targeting or acquisition of trade secrets to (2) knowingly benefit any foreign government, foreign instrumentality, or foreign agent.
Department of Defense (DoD) Instruction 5240.26-Countering Espionage, International Terrorism, and the Counterintelligence (CI) Insider Threat	Establishes policy, assigns responsibilities, and provides procedures for CI activities to counter espionage and international terrorist threats to DoD in accordance with Directives. Assigns responsibilities for the CI Insider Threat Program in support of other DoD Insider Threat programs consistent with the Secretary of Defense Memorandum. Establishes the Insider Threat CI Group (ITCIG).
CNSSD 504-Protecting NSS From Insider Threat, Department of Defense (DoD)	Establishes an integrated set of policies and procedures to deter, detect, and mitigate insider threats before damage is done to national security, personnel, resources and/or capabilities.
Navy Insider Threat Program-SECNAVINST 5510.37	Establishes an integrated set of policies and procedures to deter, detect, and mitigate insider threats before damage is done to national security, personnel, resources and/or capabilities.

continued on next page

Table 8.2. *Continued*

Law or Policy	Description
Army Insider Threat Program-Directive 2013-18	An integrated departmental effort to deter, detect and mitigate risk by employees or service members who may represent a threat to national security.
Air Force Instruction 16-1402 Insider Threat Program Management	Establishes a framework to integrate policies and procedures to detect, deter, and mitigate insider threats to national security and Air Force assets.
Uniform Code of Military Justice	Espionage, Sabotage, and Treason are defined under Sections 792–799, Chapter 37 of title 18.
NISPOM Conforming Change 2—Insider Threat	Establishes the standard procedures and requirements for government contractors interacting with classified information.

unauthorized data. Employees should especially be trained on how to recognize suspicious behavior in their coworkers that could mean a breach is occurring, and how to report such suspicious behavior.

Processes

Organizations must deploy preventative measures designed to stop malicious insiders from breaking security policies or stealing information. The organizations that are most effective at stopping malicious insider breaches are those that carefully review the logs that they generate, a practice often overlooked by most companies. Along the same lines of review logs, organizations must recognize the importance of other detection methods and should also have a strong audit process for reviewing system logs for unusual activity. Organizations must also examine the environmental issues within the company such as disgruntled employees and behavior changes to recognize when an insider attack may be taking place.

When developing security policies for trusted partners, organizations must decide what information is appropriate for their partners to access, always ensuring that partners are given the "least-privilege" possible, with access to only those systems and data that they truly need. Finally, organizations must ensure that any personal identifying information, like social security numbers and credit card numbers, are always blocked from being transferred to any network or system.

Technology

There is no one technological solution that can completely eradicate insider threats. The presence of technology alone will not keep a malicious employee from stealing information, and may not prevent highly sophisticated attacks. Organizations must combine real-time monitoring and access management technologies with good policies. The technology will then help to enforce the policies and identify and prevent unauthorized access to data. If an organization has monitoring in place and employees know they are being watched they may think twice about trying anything.

The U.S. CERT's "The Cert Guide to Insider Threats" has emerged as an industry standard for insider threat program implementation. CERT has developed a list of 19 best practices as a guide for organizations to use to mitigate the insider threat; it is recommended that these practices be implemented (Cappelli, Moore, & Trzeciak, 2012). These recommendations are:

Practice 1: Consider threats from insiders and business partners in enterprise wide risk assessments.
CERT's first recommendation is for organizations to implement risk assessments throughout the entire enterprise. This will aid the organization to identify its critical assets, the threats faced by those assets, and the impact a successful breach would have on the assets. By conducting a thorough security risk assessment, organizations will be able to implement the appropriate security controls into its environment to mitigate the critical risks. Once these critical risks are identified, the appropriate technical and physical controls can be implemented to form an in-depth defense strategy to protect the organization's critical assets from insiders.

Practice 2: Clearly document and consistently enforce policies and controls.

An organization's employees are more likely to adhere to clearly documented and consistently enforced policies and procedures. These policies need to be easy to find and also regularly reinforced. Policies must also provide the reasoning behind them and the ramifications of policy violation. It is very important that the organization have its employees sign off to confirm understanding of policies and a commitment to abide by them. Acceptable use policies should be particularly clear.

Practice 3: Incorporate insider threat awareness into periodic security training for all employees.

Properly trained employees are probably the best defense against the insider threat, or any cybersecurity threat for that matter. Initial and continuous employee security awareness training will raise awareness of insider threat risks to the organization, explain why they may be targeted, and provide methods for protecting the organization's critical assets. The training provided by organizations should teach employees how to recognize insider threat, and provide procedures for reporting suspicious behavior.

Practice 4: Beginning with the hiring process, monitor and respond to suspicious or disruptive behavior.

It is imperative that organizations do all they can to identify potential insider threat risks prior to hiring. They should conduct thorough background checks and periodic reinvestigations on prospective employees, contractors, and trusted business partners to identify insiders' personal, professional, and financial stressors. Each position should be assigned a risk level, and these risk levels should be used to trigger further investigation if warranted by the position. Just as important, organizations must ensure that they consistently enforce disciplinary actions for violations of the rules.

Practice 5: Anticipate and manage negative issues in the work environment.

Employee disgruntlement is one of the main causes of insider incidents. Therefore, organizations must work diligently to address potential issues before they actually become issues. By consistently enforcing company policies and practices, cybersecurity professionals may be able to lower the rate of incidences of insider threat before they occur.

Practice 6: Know your assets.
Many organizations are not aware of the IT assets they own. In order to effectively recover from harm due to insider threat, the organization must know what items it owns and which ones have been issued to employees. This can be an excellent deterrent because if employees know that an inventory has been conducted and they have signed for IT equipment in their possession, they may be less likely to steal these documented assets. In addition, organizations need to understand the value of their critical assets in order to implement the proper protections to be effective against insider threats.

The inventory should note who has authorized access to assets and where each is regularly located. Related to this, organizations should also understand what types of data they possess, and where the data is processed and stored. These inventories should be updated regularly, as needed.

Practice 7: Implement strict password and account management policies and practices.
In order to thwart insider threat, organizations should implement password creation policies and procedures and should enforce regular password change rules. They should also forbid the sharing of passwords. Not only should employees be required to adhere to these policies, so should trusted partners (contractors and vendors). Additionally, periodic audits should be conducted of all accounts.

Practice 8: Enforce separation of duties and least privilege.
Organizations can lessen the risks of insider threat activity by two methods: separation of duties and least privilege. Separation of duties can limit access to technical systems and physical assets by requiring at least two people (enforceable through technical or non-technical means) to participate in a task for successful completion of that activity. The rule of least privilege lessens the threat by requiring an employee to have access only to the resources needed to perform his or her particular job.

Often employees have far too much access to information that is irrelevant to their positions, especially if they have changed roles within their organization. Properly implementing role-based access control will limit access according to job function.

Practice 9: Define explicit security agreements for any cloud services, especially access restrictions and monitoring capabilities.
Organizations must ensure that cloud service providers' data protection and monitoring requirements align to their own. Just as was mentioned for organizations, requirements should include physical and technological controls, along with human resource practices for cloud provider employees. Cloud providers should also perform pre-hire and periodic background checks, have employees "signoff" to acknowledge awareness of policies and practices, and provide training on these topics. The cloud providers' Service Level Agreements and insurance should be reviewed to ensure that risks and liability are properly addressed and that their policies and practices implement suitable procedures that will protect their data's confidentiality, integrity, and availability. It is essential for organizations to constantly monitor their infrastructure, regularly review their audit logs, collect diagnostic data, and occasionally audit their cloud infrastructure to confirm that their cloud systems meet necessary security requirements.

Practice 10: Institute stringent access controls and monitoring policies on privileged users.
Privileged users are usually highly skilled individuals. Additionally, they have more access to systems, networks, and applications than a regular user, making them serious insider threats to the organization. To deal with this threat appropriate controls must be established to prevent, detect, and respond to any malicious activities they may attempt to perpetrate. These insiders must be required to sign policies that are specific to their privileged positions, including user agreements and rules of behavior that govern their IT behavior. The organization must be sure to implement separation of duties policies for privileged users, and when they resign it is critical to immediately completely disable their access to the organization's systems.

Practice 11: Institutionalize system change controls.
It is very important for organizations to have strong change control rules in place to prevent malicious insiders from making unauthorized modifications to the organization's systems. By implementing change control rules, which allow for documentation of changes, the organization will be able to provide safeguards that may protect the integrity and accuracy of the organization's systems and data. Organizations must identify and document baseline software and hardware configurations and update this information as changes are made.

The change control process must also protect change logs, backups, source codes, and other application files. Having good change control procedures in place can make it very difficult for a malicious insider to make undetected changes to the organization's systems.

Practice 12: Use a log correlation engine or Security Information and Event Management (SIEM) system to log, monitor, and audit employee actions.
Organizations often collect large quantities of log data, however, they fail to regularly review the information and correlate the data. It is important that the information is properly correlated so that the organization is able to understand its data baseline and, therefore, recognize irregular activity. To complete this function, organizations should use a SIEM system to collect and analyze the information.

Practice 13: Monitor and control remote access from all end points, including mobile devices.
With the increased prevalence of mobile devices in the workplace, malicious insiders could potentially use their mobile devices to capture and remove sensitive organizational data. Thus, organizations must be sure to closely log and audit all remote transactions and ensure that remote access is disabled when an employee is terminated or resigns.

Practice 14: Develop a comprehensive employee termination procedure.
Organizations should develop, communicate, and consistently follow a policy for dealing with voluntary and involuntary employee

terminations. Procedures should include using a termination checklist to ensure that all terminated employees' access to information resources are disabled, all organization-issued equipment returned, and all co-workers are notified of the departure. Additionally, organizations should review a departing employee's online actions during the 30 days prior to termination to identify any suspicious network activity.

Practice 15: Implement secure backup and recovery processes.
Organizations must have a secure, tested backup and recovery process and should implement their separation of duties policy to ensure that a single privileged IT administrator cannot circumvent the backup and recovery process or modify logs to conceal or delete evidence of his or her malicious activity.

Practice 16: Develop a formalized insider threat program.
Organizations should establish an insider threat program that includes clearly defined roles and responsibilities for preventing, detecting, and responding to insider incidents. The goal of an insider threat program is to develop clear criteria for identifying insider threats, a consistent procedure for implementing technical and non-technical controls to prevent malicious insider behavior, and a response plan in the event an insider does harm the organization.

Practice 17: Establish a baseline of normal network device behavior.
For an organization to distinguish normal behavior from anomalous behavior on networks, it must first know what the normal behavior is. Therefore, it is important for organizations to collect normal network behavior at the enterprise, department, group, and individual levels and establish a behavioral baseline. The longer the organization monitors this behavior, the more reliable the baseline will be.

Practice 18: Be especially vigilant regarding social media.
Social media can be an incredible risk for an organization because they may allow employees to share organizational information that adversaries could use to target current or former employees, either as victims or co-conspirators. Organizations should provide employees training

on the dangers of social media activity and develop policies and procedures, in accordance with applicable laws and regulations, to guide social media activities in the workplace.

Practice 19: Close the doors to unauthorized data exfiltration. An organization's first step to addressing insider threats is to identify its critical assets (people, information, technology, and facilities). To limit the exfiltration risks posed to critical assets, the organization must account for all devices that connect, physically or wirelessly, to its information system and implement controls that allow authorized information exchanges but prevent unauthorized exfiltration of its information assets.

Future Trends Relevant to the Insider Threat

There are a number of trends that will influence how organizations contend with insider threat in the future. Experts warn that the future will be filled with even more insider threat attacks targeting the weakest link in security—the human factor. With the continual increase of information security breaches caused by insiders, organizations and their security professionals, have to examine what is happening within the organization and consider what they can do about it. The following are seven trends that may influence the insider threat vector:

1. First, organizations must realize that insider threats will continue to be prevalent. Even as technology advances, traditional "low-tech" insider methods will remain practicable because, for the most part, insider threat stems from human characteristics. Malicious insiders will continue to exploit targets that are easiest to access in the usual security environment.

2. With the increased prevalence of attacks, malicious insiders will also become more technologically savvy, and, therefore, increasingly capable of defeating an organization's security countermeasures that remain

static, improperly scoped, or unable to keep pace with the evolving insider threat.

3. With the increased use of web-based technology the line between internal and external threats to organizations' IT infrastructure will increasingly blur, presenting more risk with which these organizations must contend.

4. It is doubtful that organizations will make the major investments needed to adequately deal with insider threat because they will continue to focus on defending against external threats.

5. Many organizations are moving their data to the "cloud" environment. This trend will provide significantly increased opportunities for insiders to systematically and repeatedly launch attacks that could exploit vulnerabilities that are susceptible insider threat vectors.

6. Attackers who perpetrate inside attacks are becoming more sophisticated, blending cyber and physical attacks. This will force organizations to use a more holistic approach to establishing security controls to deal with a much more sophisticated inside attacker.

7. Globalization and outsourcing, as they relate to an organization's infrastructure, will increase security concerns associated with employee privacy and trust issues.

Sources of Further Information

It is important for organizations to continue to explore the insider threat in order to understand how it occurs and to determine solutions for its mitigation. Unfortunately, there is very little research on the subject of insider threat; the available information on insider threat management and mitigation is particularly sparse. There is clear opportunity for future studies in this under-researched area where there are numerous frameworks and standards to use as research guidelines. The following list includes ten relatively recent resources to assist organizations to learn more about this critical area:

1. Bishop, M. et al. (2009). *Proceedings of the 2008 Workshop om New Security Paradigms*, 1–12.

2. Colwill, C. Human factors in information security: The insider threat—Who can you trust these days? (2009). *Information Security Technical Report, 14*(4), 186–196.

3. 2011 Cybersecurity watch survey by CSO Magazine (2011).

4. Hong, J., Kim, J., & Cho, J. (2010). *International Journal of Security Its Applications, 4*(3), 55–63.

5. Jones, A. (2008). Catching the malicious insider. *Information Security Technical Report, 13*(4), 220–224.

6. Pfleeger, S. L. et al. (2010). Insiders behaving badly: Addressing bad actors and their actions. *Information Forensics and Security, IEEE Transactions on, 5*(1), 169–179.

7. Sakar, K. Roy. (2010). Assessing insider threats to information security using technical, behavioral and organizational measures. *Information Security Technical Report, 15*(3).

8. Silowash, G. J. et al. (2012). Common sense guide to mitigating insider threats. Published by CERT, Software Engineering Institute, Carnegie Mellon University.

9. Widup, S. (2010). The leaking vault—Five years of data breaches. Digital Forensics Association.

10. Willison, R., & Siponen, M. (2009). Overcoming the insider: Reducing Employee computer crime through

situational crime prevention. *Communications of the ACM, 52*(9), 133–137.

Conclusion

The insider threat can never be completely eradicated, but it can be decreased if organizations implement the proper controls. Many organizations attempt to mitigate insider threat activity using technology, but technology alone is not the answer because the insider is a human being. To protect against human beings the organization must use technology that monitors traffic in and out of the network, along with processes for monitoring specific people who display suspicious non-technical behavior. This holistic, enterprise-level insider threat program must integrate and analyze both technical and non-technical indicators. The program must be robust enough to identify critical assets, including systems, services, programs, and information that, if compromised, would cause harm to the organization, individuals, national security, or others.

Insider threat has always existed in every organization and probably always will. However, as the workplace environment changes into a more mobile one where information, including sensitive information, is easily obtainable, organizations must implement strategies that will help mitigate potential insider threat opportunities using practices such as those described within this chapter.

References

Association of Certified Fraud Examiners. (2014). *Report to the nations on occupational fraud and abuse.* Austin, TX: Association of Certified Fraud Examiners.

Bautista, C. B. (2014, June 16). *AT&T data breach exposed customers' social security numbers, call logs.* Retrieved September 30, 2014, from Digitaltrends.com,http://www.digitaltrends.com/mobile/att-users-data-breach-social-security-numbers/.

Blades, M. (2010, November 1). The insider threat. *Security Technology Executive.*

Cappelli, D., Moore, A., & Trzeciak, R. (2012). *The CERT guide to insider threat: How to prevent, detect, and respond to information technology crimes.* Upper Saddle River, NJ: Addison-Wesley.

Cappelli, D., Moore, A., & Trzeciak, R. (2012). *The Cert guide to insider threats.* Upper Saddle River, NJ: Addison-Wesley.

Cummings, A., Lewellen, T., McIntire, D., Moore, A., & Trzeciak, R. (2012). *Insider threat study: Illicit cyber activity involving fraud in the U.S. financial services sector.* Pittsburgh, PA: Carnigie Mellon University.

Fritz, B. (2014, August 10). Media & marketing. *Wall Street Journal.*

Hill, K. (2013, June 10). Why NSA IT guy Edward Snowden leaked top secret documents. *Forbes.* Retrieved September 25, 2014, from http://www.forbes.com/sites/kashmirhill/2013/06/10/why-nsa-it-guy-edward-snowden-leaked-top-secret-documents/.

Hosenball, M. (2013, November 14). NSA chief says Snowden leaked up to 200,000 secret documents. *Rueters.* Retrieved September 25, 2014, from http://www.reuters.com/article/2013/11/14/us-usa-security-nsa-idUS BRE9AD19B20131114.

Kroll Advisory Solutions. (2013). *The insider threat: Why Chinese hacking may be the least of corporate worries.* New York: Kroll Incorporated.

Mazzafro, J. M. (2013). *A preliminary examination of insider threat programs in the U.S. private sector.*

McClintock, P. (2014, April 21). Average movie ticket price lowers to $7.96 in first quarter. *The Holywood Reporter.* Retrieved September 16, 2014, from http://www.hollywoodreporter.com/news/average-movie-ticket-price-lowers-697849.

Mickelberg, K., Pollard, N., & Schive, L. (2014). *US cybercrime: Rising risks, reduced readiness Key findings from the 2014 US state of cybercrime survey.* PricewaterhouseCoopers.

Office of the Press Secretary. (2007, October 11). *Executive Order 13587— Structural Reforms to Improve the Security of Classified Networks and the Responsible Sharing and Safeguarding of Classified Information.* Retrieved September 29, 2014, from The White House: http://www.whitehouse.gov/the-press-office/2011/10/07/executive-order-13587-structural-reforms-improve-security-classified-net.

Office of the Press Secretary. (2012, November 21). *National Insider Threat Policy and Minimum Standards for Executive Branch Insider Threat Programs.* Retrieved September 25, 2014, from The White House: http://www.whitehouse.gov/the-press-office/2012/11/21/presidential-memorandum-national-insider-threat-policy-and-minimum-stand.

Overview. (2014). Retrieved Septemeer 21, 2014, from CERT-Software Engineering Istitute: http://www.cert.org/insider-threat/.

Ponemon Institute. (2013). 2013 cost of cyber crime study: Global report. Traverse City, MI: Author.

Raytheon. (2014). *Securing the modern enterprise "factory": How to build an insider threat program*. Herndon: Raytheon.

Schaefer, P. (2012). *Are employees stealing from you? Tips to prevent employee theft*. Retrieved September 30, 2014, from businessknowhow.com: http://www.businessknowhow.com/manage/employee-theft.htm.

Software Engineering Institute. (2013). *Unintentional insider threats: A foundational study*. Pittsburgh: Carnegie Mellon University.

Symantec Corporation. (2013). *What's yours is mine: How employees are putting your intellectual property at risk*. Mountain View, CA: Symantec Corporation.

Verizon Enterprise Solutions. (2014). *Verizon 2014 data breach investigations report*. Verizon Enterprise Solutions.

Wilson, T. (2009). Understanding the danger within. *InformationWeek Research Report*.

Chapter 9

Cybersecurity in the C-Suite

PETER L. O'DELL

Information technology and business are becoming inextricably
interwoven. I don't think anybody can talk meaningfully about
one without talking about the other.

—Bill Gates

Introduction

Senior leadership composed of both the Board of Directors and C-Suite
for organizations have in the past largely delegated the cyber threat
to other areas of the company. Once mostly the domain of the IT
department, cyber threats to all organizations have grown in scope
and danger to the extent that boards are being forced to assume a
leadership position. Recent data breaches like Target's theft of customers' financial information through an invasion of their Point of Sale
(POS) Systems have underscored the impact to earnings, destruction
of reputation, and long-term compromise to intellectual property that
can occur and devastate an organization.

Assessment, planning, and cyber resilience are all key areas that
must be integrated into a cyber-aware culture that is set by the "Tone
at the Top," in the boardroom and C-Suite. In this chapter, we will

define the risk and explore practical avenues for identifying and aligning the entire organization to better defend and recover from this modern-day risk.

The risk to organizations of all sizes has been growing rapidly in terms of the number of incidents and the damage done worldwide. The World Economic Forum released a study in 2014 that put the cost to society at trillions of dollars; measuring not just the direct impact, but the opportunity cost from cyber efforts disrupting growth of new, innovative areas like cloud computing and the Internet of Things. There are many different studies from both technology companies and the government with the estimated cost varying greatly depending on the scope and market of their research; all, however, point toward numbers above $100 billion in worldwide impact.

Fundamental Issues Unique to Senior Leadership

The board and senior leadership are responsible for all aspects of the organization's actions and liable under the law for the initiatives that the organization takes in all areas of its operations. The board oversees hiring of senior management of the organization, and has responsibility to review, oversee, audit, and govern on a continual basis. Within others areas of the organization, the response time is predictable and relative clarity of these tasks is normally predictable; for example, the annual financial audit is done several months after the end of a given accounting period, and the results reviewed by the board weeks or months after that.

The cyber threat is a "real-time" and unpredictable organizational risk that has fully emerged in the last 10 years, and continues to grow in both scope and impact. The board and senior leadership has the unique position of being in charge, but largely unprepared to administer a comprehensive, well-constructed set of cyber defenses.

The board and senior leadership must also address a wide range of tasks that are related to a cyber attack, but are outside of the tactical mitigation and recovery process that a breach demands. For publicly traded organizations, the U.S. Securities and Exchange Commission

(SEC) has issued guidance on when disclosures to shareholders should be made in the event of a successful breach by attackers. Laws and regulations for each organization must be considered before and after a cyberevent with the board and senior leadership ensuring compliance and reporting with those statutes.

Cybersecurity Threats that Challenge Senior Leadership

Computer systems have gone from their early beginnings as artillery calculators to completely underpinning civilization in only 70 years. This incredible expansion of installed technology and the retention of and dependence on older legacy computing systems from previous decades has resulted in an environment that is fragile and vulnerable to attack. In many cases, security wasn't considered in the design of major business applications; the designers never realized they would be connected to a global public system like the Internet. Professionals who understand the problems and the long-term solutions are in very short supply, and there are many untrained and unprepared executives in charge of huge IT deployments. Organizations with these problems are at particular risk of cyber attack.

There are many groups of attackers perpetrating cyber invasion around the world, but they reduce down to three major areas of concern. The group having the greatest financial impact is cybercriminals who are driven almost exclusively by monetary gain—selling customer information and stealing credit card files. Nation-states are using cyber espionage techniques to steal a wide array of intellectual property and lay the groundwork for an attack should a cyberwar or kinetic war erupt. Hacktivists are the other major group attempting to disrupt operations or damage reputations of organizations against which they have grievances.

These threats manifest themselves through many different attack vectors. Many organizations experience attacks that are a result of malware introduced into their systems through an e-mail phishing attack or an infected USB memory stick. These threats can establish a beachhead for attackers, and give them time to pursue other attacks. Applications can be attacked through buffer overflows and SQL injection, taking advantage of computer code not designed and tested for security and durability. Insiders can be an insidious and difficult to detect source of attack, stealing sensitive information directly, or enabling privileged account access to outsiders. Hacktivists have brought operations to a complete stop with distributed denial of service (DDOS) attacks, which basically overwhelm customer-facing systems with phony transactions and information requests.

Another threat to the defenses of an organization is the continual change in information technology inside the organization. The information technology group is responsible and accountable for most major changes, but an increasing number of departments are utilizing Software As a Service (SAAS) applications like Salesforce's CRM on the Internet, often without informing the IT group. Individuals are also empowering themselves with new apps on mobile devices which can serve as a gateway into an organization's networks.

Partners in the form of sub-contractors and customers can also enable a vulnerability point into a corporate network. In the case of Target Corporation, the attackers were able to gain entry through an HVAC vendor's credentials.

Laws and Policies Relevant to Senior Leadership

Laws on cybersecurity vary widely across industries and countries around the world, and the topic is still under development in many critical areas. The U.S. Securities and Exchange Commission issued guidance about the disclosure of breaches; the guidelines center on an assessment of materiality or impact of an event, and do not mandate disclosure in all cases. NIST (National Institute of Standards and Technology), a U.S. federal agency, issued a voluntary framework in 2014 providing organizations with a comprehensive view of the problem and the major areas of concern.

Individual industries also have laws and regulations that impact their cybersecurity readiness, preparation, and compliance reporting. For instance, the energy industry has the CIP (Critical Infrastructure

Protection) standards that outline compliance steps for protecting the electrical grid. Financial services firms that process credit cards utilize the PCI (Payment Card Industry) policies as a strong set of policies and guidelines.

Another area of policy is information sharing: the exchange of information between industry partners to help bolster their threat understanding and defenses. The U.S. government has enabled the creation of ISACS (Information Sharing and Analysis Centers) for different industries like financial services, energy, information technology, and other critical areas. These centers are designed to facilitate rapid communication between participating organizations.

Current Skills of Board and C-Suite Personnel

Senior leadership outside of the Chief Information Officer (CIO) and Chief Information Security Officer (CISO) have traditionally had little to no exposure to the threat of cyber attacks and the complexity of defenses needed to defend their organizations. In many cases, the first detailed exposure comes when a major attack succeeds, and the organization is suddenly thrust into a crisis that it is ill-prepared to manage. On-the-job experience is truly a terrible way to understand the gravity of this area.

Training senior leadership to understand and be capable of full oversight of the organization's cyber strategy is very difficult when a technical approach is taken. The amount of information and understanding needed to completely comprehend the problem is daunting. It is further compounded by rapid change in both technology and in the attack techniques used by cyberattackers of all types.

The most appropriate skills that can be leveraged by senior leadership are the management skills already used to govern and oversee other complex areas of the organization. Training should focus on strategy, policy, and concrete business steps that can be taken to improve the organization's cyber awareness. Internal technical groups should distill the problems and recommended solutions into business-based decisions that can be validated by outside experts.

A good corollary to the cyber process is in the area of financial controls and auditing. Audit and compliance committees typically have set up controls and metrics for financial reporting that can be assessed and verified by outside efforts. The financial area is much more standardized and better understood, but the overall process is a good baseline for examination as senior management works to gain control of the cyber controls.

Cybersecurity Best Practices for Senior Leadership

It is incumbent upon senior leadership to take charge of the entire organization's approach to cybersecurity, and align all groups toward a common set of goals and objectives. There are several best practices that will assist your senior leadership to improve overall cyber awareness and defenses:

Honest assessment and feedback: Board members and C-Suite executives who feel overly positive about their organization's cybersecurity strategy and implementation should ensure that frank and honest feedback is being provided by internal experts, and that they are not being shielded from or deliberately uninformed about the hard truths in this critical area. It can be difficult for a mid-tier executive to deliver bad news to the board and senior executives. Organizations are going to have to work hard to ensure that they are fully in the feedback loop before an attack occurs. Finding out after the fact is very painful, and terminating the perceived guilty parties and other recriminations do little to help recovery and stimulate subsequent feedback.

Governance and oversight: This is the board's central purpose. It can be summarized as "nose in, fingers out," implying full understanding and strategic direction without micromanaging. For the cyber threat, a comprehensive overview of the organization is required and the board should be tasked with working through this issue with the full management team. The board should communicate across the organization how this oversight is accomplished, enabling individuals at all levels to contribute innovative ideas and flag potential problems before they reach massive proportions.

Hiring and development of the cyber team: This is the single crucial area where more efforts can result in a high rate of return on time invested. The board and the senior executive team are going to rely on the people and organizations that are put into place to manage, operate, and defend the organization on a 24/7 basis. The effective team will almost always be cross functional, cutting across departmental barriers and information silos, and embracing the cyber threat as the multi-headed beast that it can be. In the IT world, great people are in high demand. Organizations need to ensure the chosen defenders are the best available, verifying at the hiring point with comprehensive background checks, periodic reevaluations, and verification of capabilities through the use of outside (and thoroughly vetted) experts that can give the company a full appraisal of competence and readiness.

Prioritization: Every organization has information assets that are significantly more important than others, and the board and executive leadership team are best situated to identify these critical areas. Once identified, special care should be taken in the protection and response to these areas, even if it means lower defenses for non-critical areas. For example, a drug company may have extremely sensitive research and development systems that, if compromised, could cost the organization billions of dollars in later revenue through intellectual property theft of clinical trial information or pharmaceutical recipes. Ensuring that the leadership of the organization has clearly communicated the priorities and is aggressively following up with the operational functions is a great first step in the protection of these invaluable assets.

Balance: The cybersecurity problem being examined here is severe, immediate, and very dangerous—make no mistake. A committed approach should be taken toward these preparation and assessment efforts. In every other organization, there are dozens of other key opportunities and problems that demand attention and activity by the board and senior management. Building the base of education and understanding around cybersecurity, and having the flexibility to allocate additional leadership resources in the event of a major shortfall is also an important element of balancing critical time.

Culture of risk awareness: Almost anyone in the organization can be an entry point for a cyber attack, either maliciously or inadvertently. In most organizations, the information technology team is very risk aware and tries to sensitize everyone to the risks associated with poor cyber-hygiene. In many of the same organizations, IT is looked upon as an impediment to progress rather than the fount of wisdom on all things technology. The same risk message coming from the board instead of IT will have a different voice and be perceived differently. The board and executive leadership can sensitize and make everyone aware of the risks and impact of a major cyber incident, but they must also lead by example, adhering to the same defensive policies and actions.

Collaboration across the silos: Unfortunately, factions, silos, and fiefdoms exist within most large organizations. The board and the executive team are responsible for making these different factions work together proactively in the defense of the organization from cyber attacks. For example, the Chief Security Officer might have a full command center for monitoring the physical parts of the organizations—fences, access doors, high value areas, and video monitoring. This command center should be able to reposition its people and efforts in an emergency, assisting in the incident response called for by a cyber attack. Many of the same electronic alerting systems should be common to the physical and cyber response organizations so that personnel inside the organization are more familiar with a common method of notification. By combining these efforts and resources, organizations can realize a better overall response capability and utilization of resources.

Outside verification: No matter how good an organization's internal people are, it is very difficult to stay up to date and have a totally objective and comprehensive view of one's cyber policies, controls, defenses, responses, and future directions. Getting an independent resource to assess and verify these critical areas is a powerful cross-check that should not be skipped, skimped on, or postponed. Using an outsider can also create a trail of documentation that will out-last generations of employees, serve as a good reminder of what was important within a given time period, and what was distributed and discussed inside the leadership team. There may need to be multiple outside groups involved with this assessment and validation process. NOTE: This is not a blanket endorsement for legions of consultants taking up residence in an organization for years on end. It is incum-bent upon the board to find the right groups who can assist cyber and management team on an as-needed basis and *also* be available to surge into action in the event of an incident.

Real time response: The board needs to set the stage for a real-time response to an incident that could impact the immediate operations and future of the organization. Planning and preparation must be coor-dinated, scenarios validated, contingency agreements executed, and outside verification obtained—all supported by exercises to reinforce activities and look for gaps in the planning. This kind of rehearsal time is always difficult to schedule, execute thoroughly, and make inclusive to everyone that needs the critical understanding and preparation for the real event. Cyril Richard "Rick" Rescorla (May 27, 1939–Sep-tember 11, 2001), security director for Morgan Stanley in New York's World Trade Center, was known for being persistent and dogmatic about preparedness and evacuation drills and exercises—even with high-level executives. He is credited with saving a large number of lives in the 9/11 attacks, and lost his own life evacuating more person-nel from the South Tower. Training and preparation paid off for the individuals Rick impacted at Morgan Stanley, and he set a profound example to emulate. Apply the same efforts in your organization and the benefits will follow.

Compliance and audit: The audit committee of the board of direc-tors is typically charged with monitoring risk management activities. The committee is a subset of the board of directors and reports to the board. Some boards are establishing separate technical oversight committees as the breadth of technology continues to broaden and the organization's dependence deepens. Having a strong audit function around cyber threats and preparedness is an important oversight element. Metrics are important to gather on an ongoing basis in order to assess the success or failure of the entity's cyber efforts. If an attack happens, a good understanding of what went wrong and corrective measures are imperative.

Information sharing: Information sharing is an important defense that should be utilized to improve overall situational awareness. Because most directors are on multiple boards, there are some high-level sharing discussions that can take place between board members in terms of threats, preparation, exercises, response, and recovery. Directors are encouraged to pursue as many of these as possible—the enhanced knowledge will help all concerned. The board and executive team should also understand and promote multiple sharing efforts with the government, consortiums, industry groups, and partners to help build a more comprehensive set of defenses and awareness.

Future Cyber Trends Impacting Senior Business Leaders

The future of cybersecurity parallels the overall technology revolution and the continuing development of the Information Age that we have grown up with—the threat is expanding with every new technological capability brought to life. Where there is innovation in new services and technology, there is an attacker probing the new capability for weaknesses that can be exploited for entry, theft, disruption, or disablement of the targeted organization's operations and information assets. The primitive interconnections that exist between the many components of today's "sophisticated" enterprise systems only add to the increasing risk.

The risks from cyber attacks will likely continue their rapid rise over the coming years—there are several new areas of growth that will open up major new attack vectors. Cloud computing, Software as a Service (SAAS), and the Internet of Things (IoT) are continuing to accelerate in terms of competitive advantage and cost reduction, and increased deployment brings new attack vectors. The new capabilities have their own inherent weaknesses, but the combination with existing systems magnifies these vulnerabilities.

Several areas are especially concerning in terms of future cyber risk:

Targeted attacks: If an organization has done a good job on cyber-hygiene and layered defenses, attackers may create very specific attacks to break into its systems. One company was breached because the attackers set up a collection system at a nearby restaurant frequented by senior IT personnel, and captured privileged account information that they then used in an insider attack fashion.

Mobile/Smartphones: There have not been any public and devastating attacks on the increasingly large base of mobile phones, but most research identifies this is an imminent area of risk. A sophisticated insider attack on the iPhone infrastructure or code could leverage the rigid nature and relative standardization of all the proprietary Apple phones, enabling a widespread security event. The Android mobile operating system created by Google is much more open, making its code an open book to attackers studying how to attack the users of this technology.

Tablets: Tablets are a growing threat and a larger risk to organizational infrastructure. Many people, particularly high-level executives, are forgoing a traditional laptop and relying on a tablet for much of their day-to-day interaction with their organization, partners, and customers. This means those tablets are loaded with prizes for an attacker—confidential documents, contact databases, customer records, e-mail repositories, and—most of all—password files containing credentials to other systems. Organizations should continue to monitor this potential problem and ensure that encryption is being used wherever feasible.

Ransomware: Ransomware is a newer threat and is a significant, growing problem. The first attacks emerged out of Russia in 2005. The threat manifests through malware, and encrypts a portion of the user's storage so that it can't be used. The attacker demands a payment to unencrypt the information and release it to normal use. One highly effective version has been the Police Trojan—malware encrypts the information and sends the user a message that the local police department suspects the computer involved in illegal activity and a fine must be paid to unlock it.

Industrial Control Systems: Most industrial control systems were built as stand-alone, localized implementations. With the advent of the Internet and new generations of devices and control software, this has caused many isolated systems to be reachable via the Internet or other intruder methods like USB-based software injection. There is an increasing likelihood that major attacks will occur, causing disruption or physical damage. If an organization utilizes these types of systems, it's imperative to fund preparedness and resilience efforts. Even if an organization is not an ICS user, it may be indirectly impacted with a hit to its critical infrastructure; imagine what an extended regional power outage could do to an organization.

Cyber professionals: The creation of highly qualified, experienced cyber professionals at current levels will not meet the current and growing demand worldwide. There are many universities that have added cybersecurity and information security degree programs, and a host of certification-granting organizations has also emerged. Over time, this will help somewhat, but the experience factor is still an important element. To mitigate this negative trend, organizations need to ensure that they have good people, contract with outside providers for surge resources, continually vet and validate internal resources and work with internal teams to align organizational strategy with resource expenditures and planning. Working with educational institutions that can provide basic and advanced degrees is also recommended.

Sources of Further Information

NACD: The National Association of Corporate Directors (www. nacdonline.org) is an excellent source of board and senior leadership information. The organization puts on seminars, has an extensive library, and has over 15,000 U.S. members.

SANS Institute: SANS (www.sans.org) is a global source of training and certification programs. Their list of 20 critical security control factors is recognized as one of the most comprehensive approaches to cyber preparedness.

Ponemon Institute: Ponemon Institute does topical research and surveys around multiple areas of cyber. Information is easy to consume and understand, and is done in a manner that is useful for senior leadership.

Microsoft: Microsoft is one of the quintessential leaders in all aspects of cybersecurity. They provide automatic updating for the industry dominant software products, and also have multiple groups working with global law enforcement to stem attacks.

Global consulting firms: Global consulting firms like Ernst & Young (EY) and PricewaterhouseCoopers (PWC) are a very good source of information and research, and can provide well-vetted resources to global firms.

FireEyeand CrowdStrike: These are two relatively new firms specialize in cyber-response when a major breach occurs. Both have proactive offerings and a suite of other services, but are leaders in assembling a response and driving mitigation and recovery.

References

Lynch, S. (2014, June 10). U.S. SEC official urges broader cyber-attack disclosure. Retrieved from http://www.reuters.com/article/2014/06/10/sec-cybersecurity-aguilar-idUSL2N0OR13U20140610.

North American Electric Reliability Corporation (NERC). CIP Standards. Retrieved from www.nerc.com.

PCI Security Standards Council. (2010). PCI SSC data security standards overview. Retrieved from https://www.pcisecuritystandards.org/security_standards/.

World Economic Forum. (2014). Risk and responsibility in a hyperconnected world. Retrieved from http://www3.weforum.org/docs/WEF_Risk Responsibility_HyperconnectedWorld_Report_2014.pdf.

Chapter 10

Future Directions for Educating a Cybersecurity Workforce

KEVIN L. JACKSON

Introduction

Economic and operational advantages of highly automated information technology infrastructures, and the widespread use of automation tools like Chef and Puppet, are revolutionizing business and governmental processes. While this is mostly a good thing, organizational dynamics and responsibilities are being shifted in unforeseen ways. Previously separated work and personal lives are now being blended by 24/7 connectivity and social media interactions. The Chief Information Officers' status has been elevated by making them the center of business trends that refocus corporate resources toward technology-driven new business models. One aspect of this transition, cloud computing, is now integral to business, with 45% of executives saying they are currently running, or plan to run, their business in the cloud (North Bridge Venture Partners, 2014). The other side of this double-edged sword is being used by cybercriminals to attack and siphon off more than $400 billion dollars every year from the global economy. Cyber espionage and identity theft are believed to have affected more than 800 million people during 2013 (Williams, 2014). This not only undermines international commerce but also is detrimental to society as a whole.

Focusing on cloud, this component of the technological transition is accelerating with over 11,000 Cloud Services/APIs, and developer adoption of IaaS at 56% and PaaS at 46%. The industry is beginning to see the birth of new, re-imagined, cloud-native applications. This will result in the delivery of business value propositions that are orders of magnitude greater than what was possible before (North Bridge Venture Partners, 2014).

A recent Microsoft study confirmed this trend by showing that the vast majority of organizations of all sizes use both Software-as-a-Service (SaaS) and hosted infrastructure services. Both SaaS and hosted infrastructure services are currently being used most by organizations with less than 100 employees (Bensonoff, 2014). Government and education industries lead this shift with more than 60% of organizations reporting participation. These sectors are also more likely to utilize Platform-as-a-Service (PaaS). Small businesses lead in utilizing colocation services, which have slower adoption rates than other cloud segments (Bensonoff, 2014).

Cloud computing has also shown itself to be a strategic business move with 49% of respondents in this year's survey citing its use as a means for fueling revenue generation or new product creation. Some additional markers of this trend include:

- 45% of businesses say they already, or plan to, run their company from the cloud showing how integral cloud is to business.

- The growth of SaaS adoption from 13% in 2011 to 74% in 2014.

- 56% of businesses are using Infrastructure-as-a-Service (IaaS) technologies to harness elastic computing resources.

- 41% of businesses are using Platform-as-a-Service (PaaS) technologies to prototype and develop new applications.

- Two-thirds of respondents believe their data will come to reside in some form of cloud over the next two years as bigger data needs consolidation, collaboration, and creation go online (Bensonoff, 2014).

Of particular note is how the corporate front office is embracing cloud. Functionally, sales and marketing lead adoption rates at 51%, with customer service and analytics not far behind at 43% adoption (Kugel, 2014). With cloud dominating business IT, cybersecurity is now quickly becoming synonymous with cloud security. Although security continues to be a strong barrier to cloud transition, with 49% of respondents concerned about cloud data security, the concern is not having a significant effect on this transformative event. Even highly vocalized concerns about privacy are not having any noticeable effect. Privacy concerns actually rose to 31% in 2014 as increased tension manifested itself between the desire for anonymity and the convenience and utility of personalization (North Bridge Venture Partners, 2014).

The undeniable lesson in all of these facts is that our cybersecurity workforce must be highly educated in cloud computing and must continually expand and deepen its capabilities in this rapidly advancing arena.

Common Cybersecurity Workforce Educational Needs

Industry Vertical Knowledge

While information technology is the ubiquitous horizontal layer underlying all industry sector verticals, implementation specifics are strongly influenced by security requirements. A recent study of cloud computing adoption highlighted this by documenting the difference between regulated and unregulated industries (Kimberly Harris-Ferrante, 2014).

- Regulated Industries

    o Insurance: Private clouds are preferred because they are more secure than public clouds. By 2015 industry association community clouds are expected to increase in popularity.

    o Banking: In the banking industry, the main concern is that a cloud environment is not secure enough. This issue drives cloud use in this particular industry toward administrative functions like e-mail, file sharing, and sharing of notes.

○ Government: While opportunities to use cloud computing in a variety of ways do exist, it is also misunderstood. Today, the biggest opportunities are in public cloud computing, but many in this industry fear security problems.

• Unregulated Industries

○ Retail: In this industry, cloud implementations have been mostly IaaS or PaaS solutions. Security, availability, and vendor maturity are all aspects that retailers consider when deciding which functions they want deployed from the cloud.

○ Media: Audiences today can access content of any form in a variety of ways. This is why service providers and application developers are exploring a cloud-based visual way to enable multi-screen entertainment.

○ Manufacturing: This industry uses the cloud for logistics, sales support functions, HR, product development, and life cycle management, as well as some manufacturing operations.

A Global Cybersecurity View

Globalization of commerce driven by ubiquitous and real-time Internet-based interactions makes a global perspective on security paramount. International health IT, for example, currently supports the move toward cloud computing with governments, industry leaders, and advocacy groups keen to adopt cloud-based solutions in health care. The potential benefits, however, need to be evaluated against the significant cyber-related risks. As shown in a recent comparative study on

U.S. and EU health professionals, views on the potential benefits and risks from cloud computing vary greatly (Currie & Seddon, 2014). The results from surveying health care organizations in the U.S. and five EU countries (France, Germany, the Netherlands, Sweden, and the UK) identify differences across countries in health IT policy, incentives for adoption, privacy and security, and trust in third-party suppliers. The findings show that privacy and security are important issues for health care organizations, yet differences exist between the U.S. and across EU Member States in how these concepts are viewed. The study provides instructive insights on cross-jurisdictional approaches to personal data and privacy, regulations and rules on health data export, how countries interpret and implement different data protection regulations and rules, and the practical implementation of regulatory rules.

A key challenge for international governments keen to promote the use of advanced information technology across all industry verticals is to provide an effective legal and regulatory framework that governs trans-border data flows. In today's internationally interconnected world, personal data is likely to be held on servers that may be located in legal and regulatory jurisdictions outside the country where the data is collected and used. This is not simply an "IT challenge" for the business community, since the ramifications need to be understood and addressed within the context of the legal and regulatory framework that governs potential trans-border data flows. Cybersecurity professionals will be asked to provide direction and guidance to policy-makers, regulators, and industry leaders.

In spite of the risk, the trend toward increasing trans-border data flows will continue, albeit with serious concerns about privacy and security. Data also suggests that many organizations are concerned about working with third-party providers in the pursuit of these advanced capabilities. While this may be a trust issue, it may also stem from concerns about how to develop and execute sufficiently robust legal contracts. Corporate users are likely to enter into standard contractual clauses with IT providers, which may not fully protect the rights of all parties, including the individuals whose personal data is being stored. Unlike previous technology, which resided within a single organization, today's business landscape inevitably includes the potential for trans-border data flows across multiple legal and regulatory jurisdictions.

Global Legal Framework Knowledge

The lack of a consistent legal and regulatory environment shines a harsh spotlight on cyberspace. Our cybersecurity workforce must be educated on how to interpret international policies with respect to their own organizational policies, industry regulations, national laws and eventually, international protocols. As a start, these professionals should be taught to evaluate IT operations across these seven Business Software Alliance recommended areas:

- Ensuring privacy: Buttressing users' faith that their information will not be used or disclosed in unexpected ways. At the same time, to maximize the benefit of advanced information technology, providers must be free to move data internationally in the most efficient way.

- Promoting security: Users must be assured that information technology providers understand and properly manage the risks inherent in storing and running applications in cyberspace. Solution providers must be able to implement cutting-edge cybersecurity solutions without being required to use specific technologies.

- Battling cybercrime: In cyberspace, as in the real world, laws must provide meaningful deterrence and clear causes of action. Legal systems should provide an effective mechanism for law enforcement, and for IT providers themselves, to combat unauthorized access to data stored on interconnected global platforms.

- Protecting intellectual property: In order to promote continued innovation and technological advancement, intellectual property laws should provide for clear protection and vigorous enforcement against misappropriation and infringement of the developments that underlie the IT industry.

• Ensuring data portability and the harmonization of international rules: The smooth flow of data around the world requires efforts to promote openness and interoperability. Governments should work with industry to develop standards, while also working to minimize conflicting legal obligations on IT providers.

• Promoting free trade: By its very nature, Internet-based technologies operate across national boundaries. The ability to promote economic growth depends on a global market that transcends barriers to free trade, including preferences for particular products or providers.

• Establishing the necessary IT infrastructure: International commerce requires robust, ubiquitous, and affordable broadband access. This can be achieved through policies that provide incentives for private sector investment in broadband infrastructure and laws that promote universal access to broadband (Business Software Alliance, 2013).

The cyber workforce needs to also be internationally savvy in order to deal with global scenarios. Geo-specific IT security policies and procedures will become the norm rather than the exception (i.e., stronger identification and access management challenges for users accessing from Pakistan). Important educational topics will include:

• Multi-national Enterprise Risk Management;

• International Cyber Event Management;

• Industrialized Criminal Activity/Multi-national fraud; and

• Cloud-enabled thieves and terrorist.

Hybrid IT Infrastructure Management

The cybersecurity workforce will need to learn how to operate and securely collaborate in a de-perimeterized world. This means more training in hybrid IT infrastructure design, governance and operations, and use of new models like "Cloud Cube" reference model (The Open Group: Jericho Forum, 2009).

The Jericho Forum is an international group of organizations working together to define and promote the solutions surrounding the issue of de-perimeterization. It was officially founded at the offices of the Open Group in Reading, UK, on Friday, January 16, 2004. It had existed as a loose affiliation of interested corporate CISOs (Chief Information Security Officers) discussing the topic since the summer of 2003. One of the earlier outputs of the group is a position paper entitled "The Jericho Forum Commandments," which are a set of principles that describe how best to survive in a de-perimeterized world. The paper outlined an initial analysis process that started with the classification of data with respect to sensitivity and regulatory compliance in order to know which protection rules would be appropriate for application. A second requirement is to operate within an environment of universally adopted standards for data classification, trust level management, and standardized metadata representation for cloud security. Once these prerequisites are met, managers and operators could then be able to make rational decisions about:

- What data and processes should be moved to the cloud.

- The appropriate service models (IaaS, PaaS, SaaS) for relevant operational and business process.

- The most appropriate "Cloud Formation" to use.

The Jericho Forum identified four criteria to differentiate cloud formations from each other and the manner of their provision. The Cloud Cube Model summarizes these four dimensions:

- Dimension: Internal(I)/External (E)

  ○ If it is within your own physical boundary then it is Internal.

  ○ If it is not within your own physical boundary then it is External.

- Dimension: Proprietary (P)/Open (O)

  ○ Proprietary means that the organization providing the service is keeping the means of provision under its ownership. As a result, when operating in clouds that are proprietary, you may not be able to move to another cloud supplier without significant effort or investment. Often the more innovative technology advances occur in the proprietary domain. As such the proprietor may choose to enforce restrictions through patents and by keeping the technology involved a trade secret.

  ○ Clouds that are Open are using technology that is not proprietary, meaning that there are likely to be more suppliers, and you are not as constrained in being able to share your data and collaborate with selected parties using the same open technology. Open services tend to be those that are widespread and consumerized, and most likely a published open standard, for example, e-mail (SMTP).

- Dimension: Perimeterized (Per) / De-perimeterized (D-p) Architectures

  ○ Perimeterized implies continuing to operate within the traditional IT perimeter, often signaled by "network firewalls." As has been discussed in previous published Jericho Forum papers, this approach inhibits collaboration. In effect, when operating in the perimeterized areas, you may simply extend your own organization's perimeter into the external cloud computing domain using a VPN and operating the virtual server in your own IP domain, making use of your own directory services to control access. Then, when the computing task is completed you can withdraw your perimeter back to its original traditional position. We consider this type of system perimeter to be a traditional, though a virtual, perimeter.

o De-perimeterized, assumes that the system perimeter is architected following the principles outlined in the Jericho Forum's Commandments and Collaboration Oriented Architectures Framework. The terms Micro-Perimeterization and Macro-Perimeterization will likely be in active use here—for example, in a de-perimeterized frame the data would be encapsulated with meta-data and mechanisms that would protect the data from inappropriate usage. COA-enabled systems allow secure collaboration. In a de-perimeterized environment an organization can collaborate securely with selected parties (business partner, customer, supplier, outworker) globally over any COA capable network.

• Dimension: Insourced/Outsourced

o Insourced: the service is provided by your own staff under your control.

o Outsourced: the service is provided by a third party.

(The Open Group: Jericho Forum, 2009)

Although the Jericho Model was designed specifically for cloud computing, it also provides an excellent framework for addressing today's hybrid IT infrastructures environment. Organizations will need to develop policies that address every facet of the cube and cybersecurity professionals will be called upon to monitor and enforce those policies.

Risk Management Frameworks

Global economic stability and the integrity of governmental services will largely depend on cybersecurity; therefore, our workforce must be educated on the use and application of risk estimation metrics. "Quantitative risk analysis aspires to cede precise numeric monetary values to assets. It designates the financial risk of threats impact and frequency, costs of control and loss" (Ben Arfa Rabai, Jouini, & Aissa, 2013). Some of the more relevant risk management frameworks include:

- Single loss expectancy (SLE)—The single loss expectancy (SLE) is the expected monetary loss every time a risk occurs. It is calculated by multiplying asset value (AV) with Exposure Factor (EF) as shown in formula SLE=AV*EF, where: AV is the financial value of the asset and EF is expressed within a range from 0% to 100% and that an asset's value will be destroyed by risk (Tsiakis, 2010).

- Annual loss expectancy (ALE)—The annual loss expectancy (ALE) is the expected cumulative cost of risk over a period of one year. It is defined as the cost (loss in monetary units) of the damage resulted by a failure multiplied by its frequency in a period of one year: ALE=SLE*ARO, where: the annual rate of occurrence (ARO) is the probability that a risk will occur in this particular period of one year (Böhme & Mowey, 2008).

- OCTAVE—OCTAVE (Operationally Critical Threat, Asset, and Vulnerability Evaluation) is a risk-based strategic assessment and planning technique for security which was developed by the Software Engineering Institute of Carnegie Mellon University in the U.S. (Mayer,

2009). The method's aims are examining organizational and technological issues as well as defining an organization's security strategy and plan. It consists of three steps: making files of threat scenarios based on assets, recognizing the vulnerabilities of major facilities, and assessing the risk and developing security strategies.

• CRAMM—The CRAMM (CCTA Risk Analysis and Management Method) method has been developed since 1985 by the Central Computer and Telecommunications Agency of the UK government (Mayer, 2009). The methodological part of CRAMM is composed of three steps:

   ○ The first step identifies assets which are divided into three classes: physical, software, and data. The valuation of assets is generally done in terms of the impact coming from information potentially being unavailable, destroyed, disclosed, or modified for software and data. This estimation of assets may be done in a quantitative way by valuing them in financial terms by data owners (the business unit managers).

   ○ The second step identifies and estimates the level of threats and vulnerabilities and provides some mapping between threats and assets and between threats and impacts in a qualitative way.

   ○ The third step produces a set of countermeasures that are considered as necessary to manage the identified risks.

• Information security risk management framework for cloud computing environments—A qualitative information risk management framework for better understanding critical areas of focus in cloud computing environments and identifying threats and vulnerabilities. The qualitative risk analysis proposed method is used to approach risk assessment and rank severity of threats by using classes such as low, medium, and high of probabilities and damages for cloud providers (Zhang, 2010).

- MFC—A quantitative infrastructure that estimates the security of a system. The model measures the security of a system in terms of the loss that each stakeholder stands to sustain as a result of security breakdowns. The infrastructure in question reflects the values that stakeholders have in each security requirement, the dependency of security requirements on the operation of architectural components, and the impact of those security threats (Ben Aissa, 2010).

Key Educational Topics: Critical Threats to Cloud Security

With cloud computing dominating business IT, the cybersecurity workforce should have much more focused education on addressing the following nine critical threats to cloud security (Cloud Security Alliance, 2013):

- Data Breaches—Sensitive internal data falls into the hands of competitors. While data loss and data leakage are both serious threats to cloud computing, the measures put in place to mitigate one of these threats can exacerbate the other. You may be able to encrypt your data to reduce the impact of a data breach, but if you lose your encryption key, you will lose your data as well. Conversely, you may decide to keep offline backups of your data to reduce the impact of a catastrophic data loss, but this increases your exposure to data breaches.

- Data Loss—Permanently losing data. Under the new EU data protection rules, data destruction and corruption of personal data are considered forms of data breaches and would require appropriate notifications. Many compliance policies require organizations to retain audit records or other documentation. If an organization stores this data in the cloud, its loss could jeopardize the organization's compliance status.

- Account Hijacking—Attack methods such as phishing, fraud, and exploitation of software vulnerabilities still achieve results. Credentials and passwords are often reused, which amplifies the impact of such attacks. Account and service hijacking, usually with stolen credentials, remains a top threat. With stolen credentials, attackers can often access critical areas of deployed cloud computing services, allowing them to compromise the confidentiality, integrity, and availability of those services. Organizations should be aware of these techniques as well as common defense in-depth protection strategies to contain the damage (and possible litigation) resulting from a breach. Organizations should look to prohibit the sharing of account credentials between users and services, and leverage strong two-factor authentication techniques where possible.

- Insecure APIs—Cloud computing providers expose a set of software interfaces or APIs that customers use to manage and interact with cloud services. Provisioning, management, orchestration, and monitoring are all performed using these interfaces. The security and availability of general cloud services is dependent upon the security of these basic APIs. While most providers strive to ensure security is well integrated into their service models, it is critical for consumers of those services to understand the security implications associated with the usage, management, orchestration, and monitoring of cloud services. Reliance on a weak set of interfaces and APIs exposes organizations to a variety of security issues related to confidentiality, integrity, availability, and accountability.

- Denial of Service—Denial-of-service attacks are attacks meant to prevent users of a cloud service from being able to access their data or their applications. There is the possibility that an attacker may not be able to completely knock your service off the Net, but may still cause it to consume so much processing time that it becomes too expensive for you to run and you will be forced to take it down yourself.

- Malicious Insiders—The risk of malicious insiders has been debated in the security industry. While the level of threat is left to debate, the fact of the insider threat being a real adversary is not. From IaaS to PaaS and SaaS, the malicious insider has increasing levels of access to more critical systems, and eventually to data. Systems that depend solely on the cloud service provider (CSP) for security are at great risk. Even if encryption is implemented, if the keys are not kept with the customer and are only available at data-usage time, the system is still vulnerable to malicious insider attack.

- Abuse of Cloud Services—It might take an attacker years to crack an encryption key using his own limited hardware, but using an array of cloud servers, he might be able to crack it in minutes. Alternately, he might use that array of cloud servers to stage a DDoS attack, serve malware, or distribute pirated software. This threat is more of an issue for cloud service providers than cloud consumers, but it does raise a number of serious implications for those providers. How will you detect people abusing your service? How will you define abuse? How will you prevent them from doing it again?

- Insufficient Due Diligence—Too many enterprises jump into the cloud without understanding the full scope of the undertaking. Without a complete understanding of the CSP environment, applications, or services that are being pushed to the cloud, and operational responsibilities such as incident response, encryption, and security monitoring, organizations are taking on unknown levels of risk in ways they may not even comprehend, but that are a far departure from their current risks. An organization that rushes to adopt cloud technologies subjects itself to a number of issues. Contractual issues arise over obligations to liability, response, or transparency by creating mismatched expectations between the CSP and the customer. Pushing applications that are dependent on "internal" network-level security controls to the cloud is dangerous when those controls disappear or do not match the customer's expectation. Unknown operational and architectural issues arise when designers and architects unfamiliar with cloud technologies are designing applications being pushed to the cloud. The bottom line for enterprises and organizations moving to a cloud technology model is that they must have capable resources, and perform extensive internal and CSP due-diligence to understand the risks they assume by adopting this new technology model. This threat is specifically due to lack of education (note: low level of perceived risk and a high level of actual risk).

• Shared Technology Issues—Cloud service providers deliver their services in a scalable way by sharing infrastructure, platforms, and applications. Whether it is the underlying components that make up this infrastructure (e.g., CPU caches, GPUs, etc.) that were not designed to offer strong isolation properties for a multi-tenant architecture (IaaS), re-deployable platforms (PaaS), or multi-customer applications (SaaS), the threat of shared vulnerabilities exists in all delivery models. A compromise of an integral piece of shared technology—such as the hypervisor, a shared platform component, or an application in a SaaS environment—exposes more than just the compromised customer; rather, it exposes the entire environment to a potential of compromise and breach. This vulnerability is dangerous because it potentially can affect an entire cloud at once.

(Cloud Security Alliance, 2013)

Next Steps for Educating the Cybersecurity Workforce

There are a myriad additional new threat vectors that will comprise supplemental educational needs for new cybersecurity workers. Some of these include:

- IT supply chain management—Many of the components—including hardware, firmware, and software—that make up a technological product, contain elements stemming from a broad global market that includes nations as diverse as Germany, China, India, Brazil, and Japan. This makes it very difficult to ascertain the complete security of an end product. The market for technological goods and components grows every year and the need for cyber supply chain security grows with it.

- Shadow IT—Employees now bring their own laptops, tablets, and Smartphones to the workplace. This means that administrators are tasked with managing applications of unknown origin and inadequate security standards. Referred to as "shadow IT," the use of these alternative resources is mostly done simply out of convenience. Many of these efforts are coordinated in an effort to gain productivity advantages and streamline daily tasks. Public cloud services, for example, are often leveraged without permission of IT teams, as staff members tend to use these tools to collaborate and share files. Although shadow IT is generally aligned with overarching business goals, organizational security standards are typically ignored.

- Critical civil infrastructure—The critical infrastructure community includes public and private owners and operators, and other supporting entities that play a role in securing the nation's infrastructure. Each sector performs critical functions that are supported by information technology (IT), industrial control systems (ICS) and, in many cases, both IT and ICS. To manage cybersecurity risks, NIST has developed a cybersecurity framework designed to help professionals understand and address the security challenges and considerations specific to IT and ICS. The Framework is a risk-based approach composed of three parts: the Framework Core, the Framework Profile, and the Framework Implementation Tiers. This information should be used by organizations to determine the acceptable level of risk for IT and ICS assets and systems (National Institute of Standards and Technologies, 2013).

- Corporate social media—Conducting business and social life today inevitably involves the sharing of information. Companies outsource their business processes to partners, data and applications are moved to cloud computing based platforms, and social media has been embraced as a convenient and effective means of communication with customers and collaboration with suppliers. These changes not only increase the potential for data loss but also open organizations to the threat of infiltration and attack from the outside.

- Cloud service brokerage—A cloud server broker is a third party that acts as an intermediary between the purchaser of a cloud computing service and the sellers of that service. As these services proliferate, organizations are often using brokers to help in the transition. In the cybersecurity realm, this is yet another attack vector that must be evaluated and analyzed.

- Internet of Things—The ability to connect, communicate with, and remotely manage an incalculable number of networked, automated devices via the Internet is becoming pervasive. As organizations and individuals become increasingly reliant on intelligent, interconnected devices, cybersecurity professionals will be called upon to protect them from intrusions and interference that could compromise personal privacy or threaten public safety.

- Personal mobile devices—Smartphones and personal digital assistants (PDAs) security has not kept pace with traditional computer security. Technical security measures, such as firewalls, antivirus, and encryption, are uncommon on mobile phones, and mobile phone operating systems are not updated as frequently as those on personal computers. Malicious software can make a mobile phone a member of a network of devices that can be controlled by an attacker (a "botnet"). Malicious software can also send device information to attackers and perform other harmful commands. Mobile phones can also spread viruses to PCs with which they are connected (Foote, 2012, rev. 2013).

- Online gaming—Although online gaming is typically associated with fun and leisure, cybercriminals take advantage of that mind-set daily. A large scale, sophisticated cyber attack on an online gaming community can have huge implications. The cyber attack on the *Sony PlayStation Network* in 2011 compromised the personal data of more than 77 million users of the service by exposing their personal and financial information (Ben Quinn, 2011). Gamers who engage in massively multiplayer online role-playing games (MMORPG) such as

World of Warcraft, *Guild Wars 2*, and *Final Fantasy XIV*, and social networking games via Facebook have several common threats to watch out for, including gold keylogging, phishing, and gaming bots.

- Advance social engineering—All social engineering techniques are based on specific attributes of human decision making known as cognitive biases. These biases are exploited in various combinations to create attack techniques such as Pretexting, Diversion theft, Phishing, Baiting, Quid pro quo, and Tailgating (Crank, 2014).

- Rise of the project economy/Fall of the corporation— Work is being reduced into smaller pieces, changing the process both for companies that buy work and for professionals delivering work for pay. Whether it is outsourcing a function, engaging a consultant or consulting firm, or using freelancers, retired employees and even crowd sourcing, companies just do not need as many employees as they did five years ago. The new workforce model today includes a percentage of the workforce comprised of consultants, contractors, and freelancers. Many companies consider as much as half of their workforce as "non-employees." This brings with it a rise in the use of public cloud-based collaboration services. Technology advances also enabled workers to be remote: working from home, plugging in at Starbuck's, and even subcontracting freelancers from overseas. All are cybersecurity challenges.

- Advanced persistent threats/hacktivism/nation-state cyber terrorism—"The term APT is being commonly used to refer to cyber threats, in particular that of Internet-enabled espionage using a variety of intelligence gathering techniques to access sensitive information, but applies equally to other threats such as that of traditional espionage or attack (Sophos Inc., 2014). These processes usually target organizations and/or nations for business or political motives and require a high degree of covertness over a long period of time. Sophisticated malware is often used to exploit vulnerabilities in systems, and the persistence of these attacks is predicated upon the existence of an external command and control process that is continuously monitoring and extracting data from a specific target. APT usually refers to a group, such as a government, with both the capability and the intent to persistently and effectively target a specific entity.

• Multi-tenancy security/threat vector inheritance— Expanded use of hypervisors and multi-tenant environments adds additional security challenges. Vulnerabilities present in other users' applications now represent unknown threats to a user's security posture. Bad actors could conceivable use specialized malware to tunnel through virtualization layers in order to attack neighboring systems.

• Sector-specific IT security control points (i.e., FedRAMP)—As part of the U.S. federal government's "Cloud First" policy, all federally approved cloud service providers must adhere to security policies and procedures mandated by the Federal Risk and Authorization Management Program (FedRAMP). This specific requirement dictates automated monitoring of, and reporting on, specified cloud infrastructure security control points. Its success could lead to similar security mandates within government-regulated industries or ones that are deemed critical to national security.

• Federated identity, authorization, and access management—Organizations of any significant size will likely procure services from more than one cloud service provider. Implementation of single sign-on processes across multiple providers will inevitably drive an increased need for federated identity, authorization, and access management. Cybersecurity professionals will be called upon to evaluate, deploy, operate, and modify these systems as business models and processes evolve.

- Blended personal/corporate IT security—As society continues to move toward blended personal and professional identities in the digital world, professional identities will also continue to be blended with corporate ones. Security professionals will be charged with managing an ever-changing tapestry of internal, external, and virtual organizations, roles, and identities.

- Security-as-a-Service—"Security as a Service (Secaas) is the next generation of managed security services dedicated to the delivery, over the Internet, of specialized information-security services" (Information Systems Audit and Control Association (ISACA), 2013). While the "low cost, technically acceptable" acquisition model in this area brings its own set of concerns, normal vendor service procurement churn will also increase the cybersecurity team's breadth of responsibility.

- Cyber cartels—Harmful results posed by advanced persistent threats can be extraordinary and are rapidly increasing in scale. In fact, cyber cartels will soon surpass drug cartels in posing the largest threat to global security. Companies that are particularly in danger of industrial espionage include producers of high-tech products and those with large research and development divisions (Deloitte Center for Security & Privacy Solutions, 2011).

Conclusion

The cyber world holds both great promise and great peril. Our cybersecurity workforce will serve as our advisors, protectors, and comforters. They must be well educated, well steeled, and extremely flexible in order to deal with the unknown future ahead.

References

Ben Aissa, R. A. (2010). Quantifying security threats and their potential impacts: A case study. *Innovation in Systems and Software Engineering: A NASA Journal*, 269–281.

Ben Arfa Rabai, L., Jouini, M., & Ben Aissa, A. (2013). A cybersecurity model in cloud computing environments. *Journal of King Saud University— Computer and Information Sciences*, 25(1), 63–75. Retrieved from http:// www.sciencedirect.com/science/article/pii/S131915781200033X.

Ben Quinn, C. A. (2011, April 26). *PlayStation Network hackers access data of 77 million users*. Retrieved from The Guardian: http://www.theguardian. com/technology/2011/apr/26/playstation-network-hackers-data.

Bensonoff, K. (2014, August 30). *Infographic: Study shows cloud computing on the rise*. Retrieved from Computersupport.com ITAnyWhere Blog: http:// www.computersupport.com/blog/tag/current-state-of-cloud-computing/.

Böhme, R., & Nowey, T. (2008). Economic security metrics. In I. Eusgeld & F. C. Freiling (Eds.), *Dependability metrics* (pp. 176–187). Berlin: Springer.

Business Software Alliance. (2013). *2013 BSA global cloud computing scorecard*. Washington, DC: Business Software Alliance.

Cloud Security Alliance. (2013). *The notorious nine: Cloud computing top threats in 2013*. Cloud Security Alliance. Retrieved from https://downloads. cloudsecurityalliance.org/initiatives/top_threats/The_Notorious_Nine_ Cloud_Computing_Top_Threats_in_2013.pdf.

Crank, C. (2014, June 30). *Social engineering: How it's used to gain cyber information*. Retrieved from http://www.scmagazine.com/social-engineering-how-its-used-to-gain-cyber-information/article/358339/.

Currie, W., & Seddon, J. (2014). A cross-country study of cloud computing: Policy and regulation in healthcare. *Twenty Second European Conference on Information Systems* (p. 1–14). Tel Aviv. Retrieved from http:// ecis2014.eu/E-poster/files/0247-file1.pdf.

Deloitte Center for Security & Privacy Solutions. (2011). *Cyber espionage: The harsh reality of advanced security threats*. London, UK: Deloitte Development, LLC. Retrieved from http://www.deloitte.com/assets/ Dcom-UnitedStates/Local%20Assets/Documents/AERS/us_aers_cyber_ espionage_07292011.pdf.

Foote, P. R. (2012, rev. 2013). *Cyber threats to mobile phones*. United States Computer Emergency Readiness Team. Pittsburgh, PA: Carnegie Mellon University.

Harris-Ferrante, K., & Plummer, D. C. (2012, May 25). *Industries aim to evolve cloud computing beyond support functions to more strategic uses*. Retrieved from Gartner.com: https://www.gartner.com/doc/2027216.

Information Systems Audit and Control Association (ISACA). (2013). *Security as a service business benefits*. Retrieved from http://www.isaca.

org/Knowledge-Center/Research/Documents/Security-as-a-Service_whp_eng_1213.pdf.

Kugel, R. (2014, August 30). *Cloud computing is more than multitenancy.* Retrieved from Vantana Research Perspectives: http://robertkugel.ventanaresearch. com/2014/04/02/cloud-computing-is-more-than-multitenancy/.

Mayer, N. (2009). *Model-based management of information system security risk.* (Doctoral dissertation). Retrieved from https://hal.archives-ouvertes.fr/file/index/docid/402996/filename/Thesis_Mayer_2.0.pdf.

National Institute of Standards and Technologies. (2013). *Improving critical infrastructure cybersecurity, executive order 13636, preliminary cybersecurity framework.* Gaithersburg, MD: National Institute of Standards and Technologies.

North Bridge Venture Partners. (2014). *2014 future of cloud computing—4th annual survey results.* Retrieved from Slideshare.net: http://www.slideshare. net/mjskok/2014-future-of-cloud-computing-4th-annual-survey-results.

The Open Group: Jericho Forum. (2009). *Cloud cube model: Selecting cloud formations for secure collaboration.* Jericho Forum. Retrieved from https://collaboration.opengroup.org/jericho/cloud_cube_model_v1.0.pdf.

Tsiakis, T. (2010). Information security expenditures: a techno-economic analysis. *International Journal of Computer Science and Network Security (IJCSNS), 10*(4), 7–11.

Sophos, Inc. (2014, June 26). *APT—Advanced persistent threats—Part 1: Definition.* Retrieved from http://itsecformanagers.com/2014/06/26/apt-advanced-persistent-threats-part-1-definition/.

Williams, R. (2014, June 9). *Cyber crime costs global economy $445 bn annually.* Retrieved from The Telegraph, http://www.telegraph.co.uk/technology/internet-security/10886640/Cyber-crime-costs-global-economy-445-bn-annually.html.

Zhang, X. W. (2010). Information security risk management framework for the cloud computing environments. *10th International Conference on Computer and Information Technology (CIT),* 1328–1334.

About the Contributors

Editors

Jane LeClair, EdD, holds master's degrees in business, organizational psychology, and technical education, a graduate certificate in cybersecurity, and a doctorate from Syracuse University. She is chief operating officer of Excelsior College's National Cybersecurity Institute, located in Washington, DC, and the former dean of Excelsior's School of Business and Technology. She also has expertise in the nuclear power industry, where she worked for more than a decade.

Dr. LeClair is actively involved in multiple professional organizations, and is recognized as an advocate for attracting and retaining women in the fields of technology and cybersecurity.

Gregory Keeley, BA, MA, has significant national security, cyber, and defense expertise, deployments with both the U.S. and Australian militaries, and has held senior advisory roles with the U.S. Congress and Australian Parliament. He is the principal and founder of Ariana Partners, Inc., which operates in the defense, cybersecurity, intelligence, and homeland security spaces. Concurrently, he is chief strategy officer for Araxid, Inc., and a Visiting Fellow at the National Cybersecurity Institute.

Mr. Keeley received his undergraduate degree from Curtin University, and a master's degree from Deakin University, in Australia.

Contributors

Diana L. Burley, Ph.D. is a nationally recognized cybersecurity workforce expert. In 2014, she was selected as the cybersecurity educator of the year by the Colloquium for Information System Security Education (CISSE) and as one of the top ten influencers in information security careers by Careers Info Security magazine. She has been twice appointed (2012, 2013) to the Virginia General Assembly Joint Commission on Technology & Science Cybersecurity Advisory Committee and has served as co-Chair of the National Academy of Sciences Committee on Professionalizing the Nation's Cybersecurity Workforce. Dr. Burley is currently a Professor in the Graduate School of Education and Human Development at George Washington University. Prior to GW, she served as a Program Officer at The National Science Foundation where she managed a multi-million dollar computer science education and research portfolio and led the CyberCorps program.

Ron Carpinella is a recognized technology and digital media executive with nearly 20 years of experience leading teams in emerging technologies, digital security, and media. Currently the COO of Decooda International, he leads the company's business operations and strategy in the use of big data analytics to understand human intent, emotion, and behaviors. Prior to Decooda, Mr. Carpinella held senior leadership positions at Araxid, Equifax, Google, and other Internet technology firms.

As a leader in the field of User Centric Identity and data analysis, he has presented at numerous conferences including Burton Catalyst, and Cloud Identity Summit & RSA Security. In addition, Ron has presented before the Federal Government on the capabilities and requirements for future use in data, identity, and security. He was a founding member of the Open Identity Exchange, the Atlanta Interactive Marketing Association and has been a board member of multiple industry organizations. A veteran of the war in Afghanistan, Mr. Carpinella is a reservist in the U.S. Navy and works on the Joint Staff at the Pentagon. He is a graduate of both Purdue University and Duke University.

David E. Chesebrough, P.E., has been the President of the non-profit Association for Enterprise Information since 2001. He leads association members in collaborative engagements with government stakeholders on topics such as agile software development, IT acquisition reform, SOA implementation, and transforming enterprise architecture. Dave's career spans engineering, logistics, training, and consulting both in the U.S. and abroad. He has authored or edited a number of papers and articles dealing with evolving challenges of enterprise information. Prior to his current position, Dave was co-founder of a small consulting services company specializing in e-commerce. After a short stay in the Air Force he worked for a number of firms, from large aerospace to small tech businesses. Dave holds a BS in Mechanical Engineering from Clarkson University and an MBA from California State University.

Reg Harnish is an entrepreneur, security specialist, speaker, and Chief Security Strategist for GreyCastle Security with 15 years' experience, specializing in security solutions for financial services, health care, higher education, and other industries. Reg's security expertise ranges from Risk Management, Incident Response, and regulatory compliance to network, application, and physical security. He brings a unique, thought-provoking perspective to his work, and strives to promote awareness, establish security fundamentals, and reduce risk for Grey-Castle Security clients. Reg attended Rensselaer Polytechnic Institute in Troy, NY, and has achieved numerous security and industry certifications, including CISSP, CISM, CISA and ITIL. Reg is a member of InfraGard, the Information Systems Audit and Control Association (ISACA), and the Information Systems Security Association (ISSA).

In addition to deep expertise in cybersecurity, Reg has achieved numerous physical security certifications, including firearms instruction, range safety, and personal protection. As a frequent speaker, Reg has presented at events including U.S. Cybercrime, Symantec Vision, ISACA, ISSA, and InfraGard. Reg's successes have been featured in leading industry journals, including *Software Magazine*, *ComputerWorld*, and *InfoWorld*. Reg is a fellow of NCI, current President for the Hudson Valley Chapter of ISACA, serves on the Advisory Board for ITT

Technical Institute (a secondary business technology education institution), and a previous member of the Board of Directors for the Red Cross of Northeastern New York.

Kevin L. Jackson is Founder and CEO of GovCloud Network, a consultancy specializing in solutions to meet critical commercial and government operational requirements. Prior positions include VP & General Manager Cloud Services NJVC, VP Federal Systems at Sirius Computer Solutions, Worldwide Sales Executive at IBM, VP Global IT Project Office at JP Morgan Chase, and CTO at SENTEL Corporation. His formal education includes an MS Computer Engineering from Naval Postgraduate School; an MA National Security & Strategic Studies from Naval War College; and a BS Aerospace Engineering from the U.S. Naval Academy. Mr. Jackson is currently pursuing a Ph.D. in Applied Information Technology at the George Mason University Volgenau School of Engineering.

Through his *"Cloud Musings"* blog, Mr. Jackson has been recognized as one of *Cloud Computing Journal's* "World's 30 Most Influential Cloud Bloggers" (2009, 2010), and a *Huffington Post* Top 100 Cloud Computing Experts on Twitter (2013). He is the author of a *FedTech Magazine:* "Must Read Federal IT Blog" (2012, 2013). In 2012, he was named a "Cybersecurity Visionary" by *US Black Engineer and Information Technology* magazine. Mr. Jackson is also author of the books GovCloud: *Cloud Computing for the Business of Government* (2011) and *"GovCloud II: Implementation and Cloud Brokerage Services"* (2012); and co-author of the Intelligence and NSA whitepaper "*Cloud Computing: Risks, Benefits, and Mission Enhancement for the Intelligence Community."*

J. Thomas Malatesta, who holds a BSC from the University of Santa Clara, is CEO of Ziklag Systems LLC, a developer and marketer of enterprise level advanced mobile security products and solutions. He also advises on cybersecurity investments for SDB Partners. Thomas is former President of the InfraGard Maryland Members Alliance, a public private partnership with the FBI. In addition, he has served: on the Board of Directors of the Security Analysis and Risk Management

Association (SARMA); on the advisory team at Monument Capital Group; as CEO for Threatstorm International, Inc.; and as CEO of Cybrinth, Inc.

Earlier, Mr. Malatesta served with a boutique merchant banking group, BroadReach Management, L.L.C. and Incyte Capital Assets, L.L.C. where his focus was sourcing and screening private equity investments as a strategic counselor to both investing and business entities. Prior to that he served as VP of New Markets and Product Development for Smith Corona Corp. and as President of JTM&CO. Mr. Malatesta clearly understands the dynamics of e-commerce and the enterprise and Internet applications necessary to successfully compete in the globalized economy.

Pete O'Dell is a business and technology consultant who has been involved with information technology and business for over 25 years, working for large companies like Autodesk, Digital Equipment Corporation, Microsoft, and Micro Warehouse. He has been involved in multiple startup efforts including Swan Island Networks, Upgrade Corporation of America, and Online Interactive. Pete has been president of a high-growth software company, chief information officer of several large and small corporations, and chief operating officer for multiple startups. At Swan Island Networks, Pete had extensive interaction with the U.S. Government in the areas of homeland security, information sharing, real time situational awareness, and law enforcement. He now consults for a wide range of companies, and is on the global advisory board for BucketDream.com, an exciting new enterprise launching in 2014. He is also part of NextLevel, a growing Northwest executive and board services firm.

One of Pete's key skills is the communication and interface between technical groups and non-technical executives and board members. He has presented at National Association of Corporate Directors meetings about cybersecurity. He firmly believes that technologists must make a far better effort to translate the complexity and acronyms of information technology into understandable and actionable strategies that their executive peers and board members can understand and oversee.

Andrew A. Proia, J.D., CIPP/US, is a Privacy Policy Analyst in Washington DC. Recently, Andrew completed a postdoctoral fellowship in information security law and policy at the Indiana University Center for Applied Cybersecurity Research. Andrew's work has primarily focused on information privacy, cybersecurity, and cybercrime. He is a former author at Cybercrime Review, and his work on technology law and policy has appeared in a number of law journals and online publications. Andrew received his J.D. from the Indiana University Maurer School of Law, where he served as a managing editor of the Indiana Law Journal and was a research assistant to Professor Fred H. Cate. He received a BS in Criminal Justice from the University of Central Florida.

Drew Simshaw, J.D., is an information security policy analyst at the Center for Law, Ethics, and Applied Research in Health Information (CLEAR) at Indiana University. His work focuses on the complex security and privacy issues associated with cloud computing, big data, robotics, and new technologies. He previously served as Postdoctoral Fellow in Information Security Law and Policy at Indiana University's Center for Applied Cybersecurity Research, an NSA and DHS National Center of Academic Excellence in both Information Assurance Education and Information Assurance Research. A proud AmeriCorps alum, Drew earned his B.A. from the University of Washington and his J.D. from the Indiana University Maurer School of Law, where he was articles editor for the Federal Communications Law Journal. He is a member of the Indiana Bar and the International Association of Privacy Professionals.

Derek A. Smith is the Director of Cybersecurity Initiatives at the National Cybersecurity Institute at Excelsior College. He is also an adjunct professor in Excelsior College School of Business and Technology. Derek has years of government and military leadership experience and holds an MBA, an MS in Information Assurance, an MS in Information Technology Project Management, and a BS in Education. Derek holds the following certifications: Certified Information

Systems Security Professional (CISSP®), Certified Authorization Professional (CAP), Certified Ethical Hacker (CEH), Certified Hacking Forensic Investigator, Computer Network Defense Architect, Certified EC-Council Instructor, Certified SCADA Security Architect (CSSA), and Security+.

James Swanson, BA, MA, MIPP, has over 38 years of experience working on international issues. Currently, James is the Executive Vice President of Ziklag Systems, a developer of mobile security technologies for Smartphones. Mr. Swanson is a former Senior Vice President of Finmeccanica North America, Inc., a global defense company in Washington, DC. At Finmeccanica he handled the coordination between U.S.-based subsidiaries and Italian corporate offices for group participation in multi-billion dollar defense projects. He is a former Senior Policy Analyst and Director of Research for the congressionally sponsored U.S./China Economic and Security Review Commission. He was responsible for drafting the military, defense, and national security chapters of the Annual Report to the Congress and for providing oversight of the social and economic research for the report. For 24 years, James was a senior DoD Executive focusing on the national security threats from the global efforts to acquire weapons of mass destruction. He has extensive knowledge of technology and technology security as well as significant field experience in denying the illegal export of sensitive military technology to countries of concern. He is a retired Naval Intelligence officer with extensive experience, including assignments to duty at several major commands and deployment to Asia and the Middle East. Prior to joining the Navy, Mr. Swanson lived in Afghanistan.

Justin Zeefe is an attorney and cybersecurity expert based in Washington D C. Mr. Zeefe previously worked for a decade at the United States Department of Defense, supporting the DOD's information security apparatus. Mr. Zeefe served both in the U.S. and abroad, including tours in both Iraq and Afghanistan where he twice received the highest award available for a civilian in combat from the Joint

Chiefs of Staff. Prior to his government service, Mr. Zeefe practiced corporate law at a top firm in Washington DC. Mr. Zeefe holds a BA from The Honors College at The Ohio State University and a JD from Boston University School of Law where he graduated in 2002. Mr. Zeefe speaks German and enjoys brewing beer. He resides with his wife, son, and cat in Alexandria, Virginia.

Index

ABOUT HUDSON WHITMAN

Hudson Whitman is a small press affiliated with Excelsior College, a non-profit, online college serving primarily adult students.

Our tagline is "Books That Make a Difference," and we aim to publish high-quality nonfiction books and multimedia projects in areas that complement Excelsior's academic strengths: education, nursing, health care, military interests, cybersecurity, and for special projects that may not easily fit in one category, American culture and society.

If you would like to submit a manuscript or proposal, please review the guidelines on our website, hudsonwhitman.com. Feel free to send a note with any questions.

OTHER TITLES BY HUDSON WHITMAN

The Call of Nursing: Stories from the Front Lines of Health Care
William B. Patrick (print and e-book)

Shot: Staying Alive with Diabetes
Amy F. Ryan (print + e)

The Sanctuary of Illness: A Memoir of Heart Disease
Thomas Larson (print + e)

The Language of Men: A Memoir
Anthony D'Aries (print + e)

Courageous Learning:
Finding a New Path through Higher Education
John Ebersole and William Patrick (print + e)

Saving Troy:
A Year with Firefighters and Paramedics in a Battered City
William Patrick (e-book only)

Protecting Our Future: Educating a Cybersecurity Workforce (Vol 1)
Edited by Jane LeClair (print + e)

N21—Nursing in the Twenty-First Century
A free, peer-reviewed mobile journal available on the web or as an iOS app.

Sign up for our monthly e-newsletter for deals, events, new releases!
hudsonwhitman.com